scrapbooking *made* easy

Funny, I thought your name was Anne. But your mommy and daddy call you Magroots. So I asked your mom, "Hey, Molly, where'd ya get a nickname like 'Magroots' from?" And do you know what she said? "It rhymes with Tutti Magrooti!" Okay, so your mom is a little goofy, and that's why I love her. Anne, I know I don't live by you sweetie, and won't see you as you grow on a daily basis, but just know I love you and will always be your "Auntie" in Minnesota. SEPTEMBER 2004

MAGROOTS

Presenting over 550 of the best projects and ideas from *Simple Scrapbooks* magazine, to help you complete simple albums fast and learn easy ways to make scrapbooking a fun and fulfilling part of your busy life.

A TREASURY OF FAVORITES PRODUCED EXCLUSIVELY FOR LEISURE ARTS

Consumer Magazine & Internet Group

Editorial

FOUNDING EDITOR, Stacy Julian; *EDITOR IN CHIEF,* Lin Sorenson; *MANAGING EDITOR,* Angie Lucas; *SPECIAL PROJECTS EDITOR,* Lynda Angelastro; *CREATIVE EDITOR,* Wendy Smedley; *ASSOCIATE EDITORS,* Molly Newman, Mark Zoellner; *ASSISTANT EDITOR,* Elisha Snow; *EDITORIAL ASSISTANT,* Carolyn Jolley; *CONTRIBUTING EDITORS,* Darci Dowdle, Donna Downey, Deanna Lambson, Kris Parkin, Renee Pearson, Kathleen Samuelson, Cathy Zielske

Design

ART DIRECTOR, John Youngberg; *SPECIAL ISSUES ART DIRECTOR,* Don Lambson; *PHOTOGRAPHY,* Brian Twede, John Luke

Advertising

ADVERTISING SALES MANAGER, Becky Lowder; *ADVERTISING REPRE-SENTATIVE,* Jenny Grothe, 801-319-4168; *FAX* 801-406-0001

Publishing

VICE PRESIDENT, GROUP PUBLISHER, David O'Neil; *PUBLISHER,* Tony Golden; *PRODUCTION MANAGER,* Gary Whitehead; *SENIOR PRODUC-TION DIRECTOR,* Terry Boyer; *ADMINISTRATIVE ASSISTANT,* Kim Blackinton; *MEDIA RELATIONS,* Chantelle Turner, Bremer Public Relations, 801-364-2030 (Media Only); *WEB EDITOR,* April Tarter

Sales & Marketing

DIRECTOR OF SALES & MARKETING, Tara Green; *RETAIL MANAGER,* Stephanie Easton, ext. 226; *SPECIAL PROJECTS COORDINATOR,* Kristin Schaefer, ext. 251; *WHOLESALE ACCOUNTS,* 800-815-3538; *U.S STORES:* Becky Cude, ext. 235, Claudia Mann, ext. 244; *INTERNA-TIONAL STORES,* Tanja Rigby, ext. 250; *DISTRIBUTOR ACCOUNTS,* Tara Green, ext. 242, Kristin Schaefer, ext. 251; *SPECIAL PROMOTIONS COORDINATOR,* Jacque Jensen, ext. 577; *SENIOR PRODUCT MANAG-ER,* Dana Wilson, ext. 592; *MARKETING ASSISTANT,* Heather Ence, ext. 572; *CONSUMER SALES MANAGER,* Emily Johnson; *CUSTOMER SERVICE COORDINATORS,* Alicia Pearman, Jill Tuttle; *SUBSCRIPTION SERVICES,* 888-247-5282

PRIMEDIA Inc.

CHAIRMAN, Dean Nelson; *PRESIDENT & CEO,* Kelly Conlin; *VICE CHAIRMAN,* Beverly C. Chell

PRIMEDIA Enthusiast Media

EXECUTIVE VP, CONSUMER MARKETING/CIRCULATION, Steve Aster; *SENIOR VP, CFO,* Kevin Neary; *SENIOR VP, MFG. PRODUCTION & DISTRIBUTION,* Kevin Mullan; *SENIOR VP/CIO,* Debra C. Robinson; *VP, COMPTROLLER,* Joseph Lyons; *VP, MANUFACTURING,* Gregory Catsaros; *VP, MANUFACTURING,* Craig Donado; *VP, SINGLE COPY SALES,* Thomas L. Fogarty; *VP, MANUFACTURING BUDGETS AND OPERATIONS,* Greg Parnell

Consumer Marketing, PRIMEDIA Enthusiast Media

VP, SINGLE COPY MARKETING, Rich Baron; *VP & CFO CONSUMER MARKETING,* Jennifer Prather; *VP, RETAIL ANALYSIS AND DEVELOPMENT,* Doug Jensen; *VP, WHOLESALE/RETAIL,* Stefan Kaiser; *VP, CONSUMER MARKETING OPERATIONS,* Elizabeth Moss

Consumer Marketing, Enthusiast Media Subscription Company *CONSUMER MARKETING DIRECTOR,* Dena Spar; *ASSOCI-ATE CONSUMER MARKETING DIRECTOR,* Dana Smolik; *VP, CON-SUMER MARKETING,* Bobbi Gutman

PRIMEDIA Lifestyles Group

PRESIDENT, Scott Wagner; *VP and GROUP CFO,* Henry Donahue

Privacy

Occasionally, our subscriber list is made available to reputable firms offering goods and services that we believe would be of interest to our readers. If you prefer to be excluded, please send your current address label and a note requesting to be excluded from these promotions to PRIMEDIA, Inc., 745 Fifth Avenue, New York, NY 10151 Attn: Privacy Coordinator.

SUBSCRIPTIONS

To subscribe to *Simple Scrapbooks* magazine or to change the address of your current subscription, call or write:

Subscriber Services
Simple Scrapbooks
P.O. Box 420235
Palm Coast, FL 32142-0235

Phone: 866/334-8149
International: 386/246-3406

Email: simplescrapbooks@palmcoastd.com
Web site: *www.simplescrapbooksmag.com*

CORPORATE OFFICES

Simple Scrapbooks, 200 Madison Ave., NY, NY 10016.
Phone: 801/984-2070. **Fax:** 801/984-2080.
Homepage: www.simplescrapbooksmag.com.
Copyright © PRIMEDIA Inc. All rights reserved.

TRADEMARKS

Many product names mentioned in *Simple Scrapbooks* magazine are trade-marks or registered trademarks of their respective companies. The names are used in an editorial fashion only and to the benefit of the trademark owner, with no intention to infringe on the trademarks.

NOTICE OF LIABILITY: The information in this book is distributed on an "as is" basis, without warranty. While every precaution has been taken in the prepara-tion of this book, neither the author nor PRIMEDIA Inc. nor LEISURE ARTS Inc. shall have any liability to any person or entity with respect to any liability, loss or damage caused or alleged to be caused directly or indirectly by the instructions contained in this book.

MANUFACTURED UNDER LICENSE for PRIMEDIA Special Interest **Publications, Inc. -** a PRIMEDIA company, publisher of *Simple Scrapbooks.*

COPYRIGHT© 2005 PRIMEDIA Special Interest Publications, Inc.
All rights reserved. No part of this publication may be reproduced in any form without written permission. Readers may create any project for personal use or sale, and may copy patterns to assist them in making projects, but may not hire others to mass-produce a project without written permission from *Simple Scrapbooks.*

Scrapbooking Made Easy
Softcover ISBN 1-57486-571-4
Library of Congress Control Number 2005932076
Printed in the United States of America.

Published by Leisure Arts, Inc., 5701 Ranch Drive, Little Rock, Arkansas 72223-9633. 501-868-8800. *www.leisurearts.com.*

Leisure Arts Editorial
VICE PRESIDENT AND EDITOR-IN-CHIEF, Sandra Graham Case; EXECUTIVE DIRECTOR OF PUBLICATIONS, Cheryl Nodine Gunnells; SENIOR PUBLICATIONS DIRECTOR, Susan White Sullivan; SPECIAL PROJECTS DIRECTOR, Susan Frantz Wiles; GRAPHIC DESIGN SUPERVISOR, Amy Vaughn; GRAPHIC ARTIST, Katherine Atchison; DIRECTOR OF RETAIL MARKETING, Stephen Wilson; DIRECTOR OF DESIGNER RELATIONS, Debra Nettles; SENIOR ART OPERATIONS DIRECTOR, Jeff Curtis; ART IMAGING DIRECTOR, Mark Hawkins; PUBLISHING SYSTEMS ADMINISTRATOR, Becky Riddle; PUBLISHING SYSTEMS ASSISTANTS, Clint Hanson, Josh Hyatt and John Rose

Leisure Arts Operations
CHIEF OPERATING OFFICER, Tom Siebenmorgen; DIRECTOR OF CORPORATE PLANNING AND DEVELOPMENT, Laticia Mull Dittrich; VICE PRESIDENT, SALES AND MARKETING, Pam Stebbins; DIRECTOR OF SALES AND SERVICES, Margaret Reinold; VICE PRESIDENT, OPERATIONS, Jim Dittrich; COMPTROLLER, OPERATIONS, Rob Thieme; RETAIL CUSTOMER SERVICE MANAGER, Stan Raynor; PRINT PRODUCTION MANAGER, Fred F. Pruss

Scrapbooking—Your Way!

I'm excited to introduce you to this collection of pages and projects from *Simple Scrapbooks* magazine.

If you're new to scrapbooking, you'll find some fast, fun ideas to help you get started and complete your first page or project. If you've been scrapbooking for a while, you'll enjoy our straightforward approach to creating meaningful pages, completing projects, and learning about new approaches to the hobby that you might not have considered before.

This book, like *Simple Scrapbooks* magazine, is organized into four sections to help you find what interests you most. You'll *Learn* basic skills, *Use* fun, time-saving products, *Do* quick and easy projects, and *Share* reader stories and ideas.

No matter where you are on the scrapbooking spectrum, I'm confident that the concepts in this book will help you tell your stories and find a way to make this hobby a fun and fulfilling part of your busy life. Don't worry about scrapbooking every photo, working chronologically, making every project a creative masterpiece, or spending lots of time and money. There's no "right" way to scrapbook. Don't worry about what you should do—just do what makes the most sense to you and enjoy it.

Relax and have fun!

Lin Sorenson
Editor-in-Chief
Simple Scrapbooks Magazine

Contents

6 Learn

98 Use

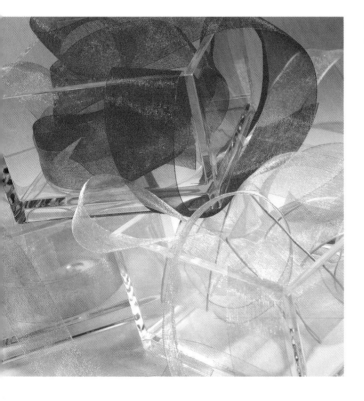

174 Do

268 Share

This is your chance to learn from "The Experts of Easy." Tips on everything from cropping photos to effectively using color in your albums. Here's how you keep it simple and make it meaningful.

Learn

Let go of the pressure

BY STACY JULIAN

"Are you sure I can do that?" I've heard these words many times as I've shared ideas for making scrapbooking less overwhelming. Oddly enough, there seem to be several unwritten laws (or at least general assumptions) concerning the preservation of memories and what's required of someone who wants to become a "scrapbooker."

I fear some of these assumptions might be keeping members of my own family and several of my friends from "getting started."

Just for the fun of it, I'll address four of these assumptions and, in case you want it, give you permission to approach scrapbooking in some new, perhaps unconventional, but very liberating ways.

Kevin and Darci

become Mr. and Mrs. Dowdle
November 20, 1999
Seattle, Wash.

Stacy, Clark & Chase
were wedding attendants.
Stacy was Darci's Maid
of honor, and the boys
and their cousins Nika &
Sonya took gifts and helped
clear tables

Figure 1. Give yourself the option of not scrapbooking all the photos from an event. You can store the rest in a slotted album (see above). *Page by Stacy Julian.* **Supplies** *Album and refill pages:* Pioneer; *Patterned papers:* Amscan, Inc. (neutral floral); Frances Meyer (plaid); Unknown (lavender rose). *Stickers:* Frances Meyer; *Alphabet rubber stamps:* Stampin' Up!; *Stamping foil:* Close To My Heart; *Pens:* Metallic Gel Roller, Pentel and Zig Millennium, EK Success. **Ideas to note:** Stacy placed organdy ribbon over the strip of plaid paper. She also used a metallic marker to color over the red berries in the stickers so they would coordinate with the page.

1. LEAVE MOST OF YOUR PHOTOS IN THE BOX.

A New Approach

Without further delay, and with the authority vested in me as founding editor of this magazine, and all the experience I have as a working mother of four, domestic goddess, life enthusiast and all-around busy person, and in accordance with the good and grand desires of my heart that make me want to celebrate every little aspect, quiet moment and unforgettable adventure of my life and the lives of those important to me, and lastly, because the most precious time is spent making memories, I hereby grant you, my fellow scrapbookers, permission to:

At least for now. I mean really, you take so many pictures, and if you expect to creatively deal with each of them in a way that will inspire your offspring for generations to come, you've placed an unrealistic expectation (not to mention burden) on yourself. Now, don't get me wrong. I'm not asking you to curb your photo-taking appetite. Shoot away. I just don't think you need the pressure of trying to scrapbook every photograph you take.

Try this instead. Set up a box, drawer or file labeled "duplicate photos" and see how good it feels to file away 19 of the 24 pictures you took at your nephew's bar mitzvah. I did something similar with photographs from my

Figure 2. Consider creating scrapbook pages that summarize a whole year of a child's life. Select one photo from each milestone or major event from the year and place them all on one layout. Additional photos can be saved for later! *Pages by Stacy Julian.* **Supplies** *Patterned paper:* Lasting Impressions for Paper; *Stickers:* me & my BIG ideas; *Letter stickers:* Provo Craft.

photos allows me to stay current on Chase's life (in his album) and scrapbook in more detail the remaining photos when I get the urge or the time (in my albums).

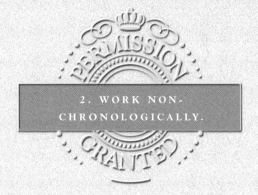

2. WORK NON-CHRONOLOGICALLY.

sister's wedding. I used just three shots to preserve the event on a scrapbook page and am storing the rest of the pictures in one of our family's large slotted photo albums (Figure 1). I saved time and we can still view all the photographs taken at the wedding. The layout I completed and others depicting special extended family events will go into my "Family Celebrations" album.

The skill of editing and choosing the most "scrap-able" photos from your stash and archiving the rest really comes in handy when you're trying to chronicle a child's life. In Figure 2, the layouts represent my son Chase's life the year he was in kindergarten. "Archiving" the extra

Some experts recommend scrapbooking your current photos first then working back in time. Others say it's better to start with older photos and work forward. I support either one of these methods. Both work well for thousands of scrapbookers. However, and I promise I'm not an anti-chronologist, whenever you organize photos in date order you automatically emphasize events and risk missing other important aspects of life.

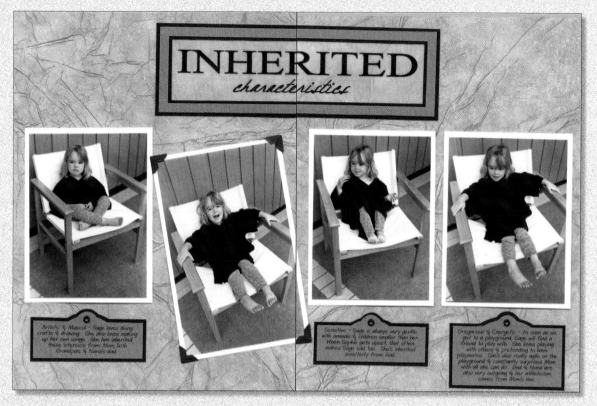

INHERITED
characteristics

Artistic & Musical - Sage loves doing crafts & drawing. She also loves making up her own songs. She has inherited these interests from Mom, both Grandpas & Nana's dad.

Sensitive - Sage is always very gentle with animals & children smaller than her. When Sophie gets upset, that often makes Sage sad too. She's inherited sensitivity from Dad.

Gregarious & Energetic - As soon as we get to a playground, Sage will find a friend to play with. She loves playing with others & pretending to have playmates. She's also really agile on the playground & constantly surprises Mom with all she can do. Dad & Nana are also very outgoing & her athleticism comes from Mom's line.

Figure 3. Seize every opportunity to capture and record personality and character traits of the people you love. *Pages by Vivian Smith.* **Supplies** *Patterned paper:* Tuscany; *Computer fonts:* Times New Roman ("Inherited"), Monotype Corporation; CK Bella ("Characteristics") and CK Print (journaling), "The Best of Creative Lettering" CD Combo, Creating Keepsakes; *Photo corners:* Canson; *Eyelets:* Impress Rubber Stamps.

Sarah and Her Daddy at Aaron & Kim's Wedding
November 4, 2000

Figure 4. Nothing is more important than celebrating important relationships. The photo on this page opens up to reveal another photo and more journaling. (above right) *Page by Emily Tucker.* **Supplies** *Computer font:* Unknown: *Other:* Ribbon.

Next time you're sorting through a new pack of prints, watch for those photographs that might help you capture and celebrate a relationship, someone's personality or a quality in a family member that you value (see Figures 3 and 4). In Figure 3, Vivian Smith of Calgary, Alberta, Canada, lists special characteristics of her daughter Sage and notes which family members she may have inherited them from. In Figure 4, Emily Tucker of Matthew, North Carolina, used this photo of her daughter and husband at a friend's wedding to create a page about a wonderful daddy-daughter relationship. She then took it a step further by drawing a connection between this relationship and the one she shares with her father.

This is what scrapbooking is all about. Don't get so caught up in chronicling the events that you skip over other memories, or miss out on the moments. You don't have to organize your photos to get started. Why not spend an afternoon sifting through decades of older photos? Randomly select several shots that make you laugh. Put them in a pile and then get them on a scrapbook page or two. They belong together—not sequentially, but emotionally.

Stacy made this layout in 18½ minutes and still had time to exercise! *Pages by Stacy Julian.* **Supplies** *Stickers:* Provo Craft; *Lettering template:* Block, ABC Tracers, Pebbles for EK Success; *Chalk:* Craf-T Products; *Pens:* Zig Millennium EK Success.

The 20-Minute Workout: Make a Page in Record Time!

What do I do when I don't have time to really exercise? My 20-minute workout, of course! It features a three-minute warm-up, 15 minutes of aerobic conditioning and two minutes of cool-down that I can squeeze into the busiest of days. I like it so much I decided to design one for composing a scrapbook layout. If you don't think it's possible to fit scrapbooking into your schedule, try my 20-minute workout—you might be surprised how good it makes you feel! I completed the layout above in just 18½ minutes!

Warm-up: Take three deep breaths. Select a handful of photographs and lay them out in front of you. Spend one full minute looking at them, and determine what it is you really want to say with this page. Now spend the next two minutes preparing yourself for some intense creative activity. Gather your materials: two or three colors of cardstock, title and journaling tools (an archival pen, alphabet stamps or a letter stencil) and a few pre-made decorative accents (a sheet of stickers, pre-printed die cuts or punches).

Creative Conditioning: Your pulse is up—set your timer for 15 minutes and get moving. Quickly decide which, if any, of your photographs need to be resized or shaped. Don't think about it for too long. Go with your first impression.

Now choose one photo to be your focal point and do something to visually emphasize it (use size, shape, color or an accent). Arrange your other photos on your workspace, being careful not to lose momentum.

Before adhering your photos to the page, think about title and word placement and make necessary adjustments. Alright now, stay strong and stick it all down. Don't give up—you're almost there!

It's time to add the journaling. This is the point in the workout where many lose their stamina—it's not always easy to get the words on paper. Think back to that first minute, remember your key message and write it down. Stay strong and focused. OK, one more big move: reach for your page protectors and slide your finished layout in.

Cool-down: Spend the last two minutes cooling down and cleaning up. Put your tools and extra materials away. Do some more deep breathing.

Walk around the room once or twice, come back to your work table and look at your completed page. Stretch your mouth into a great big smile and pat yourself on the back—you made it!

Figure 5. Watercolor patterned paper is an easy option when it comes to background choices. *Pages by Stacy Julian.* **Supplies** *Patterned paper:* Karen Foster Design; *Lettering template:* Blocky, Provo Craft; *Chalks:* Craf-T Products.

3. LET GO OF CREATIVE PRESSURE.

Remember, the essential elements of any scrapbook page are the photographs and the story behind them. That's it. You really don't need anything else. Decorative elements aren't essential, and creating custom artwork is certainly not required. We all love to drool over inspiring and mind-expanding creativity, but if trying to produce it is giving you a headache, making you feel inferior, or causing you to lose sleep, then you really need to "take a chill pill."

Scrapbooking is supposed to be fun and even relaxing. Rejoice in the fact that this industry introduces new and exciting products and page accents every day. Use them. They'll help make your job of compiling scrapbooks easier. If it's been awhile since you simply used patterned paper as a backdrop for your pictures, or just two stickers from a sheet to enhance a layout, remind yourself how refreshing

Figure 6. Look! Just two stickers from this whole sheet is all that's needed to perfectly accent these beautiful photos. *Page by Shauna Devereux.* **Supplies** *Patterned paper:* Keeping Memories Alive; *Stickers:* Frances Meyer; **Computer font:** CK Script, "The Best of Creative Lettering" CD Vol. 1, Creating Keepsakes.

Figure 7. Lots of photos and little time? Slide photos into divided sheet protectors and use a slot or two for journaling and enhancements. *Pages by Stacy Julian.* **Supplies** *Stickers:* Stickopotamus; *Divided sheet protectors:* Stampin' Up!; *Pens:* Zig Millennium, EK Success.

this can be (see Figures 5 and 6). Perhaps you could designate one of your albums as your coffee table "show book." In it you can really explore your creative side, and the execution of each page may well become as important as its message. Just be sure to take a break every now and then and take advantage of the vast array of pre-made products available online and at your local scrapbook store.

4. SPEND LESS TIME.

I have a dear friend who recently confessed, "I'd like to start scrapbooking, but I fear it would take over my life and I'd never have time for the other things I love." I've met so many women who feel the exact same way.

They're afraid of the long-term commitment. They (and maybe you) need permission to just "dabble" in scrapbooking.

With *Simple Scrapbooks*, you can become a "weekend scrapper." If you want a simpler way to record your family life, we'll teach you the shortcuts you'll need to get it done quickly (Figure 7). If you want to create an occasional gift or theme album, we'll give you all the inspiration, ideas and instructions you'll need. A theme album can offer a "slice of life" look at someone you love that can be just as meaningful as volumes of chronology.

If you're not passionate about the creative process of compiling a scrapbook, try viewing a scrapbook simply as a vehicle to capture and celebrate whatever it is you are passionate about. Imagine using your talent or interest as a unifying theme in an album all about you. Whether you love sewing, gardening, cooking or sky diving, you can weave it into your personal story so you'll leave a true-to-life record of who you really are.

There you go—permission granted to leave most of your photos in the box, work non-chronologically, let go of the creative pressure and spend less time overall. So, can you do this? You bet you can. You have my permission!

THERE ARE NO
GREAT THINGS,
ONLY SMALL THINGS
WITH GREAT LOVE.
HAPPY ARE THOSE.

———

MOTHER TERESA

What is a 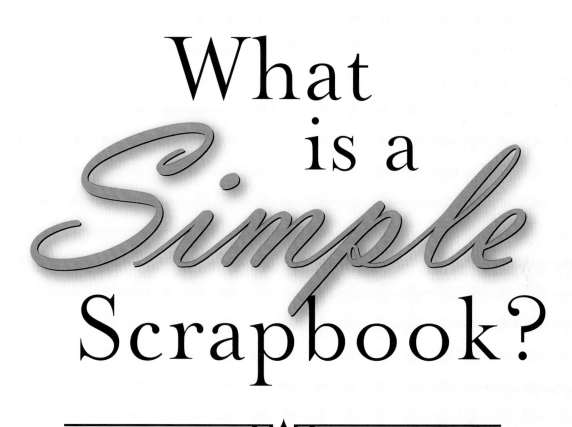Simple Scrapbook?

The "Five F's" outline this fresh approach

S imple scrapbooks. You've heard the term, seen the magazine and maybe even read the book that started it all. But perhaps you're still wondering—what exactly *is* a "simple scrapbook"? Does "simple" imply that it's just for beginners? Or lacking in creativity and content? Not at all!

A simple scrapbook isn't your everyday chronological album. Instead, it's a smaller, more manageable project that generally focuses on the "non-event" aspects of your life that can get left out of a traditional album—things like relationships, hopes and dreams, daily routines and family traditions. It helps you get back to the basics and record the less-heralded details of your life that really matter in the grand scheme of things.

A simple scrapbook is defined in terms of the "Five F's": Framework, Format, Finished, Fast and Freedom. These five elements—described on the following pages—provide a guideline for what comprises a simple scrapbook. (*Note:* Keep in mind that every simple scrapbook might not have every single element exactly as described.)

by Gayle Humpherys

Figure 1. A framework—beginning with a title page—provides the organization as well as the creative direction for an entire album. *Pages by Brenda Cosgrove.* **Supplies** *Patterned paper:* Ever After Paper Company; *Die cuts:* Pebbles in my Pocket; *Computer font:* CK Bella, "The Best of Creative Lettering" CD Vol. 3, *Creating Keepsakes.*

1. FRAMEWORK

One of the unique characteristics of a simple scrapbook is the presence of a "framework"—a group of pages, such as a title page and a table of contents page, that provides the overall structure for the album and helps define what it's all about. Framework pages are typically completed first and share a similar design that sets the tone or theme for the rest of the album.

Completing the framework pages first and defining the album's overall organization and style allows the rest of the book to come together quickly with a consistent look and feel.

Here's a brief description of the pages that make up the framework of a simple scrapbook (Figure 1):

• **Title Page.** Every scrapbook needs a title page.

This is where you give your album a name and list the date and other identifying information (such as the creator's name). The title page is also where you set the style for your entire album with the colors and design scheme you use (see "Format" on page 18).

• **Dedication/Introduction Page.** A dedication or introduction page lets you explain your reasons behind the album—it's the place to "connect" your scrapbook to another person, place or event in your life. You might also choose to dedicate it to a specific person. This optional introductory information doesn't have to be on a separate page; it's often included as part of the cover or title page.

• **Table of Contents Page.** If your album can be divided into sections, you might want to include a

table of contents page. This optional page provides a quick overview of what's included in the album, usually listing section titles. Often, the table of contents introduces a distinguishing design characteristic for each section, such as a specific color or decorative accent (die cuts, stickers, rubber stamps, etc.).

• **Section Pages.** Section pages, which simply contain the section title, are used to introduce and divide each section of your scrapbook (if you're using sections). Section pages should coordinate in design with the title and table of contents pages.

• **Filler Pages.** These pages fill up the sections; they're the "meat" of your album. Unlike the other framework pages, they don't all have to be completed at the beginning. You might only create one or two initially. The filler pages also coordinate in design

with the other framework pages, although the detail is typically simpler (sometimes only a color or design element is repeated). Here's where you can be as creative—or simple—as you like.

• **Closing Page.** This optional page is the last page of the album—it's a terrific way to add an "ending" to your book. You can include a few summarizing thoughts, a short bio about you, an inspirational quote or a parting photograph.

• **Materials File.** While not a part of the actual album, a materials file provides a place to store photos and supplies before you begin creating your scrapbook. It's also a perfect place for storing your completed "formula" (see the "A Formula for Success" sidebar on page 20) and additional information you plan to include as you update your album in the future.

Title Page

Table of Contents/Dedication Page

Section Pages

Figure 2. Establish an identifiable design scheme by using similar design elements in a consistent arrangement on your pages. *Pages by Stacy Julian.* **Supplies** *Album:* Century Craft; *Patterned paper:* Colors By Design; *Rubber stamp and stamping ink:* Close To My Heart; *Computer fonts:* CK Cursive, CK Anything Goes, CK Script and CK Handprint, "The Best of Creative Lettering" CD Combo, *Creating Keepsakes.*

Filler Pages

2. FORMAT

Every simple scrapbook follows a format of some sort. The format consists of the physical characteristics of the album, such as the album size, and the organization of its contents, such as a top-ten list or random-memories style.

One of the key aspects of an album's format is the design scheme used throughout the album— the colors and products used, the way various elements are arranged on the pages, and so on. The design scheme helps tie all the pages together, providing continuity to the album. Figure 2, for example, shows some of

Figure 3. Several colors of cardstock, coordinating patterned paper and one rubber stamp are all you need to compile a simple scrapbook! **Supplies** *Patterned paper:* Colors By Design; *Rubber stamp and stamping ink:* Close To My Heart.

the framework pages of Stacy Julian's "Family Quote Book." Her framework pages include a title page, a table of contents/dedication page, one of her section pages, and two filler pages for that section.

The design scheme for a simple scrapbook usually starts with some coordinating products, such as the blue and green cardstock, patterned paper and spiral rubber stamp Stacy used in her Family Quote Book (Figure 3). Repeating these elements establishes a design that connects the pages together. You might also repeat a design element (such as torn paper) or a lettering style on the framework pages.

In addition to specific products, the design scheme also refers to the page layout and *placement* of various elements on each framework page. For example, the section pages in Stacy's Family Quote Book follow the same design as the title page (the position of the title block fonts, torn paper strips, three spiral stamps), while the filler pages each include a circular photo over a strip of torn patterned paper.

3. FINISHED

A simple scrapbook is a project you can actually finish! Chronological albums tend to be on-going projects with an "I'll-never-be-caught-up" aspect that can add stress to our already busy lives. A simple scrapbook, on the other hand, is an album you know will be completed. This basic knowledge—before you start creating anything—removes a lot of anxiety and lets you scrapbook for the sheer enjoyment of it.

Because you're working within a framework, you know exactly how many pages you need to create. Even those scrapbooks that are occasionally updated with a filler page or two can be considered "finite" books and can easily be displayed in your home, since the completed framework pages give the book a finished look and feel.

4. FAST

One of my favorite characteristics of a simple scrapbook is that it's fast to create. Often, the most time-consuming aspect is merely deciding what format you want to use, then creating the first few framework pages. The rest of the album—including any future filler pages—comes together in a snap. All you have to do is follow the format and plug in your photos! (*Tip:* Completing a simple scrapbook formula as your very first step makes the process even faster. See the "A Formula for Success" sidebar on page 20.)

5. FREEDOM

The last characteristic of a simple scrapbook is what it ultimately gives you—freedom. Freedom to simplify chronological projects by highlighting events in a finite album, freedom to explore and record so many important aspects of your life, freedom from the anxiety of trying to stay "caught up" on your albums, and freedom to approach and tailor scrapbooking to a method that works best for you.

I've made "simple" a permanent part of my scrapbooking vocabulary. Give simple scrapbooks a try and you'll be amazed at how they can change you! →

A FORMULA FOR SUCCESS

We've designed a simple scrapbook "formula" to help you compile an album as quickly and easily as possible. The formula is simply your answers to a short set of questions that helps you determine the purpose and format of your album. Once it's completed, you can refer to the formula as you gather materials, design and create pages, and add updates in the future.

Below is the formula Robin Johnson of Farmington, Utah, completed to help her compile the beautiful friendship album featured here. The formula served as her roadmap, making completing the project a snap!

Purpose

1. **Q:** *Why am I making this album?*
   A: To capture details and memories about relationships with my friends (Figure A). I want to remember three specific things:

   Details. I want to record how and when we met and list "friendly facts" about each friend. If one of my friends is feeling blue, I want to know how I can cheer her up!

   Great Qualities. Each of my friends has contributed something to my life. I want to remember their unique qualities that inspire me to be a better person.

   Memories. I have had great friends in all the stages of my life. I want to remember what we did together and what our lives were like during that time.

Format

2. **Q:** *What size and style of album will I use?*
   A: I am using a 7¼" x 8½" Kolo binder (Figure B), so I can add more pages as my circle of friends grows.

3. **Q:** *What system will I use to organize my album?*
   A: Each spread in my album will feature a different friend.

4. **Q:** *What framework pages do I want/need in the album?*
   A: I just need a title page (Figure C).

5. **Q:** *What is my color scheme? (Attach color swatches here.)*
   A: I will use two tones of each of the following colors: green, mauve and cream (Figure D).

6. **Q:** *What decorative accents will I use? (Attach samples here.)*
   A: Sheer ribbon, vellum flower stickers, hand-made pockets and twine (Figure E)

7. **Q:** *How will I arrange my photos and journaling on the framework and filler pages to create a unified look and feel?*
   A: On each spread, the "friendly facts" list and three pockets (containing journaling on how we met, qualities and memories) will be on the left-hand page. A photo and each friend's name will be on the right-hand page. Working with my theme of a flower garden, each friend will have different flower accents and a decorative floral font (Figure F).

Preparation

8. **Q:** *Do I need to gather additional information (such as stories)?*
   A: I will interview each friend for the "friendly facts" lists and other information.

9. **Q:** *What photos do I need to complete the album?*
   A: I will need to find or take a picture of each friend.

Friendship Album by Robin Johnson. **Supplies** *Vellum:* The Paper Company; *Ribbon:* Offray; *Eyelets:* E-Z Set Eyelets, Coffee Break Design; *Album:* Kolo; *Computer fonts:* Garamond, WordPerfect; CK Flower Garden, CK Roses, CK Primary, CK Flower Power, CK Posies, CK Tulips and CK Wedding Rose, "The Art of Creative Lettering" CD; CK Script, "The Best of Creative Lettering" CD Vol. I, *Creating Keepsakes.*

C

friendship *is a*
GARDEN
whose growing season
never ends

D

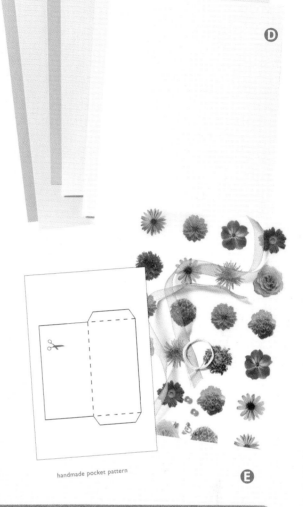

handmade pocket pattern

E

F

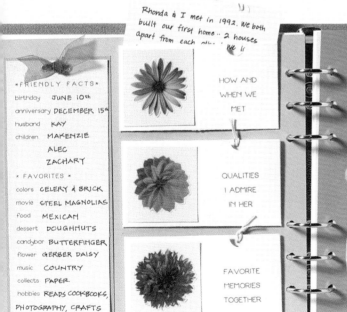

Rhonda & I met in 1992. We both
built our first home ... 2 houses
apart from each other ...

• FRIENDLY FACTS •

birthday   JUNE 10th
anniversary DECEMBER 15th
husband   KAY
children   MAKENZIE
            ALEC
            ZACHARY

• FAVORITES •

colors   CELERY & BRICK
movie   STEEL MAGNOLIAS
food   MEXICAN
dessert   DOUGHNUTS
candybar   BUTTERFINGER
flower   GERBER DAISY
music   COUNTRY
collects   PAPER
hobbies   READS COOKBOOKS,
PHOTOGRAPHY, CRAFTS

HOW AND
WHEN WE
MET

QUALITIES
I ADMIRE
IN HER

FAVORITE
MEMORIES
TOGETHER

RHONDA
salomon

moments

SOMEONE TO TELL IT TO
IS ONE OF THE FUNDAMENTAL
NEEDS OF HUMAN BEINGS.

MILES FRANKLIN

BY DEANNA LAMBSON

3 things
every album's gotta have

Wanna know a big secret? I know exactly how to make your albums more meaningful, in a day. No, I'm not a scrapbook magician. And it doesn't involve redesigning a single page. Wanna hear it? Your scrapbook needs a title, a dedication and a closing. That's it. That's the big secret.

Including these pages may seem natural for a theme album, but did you know it gives meaning and structure to a chronological scrapbook as well? Let's take a look at the albums in your scrapbook library. Perhaps you've got a chronological family album, a vacation scrapbook, or a book of heirloom heritage photos. Regardless of how you scrapbook or how many albums you have, you'd be amazed at the difference that these three simple pages can make. Just like your favorite novel, these three pages tell the reader what the book is about and why you created it, and it gives them (and you) a sense of accomplishment and completion when they've reached the end.

We've gathered a collection of pages to show you how the framework of a title, dedication, and closing can give meaning to every scrapbook. Wanna give it a try? It's easier than you think.

You'd never find an untitled book at the library. (And if you did, would you check it out?) A title tells the reader what they can expect to see when they look through your album. Surprisingly, it also gives direction to you, the scrapbook creator, as to what the scope of the album is. Is it a year in the life of your family? Is it a book about a special friend? (If you have albums without title pages, don't worry. You can always go back and add them.)

a book about me

Kim Haynes | Harrah, OK

Too often, you may be behind the camera instead of in front of it. Don't forget to tell your story too, as Kim did in this 8 x 8 album.

materials patterned paper (K & Company) • letter stickers (Wordsworth) • ribbon and heart accent (Making Memories) • Flea Market font (twopeasinabucket.com)

the rank's family album 2003

Michele Rank | Cerritos, CA

Every chronological family album deserves a title. Michele used 40 tightly cropped 1 x 2 photos of the year's highlights on her title page. What an inviting preview to what lies ahead!

materials metal rimmed tag (Close to My Heart) • CK Elegant font (Creating Keepsakes) • fibers • eyelets

ben's sports album

Jennifer Brookover | San Antonio, TX

Jennifer found this heartfelt poem on the Internet. Consider using a poem, quote or lyrics of a song on the title page of a theme album.

materials patterned paper (NRN Designs) • baseball eyelet (Making Memories) • CK Handprint font (Creating Keepsakes) • clip (Boxer Scrapbook Productions) • wire (Artistic Wire) • vellum • buttons • *photo by Kellie Ramotowski*

vacation 2003

Kathy Aiken | Minot, ND

A collage page is the perfect beginning for a vacation album. You can make one "from scratch," like Kathy's, or you can use one of the many full-page collage templates available. Notice how Kathy included photos of land-scapes, people and places from up close and from far away. Variety is the key.

materials brads • black pen

Make a dedication

2

More than any other page, your scrapbook needs a dedication. Why? First, when you look through a scrapbook you see photos and stories about whom? The subject! But a dedication is about you, the page creator. It connects you to readers with a golden thread. It allows them to see each page and each experience through your eyes.

Second, while a title page tells the reader "what" your scrapbook is about, the dedication page unlocks the mystery of "why." Why did you want to create this album? For whom did you create it? What do you hope they will come to understand through reading it? A dedication adds so much meaning to any album. Don't leave it out!

san francisco birthday

Deanna Lambson | Sandy, Utah

A dedication is the perfect place to explain your relationship to the subject of the album. I created a little gift album to celebrate a fantastic birthday spent in San Francisco with an old friend. I included a "then and now" picture on my dedication page to remind us both what we looked like in the good old days.

We met when we were 15 years old in Mrs. Moss' sophomore Kings and Queens class and discovered that we shared the same birthday. We've been best friends ever since. We celebrated all our birthdays together after that. There was the unforgettable sleepover, Miami Beach Birthday Cake, the square dancing in the driveway and the chickeroo. But since we went to college we've never lived in the same city and our birthdays were celebrated separately, sometimes with a phone call listening to Dan Fogelberg.

But our 40th birthday celebration really took the cake. Gary and Don (our sneaky husbands) surprised each of us separately with a trip to San Francisco for our birthday. Poor Ann thought she was stuck going to a family reunion all weekend! Imagine the look on our faces when we ran into each other at the Salt Lake airport. It was just the beginning of the best birthday ever!

m a t e r i a l s patterned paper (K & Company and Scrapbook Wizard) • rub-on words (Making Memories)

Simple Steps

Using rub-on words is a quick and easy way to achieve a hand-lettered look. This collection of rub-ons from Making Memories comes in a variety of themes and can be applied to any surface. Here's how to use them:

❶ Cut out the rub-on to be transferred.
❷ Remove the protective sheet and place in position.
❸ With the supplied stick, begin rubbing at one end and work toward the other. Continue until the printed design is completely transferred.
❹ Slowly lift the rub-on sheet.

Dear Aaron,

It is a couple of days before your 6th birthday. Tomorrow we will all be together to celebrate. I hope you have fun at your party with Matt and all of your friends! I'm sorry that I will miss it this year. I can't believe the time has passed so quickly because it really does seem like yesterday that we were at your mini-putt party.

The biggest thing I've noticed this year is just how much you have grown up. You are definitely not a "little" boy any more. You're getting taller each time we see you and your face has lost some of its round fullness it had when you were younger. You're off at school every day and influenced by many new people and places. You're a pretty cool and kind of goofy kid and Uncle Sean & I are having a lot of fun hanging out with you and watching you grow up. I hope you'll always be as excited to see us and spend time with us as you are now.

I've also been amazed at how much you remind me of your dad when he was little. You seem to like the same things he did. He loved playing store with me. He loved bowling. He loved game shows. He was an incredibly smart kid and you are too. You seem to really enjoy school and he did too. I guess those are things lots of kids like but your mannerisms are so similar to his that it takes me right back to when he & I were kids. You definitely look like him.

I'm so happy that you love your scrapbooks I made for you last year and I hope you'll love this one just as much as I loved making it for you. I've been very fortunate with this hobby that you've helped me find but the thing that makes it all worthwhile to me is watching you & Matt engrossed in your albums. I'm happy that you will gladly sit for hours and look through it. I'm glad that they remind you of so many good times we've had and the love we have for you. Despite your funny faces you make, you are a good sport in letting me take your picture so often and I hope you'll always be as willing to let me do so. This letter may be shorter this year but so much more of my thoughts throughout the past months have been captured in these pages. I just wish I had more time to record so many more of the moments we have shared.

As much as I am sad to see this year pass so quickly, I am looking forward to all of the adventures we will share when you are six! I love you so much Aaron! You bring so much joy and happiness to my life!

love aunt stace
xxoo

October 9/03

reminisce [rem´·e·nis] to think, talk or write about remembered events, usually with fondness

letter to aaron

Stacey Graglia | Oakville, ON, Canada

A dedication page doesn't have to include any photos at all. Just share your feelings about creating the album. Little Aaron receives a scrapbook from his Aunt Stace each year that begins with a letter especially to him. He'll never have to wonder how she feels about him. What a treasure!

materials patterned paper (KI Memories) • definition sticker (Making Memories) • Dateline font (Internet)

dedicated to BJ

Kneka Smith | Phoenix, AZ

This dedication page includes photos of the graduate's parents in their high school days. Because their photos were different (one was a color 8 x 10, the other a black-and-white 5 x 7), Kneka scanned the photos, resized them, and made them both black and white. The title on the main photo was created with letter stickers.

materials Papyrus and Lucida Calligraphy fonts (Internet) • stickers (EK Success and Wordsworth) • brads • metallic cord

3 Wrap up with a closing

Although your life will continue until the day you die, your album doesn't have to. Each scrapbook can be considered a chapter, an episode in the story of your life. A closing page gives a sense of completion to the reader and a great sense of accomplishment to you, the creator. It gives both of you a chance to pause and think about what has just been shared. Here's where you can tell the reader exactly what you hope they gain from viewing your album.

peaks and valleys

Tami Davis | Silverdale, WA

At the end of a chronological family album, Tami created a closing page that summarized some of the highlights and difficult times throughout the year. Just as a favorite novel includes a page "About the Author," don't forget to include a photo of yourself.

Dearest Family and friends,

Thank you for looking through our 2003 Family Album. It certainly has been a year of ups and downs. I was excited to move back to Washington at the beginning of the year, especially since Kris would be deployed for most of it. It's been so nice to be closer to our familes, especially to my Mom.

This year has taught me that being a Navy Wife is a very tough job when you have kids. Kris was gone for much of this year and I missed him terribly. Keeping up with the kids and the house had me busy though, and by the end of each day I was exhausted!

I was able to take a much-needed break during the summer and fly to Singapore for a few days. Kris and the USS Carl Vinson were there for a port call. I was thrilled that we could explore such a fascinating and beautiful city together.

Sadly, a month after I returned from Singapore, my Mom passed away. She had been battling congestive heart failure and during this year her health rapidly deteriorated. I was thankful to be near her this year and to be with her when she passed. I miss her so much.

I jumped for joy when we learned that the Vinson would return home earlier than planned. I appreciate Kris even more after being separated from him for eight months. I cherish the time we are all together as a "big family," in Alex's words.

I have really enjoyed putting together this scrapbook. I feel that I have found my "style" in designing layouts for you to enjoy. I have also begun to submit my layouts to scrapbook magazines and I am excited that some of my layouts have been selected for publication next year.

I am looking forward to what next year will bring and the memories that I will capture.

December 31, 2003

materials Jolee's Boutique flower stickers (EK Success) • CK Cursive title font (Creating Keepsakes) • Palatino title and Freestyle Script journaling fonts (Microsoft Word) • vellum • eyelets

next time

Christi Spodoni | Wrentham, MA

This is the closing page of Christi's album about a trip to San Diego. Like any trip to a new city, it was impossible to see and do everything. She made a list of the things she missed, so if by chance she visits again she'll know right where to start. (Gee, that reminds me of my only trip to Paris, where I never saw the Eiffel Tower. Oh well, maybe next time.)

materials Zig Millennium pen (EK Success) • postcard • chalk • colored pencil

the end

Candi Gershon | Fishers, IN

Perhaps those photos that you thought you couldn't possibly use in a scrapbook would be just perfect for "the end" of your scrapbook.

You put so much love and thought and creativity into your scrapbooks. A title, dedication and a closing are the finishing touches that make every scrapbook mean just a little bit more.

And in case you are wondering where is the closing of this article, this is it! (Don't you feel such a sense of completion?!)

materials patterned paper (Chatterbox, Inc.) • Sonnets letter stickers (Creative Imaginations) • ink (Clearsnap, Inc.) • Jolee's Boutique flower sticker (EK Success)

Here's an album that's got it all!

In 1985, Carrie Colbert took a family vacation through the Arizona desert to end up in sunny California. Believe it or not, she created all 16 pages of this 8 x 8 album in one night. The key was selecting coordinated paper that provided the entire color scheme and design, like this paper from SEI. Carrie's only other supplies were a few buttons and some rub-on words.

Even though the album is small, Carrie included a title page, a table of contents and a closing. In her closing she gives her perspective from almost 20 years after the vacation.

"I am so grateful that we all as a family were able to go on this trip together. We must always cherish these moments, because life is short. Time with family is so precious."

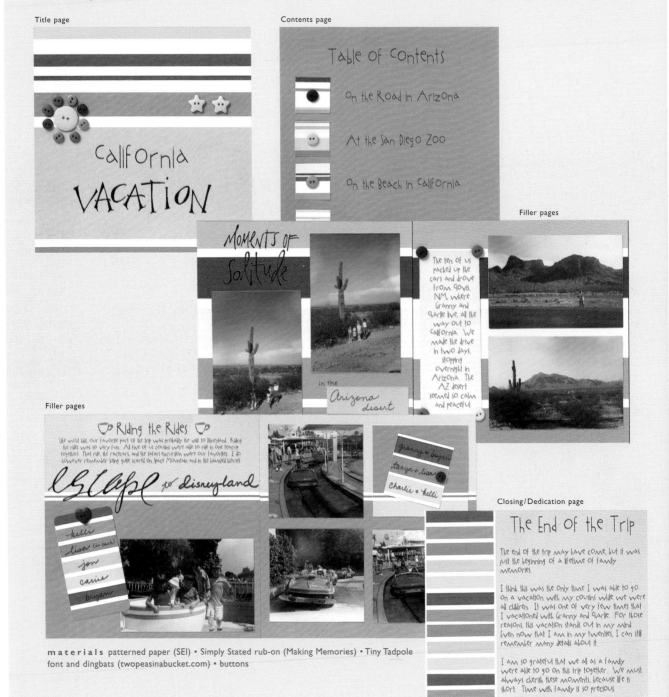

Title page

Contents page

Filler pages

Filler pages

Closing/Dedication page

materials patterned paper (SEI) • Simply Stated rub-on (Making Memories) • Tiny Tadpole font and dingbats (twopeasinabucket.com) • buttons

Simple Schemes

by Emily Tucker

Scrapbook Blueprints for Fast, Fabulous Pages

In just 48 hours, I completed an album…

When Stacy Julian first explained the concept of Simple Schemes to me, I had some reservations. Wouldn't they limit my creativity? Yet, I had to admit that sometimes I'd get so overwhelmed by having to come up with a design for my layouts, I'd often skip scrapping altogether.

And after 13 years of marriage, I had yet to begin my wedding album. Maybe this was the jump-start I needed. I studied the schemes and jotted down some ideas. Once I picked out my photos and got rolling, I was hooked. In just 48 hours, I completed an album I had been putting off for over a decade. And all it took was a few schemes!

Read on to discover the way schemes work, then see how eight designers used them to tackle weddings, birthdays, and graduations. You may find a scheme that's the perfect blueprint for building your own celebration pages.

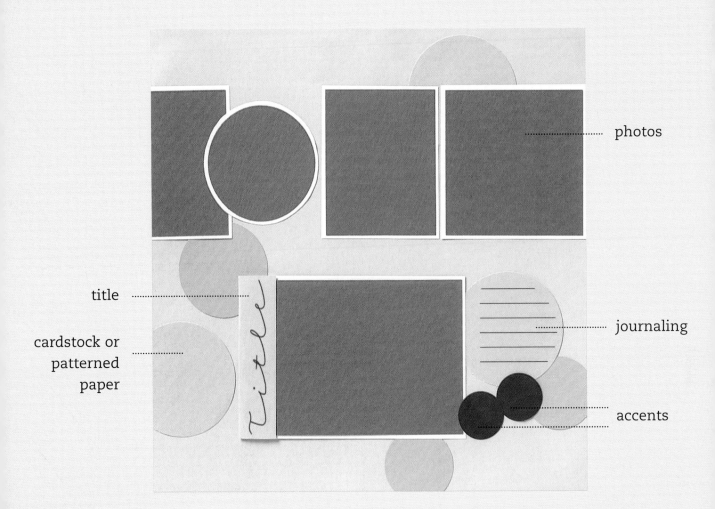

photos

title

cardstock or patterned paper

journaling

accents

 • various shades of cardstock or patterned paper

 • accents and embellishments

 • journaling

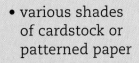 • title

 • photos, matted or unmatted

What's a Simple Scheme?

A *Simple Scheme* is a blueprint for a scrapbook page layout. The placement of all design elements is pre-determined; just plug your photos, title, journaling, and embellishments into the appropriate spots.

The beauty of a scheme is its versatility. Like blueprints for a model home, you can follow the plans exactly, or modify them to fit your needs. Either way, you'll save time and feel confident with your design.

Paper for schemes provided by The Printers Daughter (theprintersdaughter.com).

birthday date

Stacy Julian | Liberty Lake, WA

materials Alphadotz letters (Scrapworks)
• accents (Kangaroo & Joey) • colored pencils

chase is greight

Stacy Julian | Liberty Lake, WA

materials Bubble Type letters (Li'l Davis
Designs) • All About Me accents (Pebbles, Inc.)

variation on scheme

Love lies forever and belies the passage of time. It is what we take with us wherever we go.
—Flavia

scott & jenn

Allison Barnes | Las Vegas, NV

materials Jolee's Boutique rose stickers (EK Success) • Shotz letter stickers (Creative Imaginations) • CK Elegant font (Creating Keepsakes) • vellum

The four squares at the top of this scheme are a great place to include close-up photos, which can be matted together or separately. They can also be used to visually divide one photo into four equal parts. Using a strong color contrast on the title strip helps emphasize the lower photo as the focal point.

so proud

Barbara Carroll | Tucson, AZ

m a t e r i a l s   metal accents (Making Memories) • patterned paper (Karen Foster Design) • stamp (Hero Arts) • ink (Clearsnap, Inc.) • MA Sexy title font and Halvett Condensed journaling font (Internet) • Boulevard "CDO" font (two-peasinabucket.com)

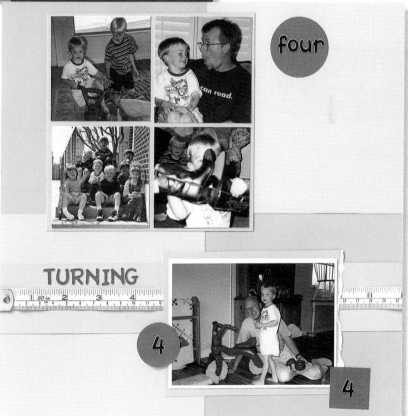

turning four

Wendy Smedley | Bountiful, UT

m a t e r i a l s   letter stickers (Scrap Pagerz)
• shape stickers (The Scrapbook Wizard)
• measuring tape

September 26, 1998.
This is the day
that I, Tonya Kay
Parkin, have chosen
to pledge my
love and devotion
to Chad LaDaw
for all time and
eternity.... in
the Bountiful,
Utah Temple.

Our family

love

Kris Parkin | Centerville, UT

materials patterned paper (Earthmade Paper Company) • silver cord • heart brad (Making Memories) • charm

Using a scheme is a great way to cure scrapper's block. Limiting design choices frees you from over-analyzing every decision, and it stimulates creativity. On this scheme, two circular photos and circular accents are placed in a visual triangle to lead the eye and establish a sense of balance, regardless of the photos and colors used.

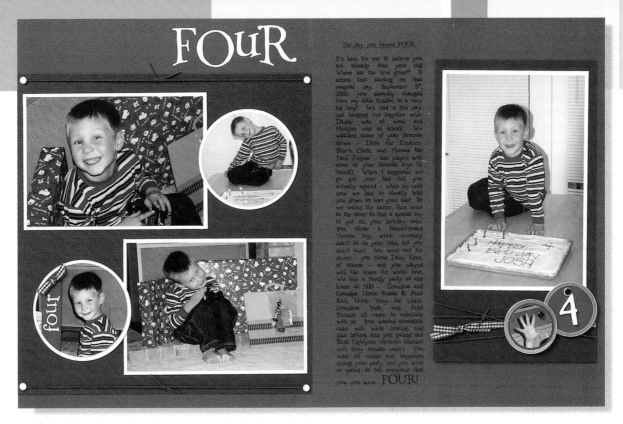

FOUR

The day you turned FOUR

It's hard for me to believe you are already four year old! Where has the time gone? It seems that starting on that magical day, September 3rd, 2003, you instantly changed from my little toddler, to a very big boy! We had a fun day, just hanging out together while Daddy was at work and Meagan was at school. We watched some of your favorite shows - Dora the Explorer, Blue's Clues, and Thomas the Tank Engine - and played with some of your favorite toys (ie trains)! When I suggested we go get your hair cut, you actually agreed - when up until now we had to literally hold you down to trim your hair. So we visited the barber, then went to the store to find a special toy to put on your birthday cake. You chose a flannel-board Thomas toy, which obviously didn't fit on your cake, but you didn't care! We went out for dinner - you chose Daisy Keen of course - and you played with the trains the whole time. We had a family party at our house at 7:00 - Grandma and Grandpa, Uncle Ruslin & Aunt Karli, Uncle Tony, the Lukes, Grandma Vida, and Aunt Rhonda all came to celebrate with us. You wanted chocolate cake with white frosting and blue letters and you picked out Buzz Lightyear icecream (sherbet with fizzy candies inside). You were all smiles and happiness during your party, and you were so proud to tell everyone that now you were FOUR!

four

Wendy Sue Anderson | Heber City, UT

materials Sonnets letter stickers (Creative Imaginations) • Flea Market font (twopeasinabucket.com) • eyelets • metal charm "4" (Making Memories) • ribbon • jute • metal-rimmed tags

troy's graduation

Kris Parkin | Centerville, UT

materials fibers • graduation stickers

Mom and Dad

Troy Parkin

June 3, 1995

Grandpa and Grandma Adkins

Troy graduated with honors from Viewmont High School on June 3, 1995, and was awarded a scholarship to Snow College. It was a privilege to celebrate Troy's successes. He excelled in his AP classes, worked at Bob's Deli and fulfilled a leadership position at church. Congratulations, Troy!

emily & ben

MaryRuth Francks | Spokane, WA

m a t e r i a l s patterned paper (C-Thru Ruler Co.)
• Scriptina title font (Internet) • CK Flourish journaling
font (Creating Keepsakes) • vellum • chalk • brads

Modify a scheme to fit your needs.
Note how Tara turned the right half
of this scheme ninety degrees so
her pictures run horizontally, while
Julie varied the sizes of her photos.
Combinations of cardstock and patterned paper replace the values of
blue in these schemes as the background of the layouts. Caution:
don't let your paper choices overpower the other elements.

happy 90th birthday!

Julie Parker | Cedar Hill, TN

m a t e r i a l s patterned paper (Colors by Design) • photo corners (3L Corp.) • Sticko number stickers (EK Success) • Bickley Script font (internet)

graduation: reflecting

Tara Cowper | Dayton, MD

m a t e r i a l s patterned paper (Kopp Design) • letter stickers (Sticker Studio) • Zig Writer pen (EK Success) • brads

title page

table of contents

filler photo

section page

filler journaling

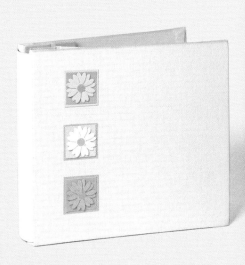

title page

table of contents

section page

filler photo

filler journaling

A Scheme and a Theme

Make a Simple Scrapbook This Weekend

While I love the professional photographs from our wedding, I find myself looking back most fondly at the candid shots taken by our family and friends. They seem to better capture the spirit of the occasion: fun, casual, and full of sentimentality. I wanted to gather those pictures to tell all the behind-the- scenes stories that made our wedding special. By using this 6 x 6 album scheme along with the *Simple Scrapbooks* formula, I was able to put together a meaningful wedding keepsake in just a weekend.

Emily Tucker | Matthews, NC

m a t e r i a l s   Zig Writer pen (EK Success) • daisy punch (Family Treasures, Inc.)

Cropping Magic

© Anne Erdman

Better photos make better pages

You know how it is: You rush to the photo lab to pick up photographs you've been dying to scrapbook. You rip open the envelopes even before you reach the car, anxious to check out the pictures—then your heart sinks. There's your daughter, way down in the corner of the photo, with a bunch of people you don't even know milling around in the background. And the photo of your son at the soccer game is so busy, your eye doesn't know where to look.

Don't despair! Most of these photos can be salvaged with a bit of artful cropping. Photo cropping is one of the fundamentals of great scrapbook design, because after all, photos are the "stars" of the pages. When you crop a photo, you select the best part and cut away the rest. You'll isolate what you wanted to capture on film, and get rid of distracting background elements. All you need to know are three basic techniques: focus, movement, and enlarging.

by lori robb

before

The more you use your viewfinder (see facing page for instructions), and learn what makes a pleasing composition, the more proficient you will become at "pre-cropping" through your camera's viewfinder.

1. Focus

Cropping a photo to remove distracting background details will focus attention on the main subject of your picture. Your focal point will then become more obvious and will attract and hold the viewer's eye.

Take a look at the "before" photo above. While I love my daughter's soccer coach, he's a distraction in this photo. Let's use an easy homemade viewfinder to crop him out!

after

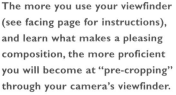

1 Place half of the viewfinder on the photo, making sure to cover the coach in the upper left corner.

2 "Ground" the subject by sliding the bottom part of the viewfinder directly under her foot, so she doesn't appear to be "floating" in the middle of the photo.

3 Look at the rest of the photo to see what else could be cropped out. Slide the top half of the viewfinder down just enough to crop out the basketball hoop sitting right above the subject's head, and slide the bottom half to the left to remove the distracting pole behind the goal.

4 With a photo-safe pen, carefully mark cutting guide-lines along the inside edges of the viewfinder.

5 Crop the photo along the guidelines.

The result? A well-balanced photo with a clear focal point and fewer distracting details in the background.

I cropped these pictures to better focus on the main subjects of the photos, and the resulting images are much more engaging.

How To Make a Viewfinder

A viewfinder is a simple tool that will help you improve the composition of your photos. Here's how to make one:

1 Cut an 8½ x 8½ inch square out of heavy cardstock.

2 Draw a line one inch in from the edge of the cardstock; repeat for all sides.

3 Cut from one corner to the opposite corner along the diagonal, dividing the card into two triangles.

4 Cut along the one inch lines, being careful not to cut beyond the pencil corners where the lines intersect.

When you are finished, you will have two L-shaped cardstock pieces that can "frame" a standard 4 x 6 or smaller photo. You'll find your viewfinder to be an invaluable tool in helping you create well-balanced compositions.

2. Movement: Suggesting the Action

Where you place the subject of your picture can greatly influence how you view what's happening. In the first cropped photo, my daughter looks as if she has just finished walking across the log fence. In the second, she seems to have just started. Placing her at the edge of the photograph instead of near the middle adds a sense of movement to an otherwise static shot. Experiment to see how cropping changes action and movement.

Do you have multiple pictures that you want cut to the same size? A square punch works well, but if you don't have one, use paper clips to hold the ends of your viewfinder window in place, and use it as a guide to mark each of your photos.

after

3. Enlarging

Occasionally I have cropped a photo, only to make it too small to be usable. If the focus of your photo is very small, use your viewfinder to frame and mark it, and then have it enlarged at your local photofinisher. I used this technique to create a lovely close-up photo of my daughter's face. It was so easy, and my viewfinder helped me decide exactly where I needed it to be cropped.

When cropping portraits, place your subject's eyes in the top third of the photo.

materials patterned paper (SEI) • brads • mini tag • *page by Darci Dowdle*

Put It To Work

Cropping is a skill that yields a big payoff with little effort. Let's look at a few well-cropped photos used in an actual layout. Not only can you use more photos on your page, but the photos themselves are more focused and dynamic. The four photos of Darci's son, Ty, clearly illustrate the benefit of removing distracting background details (extra fence, large expanses of cement or skyline, a row of rivets).

Spend some time improving your photos through cropping, and your pages will begin to look cleaner and less cluttered in no time.

color magic

CAST ITS SPELL ON YOUR NEXT PAGE

BY
STACY JULIAN

ILLUSTRATION BY
LISA ZADOR

No doubt about it, color has an irresistible power. It's the one thing that every scrapbooker needs to make her photos sing and her story come to life. Color is captivating and beautiful, it's exciting and emotional, and unfortunately, it's also a little scary.

I mean, how in the world are you supposed to know with any kind of certainty that you're selecting the best colors for your pages? We talk a lot about the color wheel. We toss around definitions and properties and formulas. And yet there's still that moment when you're ready to start a new page—your photos spread out in front of you—when you wish a little fairy would suddenly appear, wave her starry wand, and tell you just which hues you should use.

I know; I've wished for her too. And while she's never come, and I can't promise you any pixie dust, I can share three things I've learned about color that will help you turn some of the mystery into magic on your very next page. →

Figure 2. Red-orange is one third of a triadic color scheme, with yellow-green and blue-violet comprising the other two thirds. On this layout, Renee used yellow-green as her main color, and the other two colors as accents. *Page by Renee Camacho.* **Supplies** *Page accents:* Paper Fever; *Mesh:* Magic Mesh; *Glitter:* Magic Scraps; *Other:* Slide holders.

Figure 1. Red, red-orange, orange and yellow: four colors that sit adjacent on the color wheel create a vibrant, analogous color scheme. Keep in mind, if you want to use strong colors on your pages, you need strong, clear photographs. This close-up photo is visually strong enough to retain focalpoint status against a robust color scheme. *Page by Renee Camacho.* **Supplies** *Cardstock:* Canson; *Stickers:* StickyPix, Paper House Productions; *Pen:* Zig Millennium, EK Success.

1. | There's no such thing as the **perfect color** combination.

Really. Once I decided to accept this fact, I felt so relieved. You have a ton of photographs and you love to scrapbook, so grab your next focal-point photo, hold it up against several colors and pick one. It's that easy. Pick the one that makes you feel like scrapping right now, and then get busy. You may not pick the same color today that you would pick next Tuesday, and that's OK.

Renee Camacho of Nashville, Tennessee, created the beautifully bold page in Figure 1 and submitted it for publication. I loved it so much, I called and asked her to use the same picture again, only this time with a totally different color scheme (Figure 2). Renee actually liked the new version better!

If you're spending too much time trying to discover the one "perfect" color combination, relax a little. Let yourself experiment with lots of different colors, and be careful limiting your palette (and your creativity) with statements like "I just don't use bright colors" or "Neutral colors are boring." Your confidence with color will increase as you allow yourself to play and have fun. The good news is, color is a personal decision and no matter what anyone tells you (me included), you don't have to like or dislike any one combination. Listen and learn, and then be true to yourself!

Try This: Each time you begin a new page, ask yourself "What is my key message?" Jot down the first two descriptive words that come to mind. Use these words to gauge the effectiveness of each color you introduce to your design. If a color enhances the mood you're trying to convey, it passes the test; if not, try again!

King Triton's Carousel is the most beautiful ride to look at in the park. The animals on the ride are exquisitely painted. I love the rich, bright colours and I love to watch the girls ride round and round as the beautiful colours swish by!

2. | Color communicates.

This we know. So, what is it you really want to say with your photos? Remember, each color you introduce to your design will either add to or detract from this key message. In my opinion, there are two properties of color that most strongly influence its ability to communicate an emotion or mood. One is value, how light or dark a color is, and the other is temperature, the general feeling of either warmth or coolness in a color. The more comfortable you are identifying these properties in colors, the better you will be at selecting the colors you need to communicate a particular message (see the sidebar

"What Are You Trying to Say?" on pages 50 and 51).

When Debra Wilcox of Farmington, Utah, sat down to scrapbook photos of her daughter riding King Triton's Carousel, she wanted to celebrate the excitement of a child in the midst of an enchanting theme park. The mixture of warm and cool in the carousel's bright blues, pinks and yellows, along with the playful polka dot and swirl patterns, communicates the commotion of such a thrilling ride (Figure 3).

Figure 3. Use color and pattern to communicate the emotion of your photos. Here, repeating the bright colors and varied patterns in opposite locations on the workspace provides a sense of balance. *Pages by Debra Wilcox.* **Supplies** *Patterned paper:* Kangaroo & Joey (blue and yellow polka dot), Paper Fever; *Paper frame:* My Mind's Eye; *Buttons:* Buttons Galore; *Fibers:* On the Surface; *Computer font:* Brush Strokes, Chatterbox.

what are you trying to say?

The cool gray on this layout has underlying tones of blue. Neutrals like this provide a low-contrast backdrop for the simplicity of black-and-white photos. *Page by Donna Downey.* **Supplies** *Cardstock and vellum:* Bazzill Basics; *Envelope die cut:* Ellison; *Duck punch:* Paper Shapers, EK Success; *Fasteners:* Boxer Scrapbook Productions (brad), Making Memories (square eyelet); *Pen:* Gel Stylus, Y&C; *Computer fonts:* Think Small and Bad Hair Day, downloaded from *two-peasinabucket.com; Dog tag and chain:* Chronicle Books.

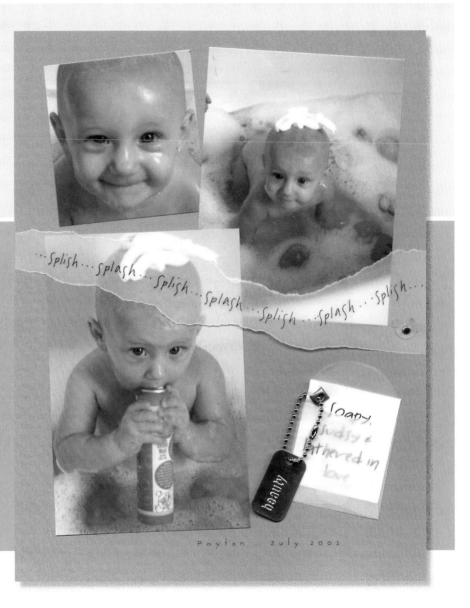

The value and temperature of a color go a long way in determining what message it will convey on your page. When working with color, keep these guidelines in mind:

Warm colors denote warmth, and bring a cheerful exuberance to a composition. Edgy and energetic, they come forward with vibrancy.

Cool colors denote coolness, and look calm, clean and inviting. Reflective of nature, they recede and are restful.

Mixed colors lend a smart, stylish feel to the simple lines of this layout. *Page by Donna Downey.*
Supplies *Cardstock:* Bazzill Basics; *Vellum tag:* Making Memories; *Computer fonts:* Dragonfly, Think Small and Picnic Basket, downloaded from *twopeasinabucket.com*; *Dried flower:* Botanicals, SEI.

Neutrals, such as white, cream, beige, gray, brown and black, often have undertones of color that influence whether they appear warm or cool (see layout at left). Neutral colors can add subtle interest and stability to nearly any color combination.

Mid-range values are strong and confident. They denote youth and action. However, mid-range colors combined with black and white make a bold statement that may overpower a weaker photograph. Gray, taupe and off-white are pleasing neutrals for this range.

Light values, or pastels, open up a space and make it seem larger. They are restful, light and airy. They seem soft and are often associated with newness (think babies and spring).

Dark values, or jewel tones, are considered conservative, powerful and authoritative. They close up space and make it seem smaller. Black and charcoal are good choices for neutral additions to these traditional colors.

Mixed colors, or tertiary colors, are the result of combining a primary color with a secondary color. The more colors that are mixed with each other, the more sophisticated or chic they become. Mixed colors enjoy the crisp, clean contrast of neutral accents in white or black (see layout above).

Color combinations that are balanced on a color wheel will add a sense of balance to your scrapbook page. Colors that share the same value range on a color wheel are in harmony with each other and will lend a harmonious feeling to your composition as well.

Figure 4. The subtle contrast between warm analogous colors creates an inviting mood. *Page by Debra Wilcox.* **Supplies** *Patterned paper:* Scrap-Ease; *Stickers:* Hallmark; *Computer font:* Vivaldi, downloaded from the Internet.

Figure 5. Brrrr. Carolyn's monochromatic blue color scheme evokes the icy feel of these photos. *Page by Carolyn Davis.* **Supplies** *Specialty papers:* Paper Adventures (vellum and velveteen); *Square punch:* Fiskars; *Computer font:* Fancy Footwork, package unknown; *Other:* Organdy ribbon.

Contrast the feeling of this layout with the page Debra created about a special place her daughter loves to visit (Figure 4). Here, the values of the yellow, orange and green are toned down to a rich, earthy range that says this is a warm, friendly place to be. The white journaling block and light-yellow mat provide just enough contrast to emphasize the words and photo, supporting the bright, yet comfortable feeling of sunlight streaming in through a window.

I start to shiver just looking at Carolyn Davis's "Snow Baby" layout in Figure 5. She used a monochromatic color scheme that stems from the medium blue in her baby's pants and features a range of light, icy values that create a chilly feeling well-suited to her photos' wintry theme. The cool blues are a perfect contrast to baby's pink, wind-kissed cheeks.

3. | Using a color wheel can help!

The colors on a color wheel have a scientific basis. Their sequence isn't haphazard, but rather an ordered placement that occurs naturally in a spectrum of light. When you use a color wheel to guide your selection of color combinations, you can rest assured that your choices will be based on proven principles of balance and harmony.

Figure 6. A light yellow-orange completed this triadic color scheme. Stacy used it in her decorative accents to bring a sense of balance to the design. *Page by Stacy Julian.* **Supplies** *Cardstock:* Paper Reflections, DMD Industries (white corrugated), Close To My Heart (blue and lavender); *Tag:* Paper Reflections, DMD Industries; *Rubber stamp and stamping ink:* Close To My Heart; *Pen:* Zig Millennium, EK Success; *Buttons:* Making Memories; *Craft wire:* Stampin' Up!; *Metal letter tiles:* Global Solutions.

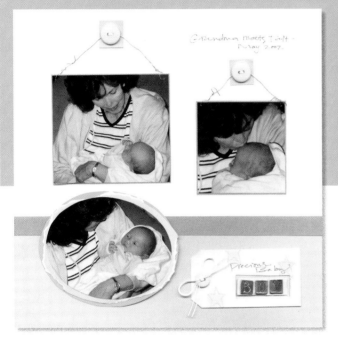

Figure 7. A good color wheel features a spectrum of 12 colors in several different values, as well as a guide to help you create successful color combinations for your pages. **Supplies** *Color wheel:* Rainbow Color Selector, K1C2, EK Success.

And using a color wheel isn't difficult. After I've selected a color or two from my photographs that I know I want to repeat on my page, I find those colors on my color wheel. Then I can easily see if and how these colors are related to each other, and discover other colors that might work well in my composition.

When I created the page in Figure 6, I knew I wanted to repeat the soft colors in my mom's and son's clothing. I started by placing my photo under various windows in my color wheel until I found the blue-green and red-violet families that most closely matched them. The movable guide on my color wheel (Figure 7) helped me see that the colors in my photo are part of a triadic, or three-color, combination. The color that completes this triad is a yellow-orange, also in the pastel range. Blue-green, red-violet and yellow-orange are each separated from each other by three other colors. They are equidistant on the wheel. When I introduce a

yellow-orange as an accent on my page, it adds a sense of balance to my design. These touches of yellow also bring a warmth to my composition that mimics the warm skin tones in my photos.

The color wheel truly is a handy tool that can assist you in selecting color schemes, both for individual pages and entire albums. Be sure to read the information on your specific wheel and become familiar with its markings and guides.

The next time you find yourself wishing for a visit from the color fairy, remember these three things:

1. There is more than one color combination that will work on any page.
2. Color will help you communicate what is really in your heart.
3. You can use your color wheel to take the guesswork out of combining colors.

Color is magic! It can make a page pop, sizzle, soothe or charm. It's the easiest way to express your personal style and communicate the mood and emotion of your photographs. Sure, there is much to know, but it needn't be scary. We're out to ease your color fears and teach you tips and tricks for creating spellbinding pages every time. →

using a color wheel

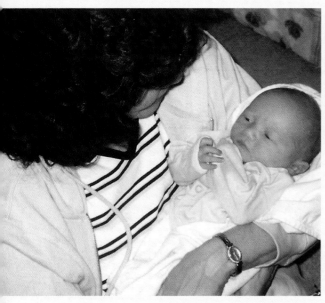

Step 1. Select one or two colors from your photos. I chose to repeat both the light turquoise color in my son's nightgown and the lavender in my mom's jacket.

Step 2. Locate your colors on the color wheel. My colors fall into the blue-green and red-violet families, in the pastel range.

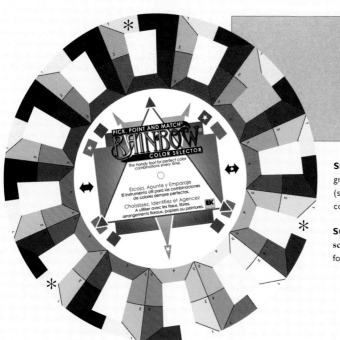

Step 3. Determine the relationship between these colors. Blue-green and red-violet are two parts of a three-color triadic scheme (see stars on color wheel). A pastel yellow-orange is the color that completes the triad.

Step 4. Choose papers and decorative elements in your color-scheme. Don't fret if you can't find the exact values you're looking for—most of the time, close is good enough.

Ready

Set

Click!

MAKE YOUR

FIRST DIGITAL PAGE

IN 30 MINUTES

OR LESS.

by Renee Pearson

What's the most-used item in your scrapbooking toolbox? A favorite set of pens? Your Xyron machine? How about that essential paper cutter? For me, it's my computer.

As a freelance graphic artist, I spend my days creating digital designs for business clients. So it's natural for me to think of my computer first when working on my own scrapbook pages. While digital page layouts are great time- and cost-savers, I get the biggest kick out of combining both scrapbooking worlds—digital and traditional—to make my own one-of-a-kind page elements.

If you've felt limited to using your computer for page titles and journaling, read on. I'll show you how to make your first digital page using simple shapes and tools in Adobe Photoshop Elements 2.0.

These instructions work the same for Windows or Mac. They'll also work in Elements' big brother, Adobe Photoshop 7.0. This exercise is designed to teach you some of the basics of digital design—use the tools you learn here to experiment with your own layouts. Ready? Let's get started!

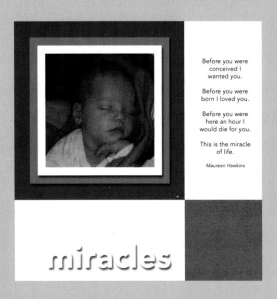

Make this simple
page in four easy steps.

What you need:

One digital photo
    (At least 300 dpi, 3½" x 3½")
Adobe Photoshop Elements 2.0
    (Download a free trial version at adobe.com)

Step 1: Make the color-blocked background

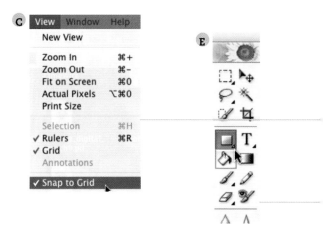

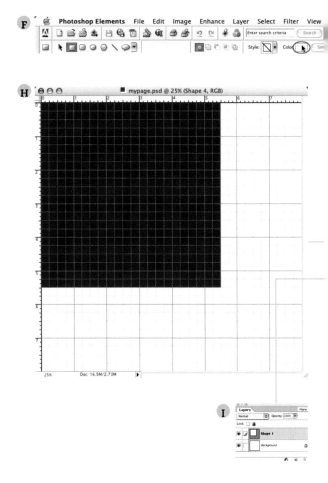

The page you're about to build is called an "image" in Adobe Photoshop Elements 2.0. To start, choose File > New from the menu bar (A). In the dialog box (B), give your image a name. Then, make sure Width and Height are displayed in inches (not pixels) and enter an "8" in both boxes. Your Resolution should be 300 pixels/inch, and your Mode should be RGB Color. Click OK.

Rulers and grids help to precisely position items. Make sure rulers and grids are visible by choosing View > Rulers. Then, choose View > Grid and, finally, choose View > Snap to Grid (C). These commands toggle; to turn them off simply choose them again. Your image should look like figure D.

Use Photoshop Elements' shape tools (E) to draw rectangles, ellipses, circles and other shapes in your image. To draw the first color block, choose the rectangle shape tool from the toolbox. Click the color box (F) in the options bar (just below the menu bar) and enter the color's RGB values in the Color Picker window (G). Enter R:34, G:63, B:66. Click OK.

Tip: You can also choose colors by clicking inside the color field or the color slider in the Color Picker window. The numerical color values will automatically change to reflect the new color selection.

Beginning at the upper left corner of the image, draw a 5 ½-inch square (H) with the rectangle tool. You should have two layers in the Layers palette (I), and your image should now look like this. (If you don't see a Layers palette on your screen, click Window > Layers.)

Draw a 2 1/2-inch square in the lower right corner of your image (J). Click the color box again (K) and enter R:255, G:65, B:5.

Your color-blocked background is now complete (J). Save your file by choosing File > Save.

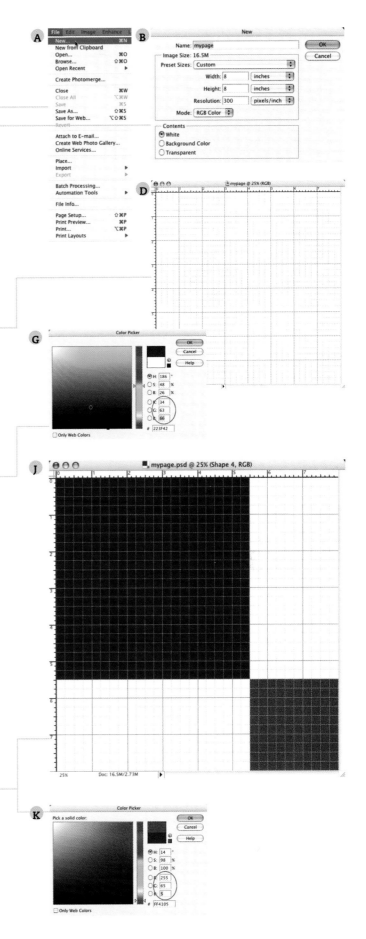

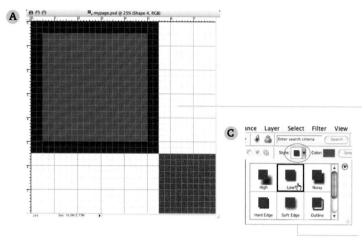

A

C

Step 2: Create the two '3-D' photo mats

With the rectangle tool still selected, draw a 4½-inch square beginning ½ inch from the top left corner of the image (A). Click the color box in the options bar (B) and enter R:67, G:120, B:126.

Now let's apply a drop shadow to the mat. Click the down arrow next to the Style box in the options bar (C). (If your choices don't look like ours, click the round arrow button on the right and choose Drop Shadows.) Then choose the shadow style you prefer. I chose Low. *Voilá!*—instant depth.

Draw a 4-inch square beginning ¾ inch from the top left corner of the image. Click the color box and enter R:255, G:255, B:255. Notice that the drop shadow is still selected on the options bar, saving you a step. Your image should now look like figure D.

Save your file by choosing File > Save.

B

Color Picker

Select background color:

OK
Cancel
Help

H: 186 °
S: 47 %
B: 49 %
R: 67
G: 120
B: 126

43787E

☐ Only Web Colors

D

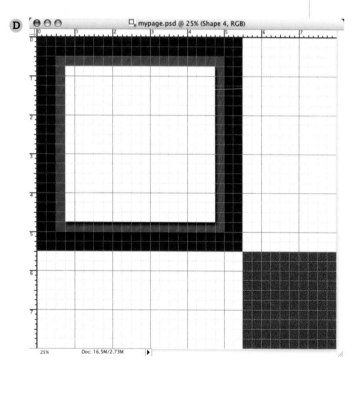

K

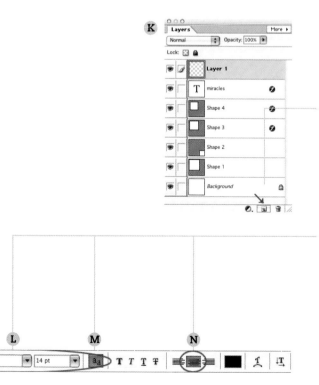

L **M** **N**

Step 3: Add the title and journaling text

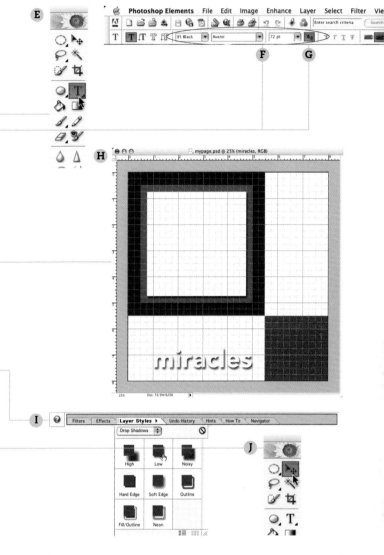

Choose the horizontal type tool from the toolbox on the left of your screen (E). Then, in the options bar (F), choose a font and size. (I used Avenir 95 Black at 72 points.) Also, click the anti-alias button (G); this feature produces smooth-edged type. Change the text color to white by clicking the color box and entering R:255, G:255, B:255.

Type your page title in the image window near its final position (H). If you clicked inside the white area, you won't see your title yet because it's the same color as the background—white. Next we'll add a drop shadow to the title.

Click the Layer Styles tab in the palette well in the upper right below the menu bar (I). Select Drop Shadows from the menu. Click Low.

Choose the Move tool from the toolbox (J). To position the title, click and hold the left mouse button while moving the title. Your title now has just enough emphasis without overpowering the focal point, your photo.

The journaling is next. First, add a new layer by clicking the New Layer button at the bottom of the Layers palette (K). (If your Layers palette doesn't show on the screen, click Window > Layers, then click the New Layer button.)

Next, make sure the horizontal type tool is still selected. In the options bar, select the font and size. I used 14 point Avenir 45 Book (L). Also, click the anti-alias (M) and the center text (N) buttons. (For black text, enter R:0, G:0, B:0 in the color box.)

Now start typing your journaling text in the image window (O)—Elements' type tool works much like a standard word processor. Use your enter/return key to control the line lengths. When you're finished typing, choose the Move tool from the toolbox (J) and position your journaling text if necessary. Now all you need to do is add your photo.

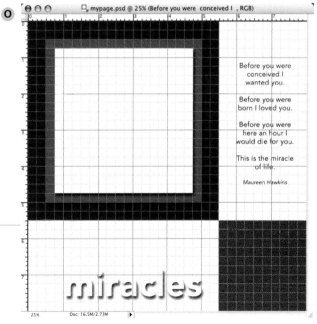

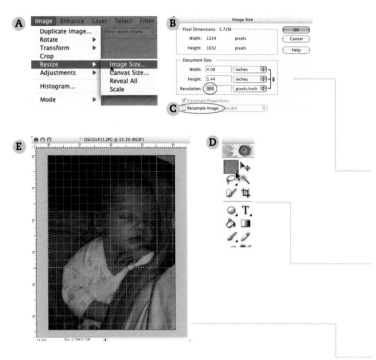

Step 4: Drop in your photograph

To drop in a photograph, choose File > Open and browse for your desired image. Your photo will open in a separate window. Now check the resolution by choosing Image > Resize > Image Size (A). Set your Resolution to 300 pixels/inch (B), and make sure Resample Image is off (C).

If your image is larger than 3½ inches square, you'll need to digitally lift a portion of it for your new page layout. To do that, choose the Rectangular Marquee Tool in the toolbox (D).

Using the ruler and grid as guides, draw a 3½-inch square, starting in the upper left corner (E). You should now have a 3½-inch square selection of "dancing ants." Now, with the marquee tool still selected, move the selection with your mouse or the arrow keys until it's positioned over the area of the photo you want to use (F).

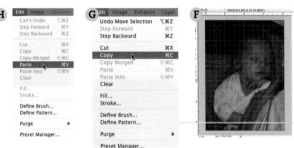

Copy just that portion by choosing Edit > Copy (G). Close the photo window and go back to your page layout. Paste the photo in your image window by choosing Copy > Paste (H). (If your image ends up behind your color blocks, go to your Layers palette and drag your photo layer to the top of the list.)

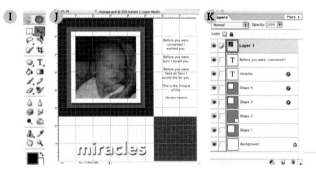

Now, choose the Move tool from the toolbox (I) and move the photo until it's centered over your mats, as pictured (J). Your Layers palette should look similar to figure K.

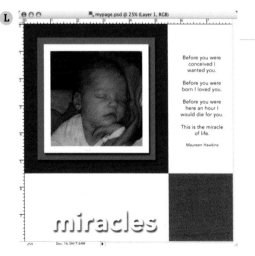

Choose View > Grid to turn off the grid and admire your handiwork (L). Save your file. That's it! You're done!

Use these techniques to create your own custom color-blocked pages. Experiment with the various shape tools to add interest and variety to your digital page layouts. With digital scrapbooking, the possibilities are truly endless.

materials: Adobe Photoshop Elements 2.0 (Adobe Systems Incorporated) • Avenir title and journaling font (Linotype Library) • *page by Renee Pearson*

Fontastic!

TYPE THE WORD "FONT" into any search engine and you'll be bombarded with thousands of Web sites, each one containing hundreds of type families. At *Simple Scrapbooks,* we love to make your life easier, so we navigated our way through all the "type hype" and found fifteen versatile fonts. These multi-use varieties—with serif and *sans*—will work for most any scrapbook topic, from birthdays and retirement parties to vacations and heritage pages. We've even created an exclusive font just for you. Make it yours at *simplescrapbooksmag.com!* Take an afternoon to download this and the other free fonts to your collection. Your design work will be letter perfect.

FONT	SOURCE	USAGE
Girls are Weird	momscorner4kids.com	whimsical headline
Space Toaster	scrapvillage.com	playful headline
Beautiful	dafonts.com	elegant headline
Little days	momscorner4kids.com	delicate headline or journaling
Caslon Antique	abstractfonts.com	heritage headline and journaling
COLLEGIATE	mouserfonts.com	masculine, sporty headline
Modern	Microsoft Word	classic, traditional journaling
CAC Shishoni	scrapvillage.com	fanciful headline
Garamond	Microsoft word	versatile journaling
Impact	Microsoft word	dynamic headline
Butterbropapier	scrapvillage.com	vintage headline and journaling
PUNCH LABEL	abstractfonts.com	contemporary headline
Marydale	scrapbookvillage.com	casual headline and journaling
LD Reversed	inspiregraphics.com	funky, playful headline
SS Whimsy	simplescrapbooksmag.com	casual headline and journaling

sometimes

I'll admit it—many a day passes when I feel as though I may truly lose my mind as a stay-at-home mom. I can almost hear the sirens wailing as they approach Sheldon Street to take me to my new home, complete with padded walls, group therapy and three hot meals a day...

But more days pass when I think—no, I know—that I am absolutely the most fortunate person to ever be placed on this planet because I get to bask everyday in the glorious, sometimes insane glow and noise that is you, Coley.

How's that for blessed and lucky?

Straight to the Point

Follow these concise Typography 101 pointers for a professional look:

- Use 11 to 13 point for journaling.
- Use 60 point for title.
- Keep the title short for readability.
- Include no more than three font types on a page.
- Select 1.5-inch line spacing.

materials patterned paper (KI Memories)
• Details Four ribbon charm (Making Memories)
• Marydale font (Internet) • *page by Cathy Zielske*

Simple Scrapbooks editorial board member Cathy Zielske, font expert and writer of our Font 411 column, says: "Typography is as much a part of the artistic process in scrapbooking as choosing your paper and embellishments. It truly has the power to transform your layout."

materials Times New Roman font (Microsoft Word)
• paper flowers (Savvy Stamps) • *page by Cathy Zielske*

"I wish there was no such things as bedtime or school so you could play every second of your life!"—*Miss Aidan at seven*

And Aidan, I wish I could capture every fabulous thing you say, but if I attempted to, I would have volumes of notebooks and papers in my efforts to keep up with all of the clever, funny and original things you say! And it's not just what you say, it's how you say it. You are the queen of the overstatement, and I absolutely love that about you. Still, I need to do exactly what I did today: you said it, I scrambled to find a piece of paper to write it down. These are the little pieces of you that I never, ever want to forget.

I wish

10.28.03

The Rules of Alignment

YOU'VE JUST TYPED IN YOUR JOURNAL-ING BLOCK, and now the moment of truth: Do I center it? Justify it? Align it to the left? The alignment you choose will affect how someone reads your words. Here are some general guidelines to help you decide.

Align to the left when you have a large journaling block. Why? A left aligned text block, (also called "ragged right") is the easiest of all alignment styles to read, especially when you have lots of text. For this reason, most magazines format their text using a left alignment. When in doubt, align to the left. The journaling on my layout here has many lines, so I used a left alignment to enhance readability.

Centering your text is OK if you have brief text. Centering is great when you are using a quote or other journaling with eight lines or less. Pay attention to your line lengths. Centered text blocks look more appealing when the line lengths vary, fully emphasizing the centered alignment.

Justify your text with caution! Justifying text, or forcing each line to be the same length, is tricky. Why? Because inevitably some lines will have fewer words, thereby causing them to appear more spaced out than others and allowing for larger gaps between words. This creates an uneven, discordant look. If you have similar-sized words, or you're comfortable shifting words from line to line to adjust the number of words per line, give it a try.

you don't like to smile for pictures

you bellow for glass after glass of chocolate milk

you rarely add in a "please" or a "thank you"

you get boiling mad over pretty much anything that doesn't go your way

you refuse to poop in the pot, no matter how many bribes we offer

your room looks like it was hit by a hurricane, and yet most nights, when we tuck you in, you ask us to clean your room before you'll go to sleep

you make dramatic statements like, "This is my absolute worst day ever"

but you are, despite this newly-acquired feisty nature, the sweetest, most adorable, softest, cuddliest little four-year-old in the entire history of the world. And that's all that matters.

PHOTO TAKEN IN SEPTEMBER 03

four *and* feisty

Photo: Special Effects Illustration, Title: Carrie Owens

Left Aligned
A left aligned text block, (also called "ragged right") is the easiest of all alignment styles to read, especially when you have lots of text. When in doubt, align to the left.

Centered
Centering is great when you are using a quote or other journaling with eight lines or less. Pay attention to your line lengths.

Justified
If you have similar-sized words, or you're comfortable shifting words from line to line to adjust the number of words per line, give it a try.

materials patterned paper (Chatterbox, Inc.) • Bell Gothic font (Adobe Systems) • Carpenter font (Eyewire)

Timeless Type

CLASSIC, OLD-STYLE TYPEFACES are to your font collection what the basic black dress is to your wardrobe—enduring, timeless and always appropriate. Fonts such as Times, Garamond and Goudy are truly workhorse fonts with a long, rich tradition in typesetting. Far from trendy, classic typefaces will lend a certain stability and timelessness to your scrapbook pages.

There is actually something fresh about old-style typefaces. Here are just a few good reasons to use classic fonts:

- They're easy to read.
- They're perfect for journaling blocks.
- They won't detract from or overwhelm your photos.
- They will never look dated.

But does classic mean boring? Hardly! This page includes one classic typeface, Adobe Garamond, for the entire layout. It's one of my favorites. By varying size and weight, you can create a dynamic type relationship on your page with classic old-style fonts.

Take stock of your classic typefaces today and experiment with the versatility they afford and the timelessness they impart. Like the basic black dress, your pages will never look out of style. ⑤

FONT SCHOOL

A serif is the little extra stroke found at the end of main vertical and horizontal strokes on a letterform.

Serif

Serif

Serif

These are classic old-style serif fonts:

Adobe Garamond
Adobe Systems

Goudy
Adobe Systems

Times
Usually included with most word-processing programs

smile
though your heart is aching

smile
even though it's breaking
when there are clouds in the sky
you'll get by if you smile
through your fear and sorrow

smile
and maybe tomorrow
you'll see the sun come shining thru for you

light
up your face with gladness
hide every trace of sadness
although a tear may be ever so near
that's the time you must keep trying

smile
what's the use of crying
you'll find that life is still worthwhile
if you just smile

MATERIALS Adobe Garamond font (Adobe Systems) • patterned paper (Pebbles in my Pocket) • buttons (Making Memories) • glue dots • tag (Avery)

by Cathy Zielske

Sans serif typefaces are great for

clean and simple designs. Sans serif literally means "without serifs." Serifs are the tiny strokes that adorn letter forms in typefaces like Caecilia (the font you're reading now) or Times Roman. Sans serif typefaces are free of extra adornments. Think Interstate (the font used on my layout below) or Arial. Sleek and simple, they add a crisp, contemporary feel to any layout.

Sans serif fonts often feel more understated, allowing your photos and design to shine. Understated does not, however, mean boring. For example, sans serif typefaces are used on the covers of many popular home and lifestyle magazines (think *Real Simple, Martha Stewart Living,* even *Simple Scrapbooks*). They often make for some of the most attractive, inviting covers.

Look for pre-made products that use sans serif fonts, like the tin letter "M" from Making Memories on my layout at right. For a unified look, I simply chose a similar sans serif font, Interstate, for my title and journaling.

Add a little understated, graphic flare to your next scrapbook page by using a sans serif font.

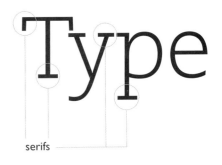

serifs

Favorite sans serif fonts

Zurich

Universe

Bell Gothic

Letter Gothic

Helvetica

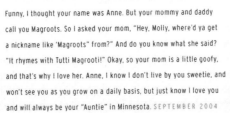

Funny, I thought your name was Anne. But your mommy and daddy call you Magroots. So I asked your mom, "Hey, Molly, where'd ya get a nickname like 'Magroots' from?" And do you know what she said? "It rhymes with Tutti Magrooti!" Okay, so your mom is a little goofy, and that's why I love her. Anne, I know I don't live by you sweetie, and won't see you as you grow on a daily basis, but just know I love you and will always be your "Auntie" in Minnesota. SEPTEMBER 2004

MAGROOTS

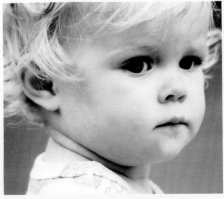

materials patterned paper (SEI) • mailbox letter (Making Memories) • 3-D adhesive • Interstate font

Pen & Paper

REDISCOVERING THE ESSENTIAL ELEMENTS

text and samples by Emily Tucker

When I first began scrapbooking in 1997, supplies were limited. I remember being able to fit all my "stuff"—cardstock, trimmer, adhesive and pens—into a small plastic sweater box that I carried with me to crops. Because choices were few, I didn't spend a lot of time fretting over what accents to use or which computer font to try. I worked with what I had and completed pages relatively quickly.

Fast forward to 2003—a time when my scrapbook stuff takes up an entire room in my home—and I can't help noticing how much longer it takes me to finish a page, not to mention the number of decisions I have to make; should I decorate my title with brads or nail heads?

Meet three designers who have rediscovered the simplicity, classic style, and freedom offered by working with the essential elements of pen and paper. Sarah Champion, Shelley Sullivan, and Tara Whitney have made the conscious choice to limit the supplies used on their pages, and their resulting layouts are genuinely beautiful, with the focus on the photos.

I would never want to completely limit myself to using only the supplies I had in 1997. (I would miss my eyelet setter and paper yarn too much!) Still, it's nice to know that I can create fresh, stylish scrapbook pages quickly and easily using just the essentials.

Meet

Sarah Champion
OREM, UT

BUSY WOMAN: single, works full time in the scrapbooking industry

FAVORITE PEN: Slick Writers by American Crafts, because they write on vellum, dry quickly, and come in various tip sizes.

FAVORITE PAPER: Well, I'm biased because I helped design it, but I love American Craft's Made to Match paper. It's patterned on one side and solid on the other. My favorite colors are red, gold, and celery.

WHY I LOVE PEN AND PAPER LAYOUTS: The longer I scrapbook, the more I focus on the photos. I find using my own handwriting to actually be quicker, and it provides such a personal touch.

beach
b o y
mitch
bear lake
7.02

beach boy

PEN TIP: Want a great title in minutes? Skip the scissors! Instead of cutting out template letters, trace them directly onto your page with a fine tip gel pen for a cool, crisp look.

materials white and black Ultimate Gel pens (American Crafts) • Spunky lettering template (C-Thru Ruler Co.) • square punch (Emagination Crafts)

PEN TIP: Write the title with the thick tip of a calligraphy pen. When the ink dries, go back with a gel pen and doodle dots, squiggles, etc.

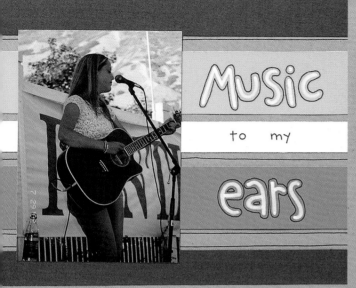

Music to my ears

Drew, Maren, Jenny & me

I love going to Maren's shows. It's always a lot of fun. This night was so beautiful—perfect for an outdoor concert. It was set up by a friend of Maren's & she performed at King Henry Apartments in Provo. There was such a huge crowd, including some members of "The R.M." crew since it was during filming. It was such a lovely evening & I had fun spending time with Drew & Jenny.   July 29, 2002

Drew & Jenny lipsynching
before the show

tali
and
ALLI

cousins
are Flowers
from the
SAME
garden

music to my ears

PEN TIP: Handwritten journaling adds a personal touch—be sure to include it on at least some your pages. If you're worried about mistakes, write on a separate sheet of cardstock and then adhere it to your layout.

materials Galaxy Marker and Ultimate Gel pen (American Crafts)

cousins

PEN TIP: Experiment with different styles of pens. Using a variety of tips changes the look of your writing and adds visual interest.

materials patterned paper (Colors by Design) • Slick Writer pens (American Crafts) • Paper Shapers mini flower & circle punch (EK Success) • large flower designed by Sarah

Meet

Shelly Sullivan
ABBEVILLE, SC

BUSY WOMAN: single mom of one, homemaker, student

FAVORITE PEN: Zig Writer (fine tip)

FAVORITE PAPER: Anything with texture. I love Bazzill's new line, for instance. My favorite color combinations are blues and greens with khaki, or vibrant hues paired with white and black. I like to experiment with unique, funky combinations, too.

BEST PAPER TIP: Pull the colors from your photos carefully. For example, matching the right shade of blue might be just the thing that makes your photos really pop off the page.

BEST PEN TIP: Outline titles, journaling boxes and mats with a fine black pen. It really adds a finished look to your layouts.

car wash

Dear Chandler,
These pics were taken on a surprisingly warm day in late January. You & Cassie got more soap and water on each other than my car, but that's okay. The cold weather returned the next day & the sandals were put away. But it was nice to get a little taste of spring.
Love,
Mom

car wash

PEN TIP: Jot handwritten notes on the backs of your layouts: You'll save space for more photos while providing hidden treasures for your family to discover!

materials Le Plume pens (Marvy Uchida)

PEN TIP:
❶ Using the bullet tip of the Zig Writer and a ruler, draw a box around your photo, title, or page.
❷ Using the fine tip of the Writer, draw a squiggly border. While making the squiggle, it helps to think "front loop, back loop, front loop, back loop…" and just let it flow. Add dots as desired.
❸ Using the brush end of the Zig Scroll and Brush pen, add leaves to your vine. Hold the pen almost parallel to the paper and press down gently, starting from the tip, to form a leaf.

san diego

Your slumber party for your 8th bday was a blast!

...musical chairs... memory game... makeovers... 8 zany girls!

the party g[i]

fave party game

party girls

PAPER KNOT TECHNIQUE: Who needs ribbon when you've got paper? Tie a thin strip of cardstock as if you're tying a knot. Pull tightly until just before it feels as if the paper will tear. Press the knot flat with your thumb and forefinger.

materials Zig Writer (EK Success)

Precious jewel,
you glow, you shine,
reflecting
all the good things
in the world.
- Maya Angelou

precious jewel

PEN TIP: A simple series of lines are the perfect enhancement for a striking photo. Using pens from a pre-packaged set ensures your color choices will match one another. Don't use a ruler to keep your lines perfectly straight; instead, draw them by hand for a touch of homemade charm.

materials Le Plume pens (Marvy Uchida)

Meet

Tara Whitney
VALENCIA, CA

BUSY WOMAN: Married, Homemaker, Mother of four kids, ages seven, five, three and two months. Tara's oldest daughter is autistic.

FAVORITE PEN: Black Zig Writer

FAVORITE PAPER: Bazzill Basics, Canson Mi Tienes

WHY I LOVE PEN AND PAPER LAYOUTS: Because I'm lazy and impatient! I don't have time to mess around with the computer, trying to get fonts and journaling right. I'm busy with family life, house stuff, etc. I need to take as little time as I can with each layout. I *love* scrapping, so the easier I make it, the more I can do.

I also like the classic simplicity of pen and paper. I think when I look back in a few years, I won't be as "amused" as I am with some of my older pages that have "stuff" all over them.

The main reason I limit my supplies is I want my photos to shine. My pages changed dramatically after I got a good camera and took some photography classes. Now, instead of taking pictures to match some great patterned paper I bought, I scrapbook because I have photos I love.

dolphins

PAPER POINTER: Line up strips of torn paper to match the scenery in your photos, as Tara did with the shoreline in this layout.

materials Zig Writer (EK Success)

PAPER POINTER: Tear paper into desired shape. To make the paper wisps, cut a thin strip of paper using a trimmer. Wrap the paper strip around a pencil to make it curl. In addition to accenting strawberries, paper wisps are great for vines on grapes and pumpkins.

PEN TIP: Define torn shapes by adding pen stitching or wavy lines around the edges.

kind of smile

PAPER POINTER: Great photos speak for themselves. Sometimes all that's needed is a little contrast (provided here by the large circles and bright cardstock).

materials Zig Writer (EK Success)

you can always make me smile

PEN TIP/PAPER POINTER: Not every edge needs to be straight. Cutting paper into asymmetrical lines gives this layout a fun, funky feel. The uneven pen stitching further adds to the sense of movement and playfulness.

materials Zig Writer (EK Success)

©CORBIS

"TO LOVE AND BE LOVED IS TO

FEEL THE SUN FROM BOTH SIDES."

————

DAVID VISCOTT

BY CARRIE OWENS

Handwriting *with* Confidence

ABOUT TWO YEARS AGO, I went font-free. I made the decision to use my own writing—aside from an occasional stamp or sticker—on every page I created from then on. I haven't looked back.

Most people say, "It's easy for you, you've got great handwriting." Well, I *do* have nice handwriting, but it's not just raw talent. I was trained as an interior architect, and I took calligraphy classes as a child and young adult, so from my point of view I was taught how to write well. I learned letter-forms, the art of spacing, and patience.

Even more important than my training, I write every day. Sure, there's an element of talent involved in good handwriting, but the rest can be learned, practiced and put into action with just a little effort on your part. So, grab a pen and your sketchbook and get ready to give your scrapbooks the personal touch of handwritten journaling.

LEARN HOW!

1 Practice

EVERY TIME I sit down with a magazine, every time I'm on the phone, every time I wait at the doctor's office, I am writing. I have about six sketchbooks scattered around my house, car and purse, just waiting to be used. And used they are. Practice makes perfect. Think back to your days in high school, with your doodle-covered PeeChee. This is where you need to be again.

Every time you write a shopping list, a to-do list, a check, or a note to your husband, do it with style and patience. This is your practice time.

As someone who has played the weight loss game once or twice, I've often heard the phrase, "Every little bit helps." The gurus tell us to "park in the farthest parking stall," "take the stairs," etc., to get in a little exercise here and a little there. Well, the same holds true for handwriting. Every little bit helps. When you see a font you like, try your hand at it even as you're downloading it. Practice. Practice. Practice. You'll get better.

> " SCRAPBOOKING IS A PERSONAL EXPRESSION, NOT PERFECTION. NOTHING SAYS YOU LIKE YOUR HANDWRITING. "

Process

MANY PEOPLE HESITATE to use their own handwriting on their pages. *What if I ruin my layout? My letters always run uphill. I can't format my text like I can on my computer. There isn't enough room to include everything I want to say.* These are all very nice excuses, but I'm not buying them! There is a way to get your lettering the way you want it. It's a process, consisting of four steps. Follow them every time and you'll get results that even your toughest critic (you) will be proud of.

SIMPLE STEPS

- **Plan it**

  What do you want to say? Where should it fit on your layout? What lettering style communicates the mood you want to create with your photos? Answer these questions by practicing on a sheet of scratch paper. This will give you an idea of the amount of room you'll need.

- **Follow the lines**

  I use guidelines, every single time. Even if I'm doing whimsical, bouncy lettering, I need guidelines. You'll need them too. They'll help you "format" your text, just like you would on a computer.

- **Pencil first, pen second**

  Using a pencil first allows you to test your text, reconfirm what you are going to say, and see if it will fit where you want it. Now is the time to determine line, word and character spacing—and to check for spelling errors. When you start writing with your pen or marker, DO NOT trace your letters. The penciled text should serve only as a guide for writing with your pen. If you trace millimeter by millimeter it will look stiff and contrived, and not at all like you have the confidence to be writing on your page.

- **Clean it up**

  Erase, and fast! Once your ink is dry, use a white (or art gum) eraser to gently erase your pencil marks. I promise, there will be times when you will prefer the penciled text to your final copy. This is why you need to erase the pencil fast. Once it's gone, you can't compare.

3 Pride

THINK BACK a few years to high school. How did you feel about yourself? Did you feel fat, out of style, gangly and awkward, or otherwise not so perfect? When you look back at high school photos now, what do you see? Someone who really wasn't that bad, right? I always thought I was heavy (remember the dieting story?), but now when I look at my pictures from high school, I think, "Hey, I wasn't so bad!" Actually, I think, "What I wouldn't give for those legs now!"

Your handwriting is like that too. You never think it's good enough, but you just need to take a step back and look at it with a less critical eye. Scrapbooking is a personal expression, not perfection.

Nothing says you like your handwriting. Practice and follow the process, but more than anything else, take pride in your own hand.

everyone needs their own...

Where do you go when you're blue? Or Red? Or when you're bored? Or just want to escape for a bit? There's a chair in my living room that I go to... when I need to center myself. I have a great view of the front yard... the leaves blowing in the wind... the cars driving by... the peacefulness of our street. I have a great view of the 50 year old piano, the entry table, a small slice of the kitchen and the hall. I'm nestled back into the corner of the living room... the clean room. I love it there, in that chair, that twenty year old chair from Grandma Nokelby that is still so very comfortable...

Spot

The chair that's arms are still dotted with formula from holding the babies as they sipped on their bottles so late at night... The chair that I sit in on happy days and sad days... The chair that we wave bye-bye to Daddy from as he heads off to work in the mornings... The chair that I will be waiting in... watching from... as my kids will walk home from school one day...

my views

daddy's
nicer
than you are...

"Oh, really?" I asked, "and why is that?"
"Because he's just nice..."
"Well, Jack, that probably is true. Daddy is often much nicer than Mommy."
"Yeah, he's just nice."

Well, I guess our Good Cop - Bad Cop roles have been established, and Mommy has officially made it as the
bad cop...

started · May 11th · 2004.

photos · december 24, 2003.

Carrie recommends these tools in the handwriting course she teaches:

TOOLS OF THE TRADE

❶ Zig writers in black and platinum for large lettering. Try "shadowing" your text by writing first with the Platinum, then again slightly above and to the right with Black. (See "Everyone Needs Their Own Spot" layout.) ❷ Archival pens like Close To My Heart Legacy Writers or Zig Millenium pens for smaller lettering. Point sizes range from .01–.08.

❸ A mechanical pencil (.5 or wider lead width) for planning and practicing. ❹ A dusting brush to remove eraser squirmies without smudging or wrinkling your page. ❺ A pencil eraser. Carrie's favorite is the Staedtler white vinyl, in either the pen or block version. ❻ The Ames Lettering Guide, for quickly and easily creating straight, equally spaced lines. Visit the e-store at MasterG.com to find the guide and other useful hand-lettering supplies.

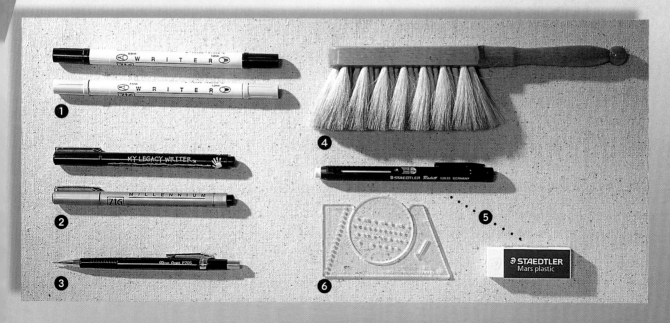

ONE MAN PRACTICING SPORT IS BETTER

THAN FIFTY PREACHING IT.

KNUTE ROCKNE

BY LYNNE MONTGOMERY

How Valuable Are Your Scrapbooks?

ARE YOU SCRAPBOOKING what really matters most to you? I have a friend who won a battle with cancer. During the uncertain months of her treatment, she scrapbooked night and day in an effort to leave her family a legacy of what was in her heart. Her experience has caused me to take a close look at my own albums. Do my pages reflect the values I hold most dear? Am I recording the lessons I've learned and the principles I've honored that have made me the person I am?

3 ways to share what matters most

It's easy to talk about putting more values-based sentiment into your scrapbook pages, but how do you start doing it? Here, I'll share three ways to begin recording the values that guide your life, so you can rest assured you're passing on what matters most.

Record where a value came from.

I want my children to go to college. When they ask me why, I tell them about my grandfather, Joseph Walker. At the age of 10, he emigrated from Austria to the United States, where he was sent all alone to live and work. He didn't speak any English, and later ran away from his caregiver.

Despite his hardships and lack of education, he married, raised seven children and developed a successful logging company. →

Figure 1. Combine photos of your ancestors with current photos to trace where a value has come from and how it has impacted your life. *Pages by Lynne Montgomery.* **Supplies** *Patterned papers:* Bravissimo!, Emagination Crafts; Memory Lane Paper Co.; *Computer font:* CK Bella, "The Best of Creative Lettering" CD Vol. 3, *Creating Keepsakes; Tags:* Avery Dennison; *Paper clips:* Clipiola; *Beads:* Beads by Pamela; *Chalk:* Craft-T Products; *Other:* Fiber and safety pin.

Figure 2. What values are you teaching your children? Reinforce a value or character trait by dedicating a scrapbook page to it. *Pages by Lynne Montgomery.* **Supplies** *Embossed paper:* Source unknown; *Computer font:* CK Journaling, "The Best of Creative Lettering" CD Vol. 2, *Creating Keepsakes; Tags:* Avery Dennison; *Pressed flowers:* Nature's Pressed; *Rubber stamps:* PSX Design; *Stamping ink:* Ranger Industries; *Circle punch:* Family Treasures; *Paper clip:* Clipiola; *Word tiles:* Limited Edition Rubber Stamps; *Glassine envelopes:* Source unknown; *Other:* Watch crystal, fibers and buttons.

As my grandfather raised his children, he taught them the value of mastering a skill and obtaining an education. My father, the youngest of my grandfather's children, was the first to graduate from high school and college. In turn, my father inspired and encour- aged me to do the same.

Receiving my degree has given me greater confidence, more opportunities and peace of mind; it's a lesson I want to pass on to my own children. In Figure 1, I paired my graduation photo with photos of my grandfather and father to help my children understand the origin of my love for and commitment to learning.

Think about something you value. Who instilled this value in you?

WRITE NOW

Did you know that Benjamin Franklin created a list of 13 personal virtues (below) that he wanted to develop in his lifetime? These governing values guided his decisions and surely helped him deepen his character. What values would make your list? Write them down and create a scrapbook page around the entire list, or dedicate a layout to each value. They'll be a meaningful addition to your scrapbook.

- Temperance
- Silence
- Frugality
- Order
- Resolution
- Industry
- Sincerity
- Cleanliness
- Tranquility
- Chastity
- Justice
- Moderation
- Humility

For values-related quotes and information, check out these web sites:

humanityquest.com. Lists over 500 human values and links to famous quotations supporting each value.

franklincovey.com/missionbuilder/index.html. Takes you through an interactive quiz; in the end, the company formulates a mission statement for you.

selfgrowth.com. More of an all-inclusive site to encourage and support you through goal-centered changes.

What experiences have strengthened your resolve to pass this value on? Gather a few photos that will help you draw a connection and show where this value came from.

Make a value the theme of your page.

Through the years, my husband and I have watched our children as they've pored over their scrapbook pages. They ask questions about the places we've been and the events we've celebrated. We've noticed how much they're learning about who we are as a family.

Over the past year, I've been jotting down many of the sweet things my daughter Emily has said in her bedtime prayers. I never want to forget her innocence and sincerity. As I was re-reading her words recently, I realized that I diligently scrapbook her birthday every year. Why shouldn't I also design a layout about her daily prayers? (See Figure 2.)

The next time you come across a loved one's photo that doesn't really belong to an event, take the opportunity to share a belief or value you want to instill in that person. A personal message recorded on a scrapbook page just might motivate and inspire him at a time when he really needs it.

Add "value" to everyday event pictures.

We practice living core values every day. As we go about our daily routines, life teaches us the skills we need to be successful. You don't need to conduct a special photo shoot or use professional photos to create a scrapbook page about values.

In Figure 3, Julie Turner of Gilbert, Arizona, took ordinary photos of her daughter playing T-ball and put a unique "value-added" twist on the journaling, sharing with her the importance of being a team player. Instead of focusing on the traditional who, what, where and when, she chose to highlight the skills her daughter is learning: do your best, listen to the coach, follow instructions, encourage others and enjoy the game. The abilities she learns on the ball field will help build her character, and they'll transfer over to other areas of her life. This layout will serve as a reminder of these early experiences.

The next time you're at a loss for words, think about the lessons your photos might illustrate. Reinforce through your journaling the things everyday life is teaching you and those you love. 🅢

Figure 3. Let photos from everyday events communicate the principles you value most. *Pages by Julie Turner.* **Supplies** *Patterned papers:* Bravissimo!, Emagination Crafts; Ink It; *Computer font:* Garamouche, P22 Type Foundry; *Beads:* Westrim Crafts; *Chalk:* Craft-T Products; *Eyelets:* Coffee Break Design; *Craft wire:* Artistic Wire Ltd.; *Square punch:* Marvy Uchida; *Other:* Mat board and twine.

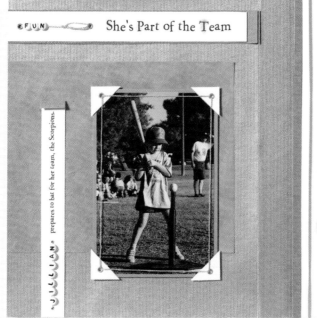

She's Part of the Team

The People We Love

WHEN IT COMES TO WRITING ABOUT PEOPLE WE LOVE, EVEN EXPERT WRITERS GET STUCK. Why? There's just too much to say. People are complex, as are our relationships with them. Trying to incorporate all your memories, feelings, and intimate knowledge of a person into just a few paragraphs can be overwhelming.

Don't feel bad if you've buckled under the pressure. While scrapbooking, I have been known to cop out with a lame caption and the date, while trusting my true feelings to my memory. Great loves and life-altering events have been erased from history in this way.

The truth is, not many people—except maybe immediate family members—get that much space in your scrapbooks. So when you make pages about the community of souls who really matter in your life, it's important to do right by them in your journaling. Here are three ideas that will make writing about the people you love easier and more fun.

Say it in a letter

Letters create intimacy, because they are directed to specific people, not an unknown audience. You can also get away with saying things you might not say in person. Use a letter to praise (or gush about) your loved one's good qualities, tell them how you feel about them, and reminisce about some of your favorite shared memories.

A letter is also a form of dialog with another person, albeit one-sided. Your own voice and style can shine through without being hampered by the constraints of traditional composition. In Laura Nicholas's letter to her Gramps (below), her love for him is evident in the way she talks to him. The examples in Laura's letter make his personality and presence feel close and real.

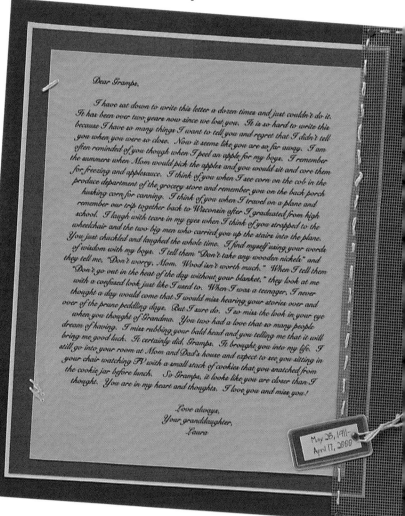

materials metal rimmed tags (Making Memories) • CK Footnote title font (Creating Keepsakes) • screen • brads • fiber • vellum • page by Laura Nicholas

Write an Ad

Another fun way to write about people you love is to pretend that you're an advertising copywriter hired to write an ad about them. It's easy to get ideas; they're all around you—in magazines and newspapers, on billboards, trucks and T-shirts. Decide what type of ad would work best for your subject, and then be creative with the journaling.

In my page below, I wrote a press release for my friend Todd. I started with a list of all the qualities that one could love about him, like spontaneity and a good sense of humor, and then gave examples of those qualities in action. In your own writing, try to do the same thing. Words like "spontaneous" or "funny," if left to stand alone, are vague and can be interpreted in different ways. If you back up these terms with specific examples, your subject will feel more realistic to readers.

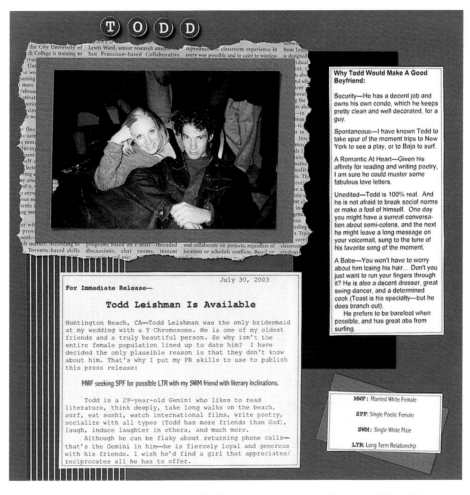

materials Paper Reflections collage papers (DMD Industries, Inc.) • Courier New and Arial fonts (Microsoft Word) • *page by Felice Austin*

Try writing a personal ad, celebrity profile or TV commercial for someone you love.

Draw a Comparison

Write about people you love by comparing them to something else. What person, place, or thing do they remind you of?

When I was a kid and my family played "Guess the Animal," my brother was always a rhinoceros. He would get on all fours, and then charge whatever was in front of him. He rammed his head into the wall so many times, I'm shocked he still has any wits.

Ironically, a rhino is a fitting animal for comparison with the person my brother has turned out to be. He still butts his head into real and figurative walls, but I have learned to admire his persistence.

When Michelle Christensen dared to compare her husband to something, she opted for his Chevy Chevelle. Both of these classics, it seems, have more than good looks going for them.

Now that you have three great ways to write about people you love, open up those storage cells in your brain and start unpacking the valuables. Take these comparisons and run with them, using specific examples to back up your writing along the way.

write from the heart

Good descriptive writing often begins with the urge to compare your subject to something else. Michelle uses a tried-and-true device—the extended metaphor—to vividly describe her husband's remarkable qualities.

Her Objectives: 1) Introduce the object of comparison straight away; 2) Convey the abiding feeling her husband has for his classic car, and how she has come to love the Chevelle; 3) List and elaborate upon the traits shared by spouse and vehicle; 4) Conclude with a specific, memorable incident involving couple and car.

Why it Works: Did she love the car first—or the man? When Michelle slides across the seat of that "glistening gold, roaring Chevy Chevelle" on a first date with her husband-to-be, we sense her immediate bonding with both of these very similar forces.

The qualities of the car—sleek, accommodating and dependable—are the qualities she also loves in her man. Just as the Chevelle represents a shining era of sturdiness and understated design, Michelle sees in her husband a man who stylishly withstands life's rigors while avoiding being "too flashy or evident." And as he meticulously restores and maintains his vehicle, so too does he look for ways to fine-tune himself.

A good car—in particular, a 1966 Chevelle—is built to endure, and one might argue that a good marriage should be similarly constructed. How fortunate for her husband that Michelle understands the maintenance contract: with "a little extra care" and "a little tuning here and there," they will hum like new! –MZ

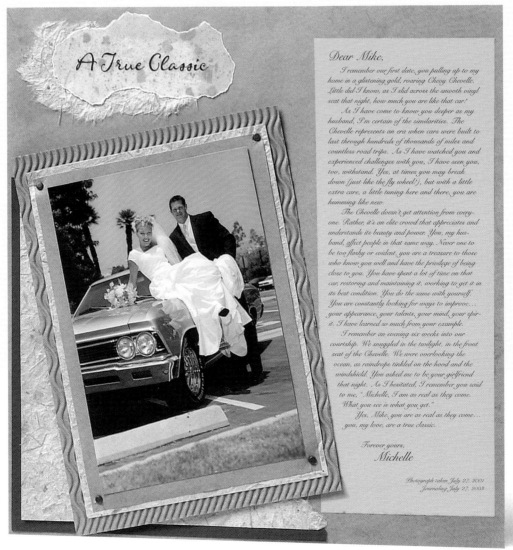

A True Classic

Dear Mike,

I remember our first date, you pulling up to my home in a glistening gold, roaring Chevy Chevelle. Little did I know, as I slid across the smooth vinyl seat that night, how much you are like that car!

As I have come to know you deeper as my husband, I'm certain of the similarities. The Chevelle represents an era when cars were built to last through hundreds of thousands of miles and countless road trips. As I have watched you and experienced challenges with you, I have seen you, too, withstand. Yes, at times you may break down (just like the fly wheel!), but with a little extra care, a little tuning here and there, you are humming like new.

The Chevelle doesn't get attention from everyone. Rather, it's an elite crowd that appreciates and understands its beauty and power. You, my husband, affect people in that same way. Never one to be too flashy or evident, you are a treasure to those who know you well and have the privilege of being close to you. You have spent a lot of time on that car, restoring and maintaining it, working to get it in its best condition. You do the same with yourself. You are constantly looking for ways to improve... your appearance, your talents, your mind, your spirit. I have learned so much from your example.

I remember an evening six weeks into our courtship. We snuggled in the twilight, in the front seat of the Chevelle. We were overlooking the ocean, as raindrops tinkled on the hood and the windshield. You asked me to be your girlfriend that night. As I hesitated, I remember you said to me, "Michelle, I am as real as they come. What you see is what you get."

Yes, Mike, you are as real as they come... you, my love, are a true classic.

Forever yours,
Michelle

Photograph taken July 27, 2001
Journaling July 27, 2003

materials Metallic Splash velum (Colorbök, Inc.) • Shestnit accent patterned paper (K & Company) • natural fiber paper • Scrap Cursive font (Lettering Delights) • Papyrus font (Microsoft Word) • brads • *page by Michelle Christensen*

Can I Quote You on That?

IF YOU WANT TO MAKE YOUR JOURNAL-ING MORE MEANINGFUL, start thinking like a reporter—listen for and record the sound bites! When you take habitual note of words or phrases spoken by the subjects of your pages, you'll find you have a treasure trove of journaling jump-starts to work with.

Moreover, when you make an effort to record the dialogue of your subjects, you reveal a tremendous amount about who they are. From the mundane to the disarming, these insightful bits of commentary often accurately tell more about your subject than page after page of text could ever convey.

Let's put a hold on bland descriptive passages and get to the meat of what was said. Take this journal entry, for instance: "Aidan went trick or treating and made quite a haul. She was reluctant, however, to share her candy with Mom." Why shouldn't I try using my daughter's actual words? "Way no fair, Mom! It's MY candy, not yours!" The latter gets the point across in a more authentic way.

I think you'll see that this approach can propel your journaling to more meaningful heights.

Have pen, will quote

First things first: Keep a notebook handy to record the silly, quirky, tender and endearing things the people in your life say. When one of my kids says something uncannily wise—or gut-wrenchingly funny—it goes into the notebook for use at a later date. Building a collection of personal quotes is a great resource for scrapbook journaling.

Have quote, will scrap

Once you've disciplined yourself to the journalist's skill of getting the good quote, there are two methods for incorporating these spoken words into your journaling. The first is to start with a quote and then find pictures and devise text to support the layout, as I did at left. Record on a scrapbook page whatever memorable wordplay transpired, and then find pictures to support the journaling.

When Aidan was three, her Great Grandpa Harry passed away. It was important to Dan and I to include her at the funeral, because despite her youth, we wanted her to know that saying goodbye to someone you love is a part of life, and that it is also a way to celebrate that person's completed life. She seemed to handle the funeral well, and I'm sure she didn't understand alot of it, but we felt glad to have included her.

A few nights later, Aidan and I were lying in her bed, when she asked me, "Mom, is Grandpa Harry in Heaven?" To which I replied, "Yes, honey, he is." She paused for a moment, remembering our cat that had recently died, and asked, "Is Emmit in Heaven?" To which I replied again, "Yes, honey, I believe that animals have a place in Heaven, too." Finally, she asked, "Mom, will I go to Heaven some day?" And I told her absolutely, but not for a very long, long time.

I always wonder how kids truly process things. Sometimes, I think it's easy to forget they take little pieces of information, and put them together in ways that are so very different from our adult comprehension. What they isolate and focus on can seem so unexpected at times.

This was so clear to me with her final question: "Mom, will I have skin in Heaven?" I smiled at her, pulling her close to me, and said, "I think you probably will, sweetie. I think you probably will."

"Mom, will I have skin in Heaven?"

A conversation with Aidan I will never forget.

materials Caecilia font for title (Adobe Systems) • Garamond font for journaling (Adobe Systems) • paper flower

This approach isn't stressful, as the pictures do not have to be from the time the words were actually spoken.

For the layout on the preceeding page, I recount a conversation I had with my daughter about Heaven when she was four years old. The pure innocence of her bedtime question, "Will I have skin in Heaven?" stayed with me long after she had fallen asleep. Two years later, her words became a scrapbook page, recounting the endearing conversation that so aptly depicted who she was at the time.

Recording a brief portion of actual dialogue sometimes eliminates the need to write extensively to capture the memory. There are occasions, of course, when the captured dialogue triggers in me the desire to extend the experience. In remembering and reporting this conversation, I found myself wanting and able to expound on how it affected me.

Have pics, need quote

The second method for journaling dialogue? Choose your photos and then supply appropriate quotes. How many times have you sat staring at a series of photos from a particular event, and wondered, "Okay, now what do I say?" My solution (below) was to keep track of some of the things my daughter actually said on her seventh birthday. I wanted to go beyond the usual, "Aidan got a bike for her birthday. It was really fun!" and capture more of who she truly is.

Let's face it, the urge to write something descriptive and sweet is fine, but often not very illuminating. By keeping the journaling in my daughter's own words, I skirted the problem. And believe me, the people in our lives provide a wealth of journaling material—if only we are aware enough to listen!

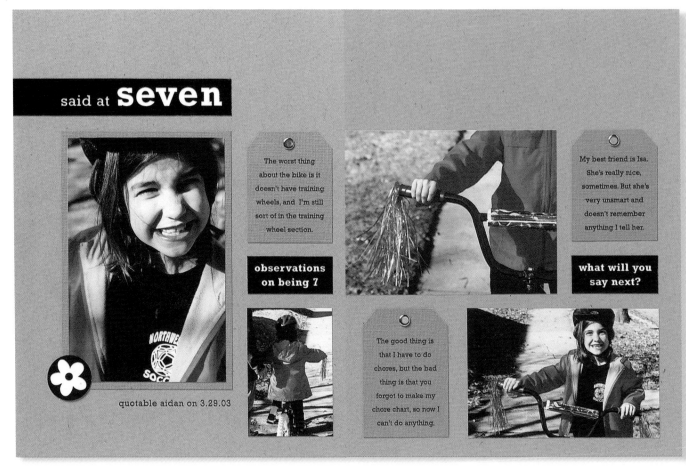

said at seven

The worst thing about the bike is it doesn't have training wheels, and I'm still sort of in the training wheel section.

observations on being 7

My best friend is Isa. She's really nice, sometimes. But she's very unsmart and doesn't remember anything I tell her.

what will you say next?

The good thing is that I have to do chores, but the bad thing is that you forgot to make my chore chart, so now I can't do anything.

quotable aidan on 3.29.03

materials Rockwell font (Adobe Systems) • snaps (Making Memories) • circle die cut (KI Memories)

Editor's note: Mark Zoellner, our Associate Editor, appreciates a well-tooled paragraph like I appreciate a well-designed scrapbook page. I've invited him to share his insight each issue on good journaling by critiquing one layout in this column. —Stacy

because yeah

One of the millions of ways you melt my heart is with your original interpretation of the English language. Case in point:

Mom: "Coley, why did you pour the entire pitcher of orange juice all over the kitchen counter?"
Coley: "Because yeah."

Mom: "Coley, why did you hit your sister over the head with that baton?"
Coley: "Because yeah."

Mom: "Coley, just how did you get so cute?"
Coley: Because yeah.

Daddy and I think it's a pretty sound response to just about anything this world can throw at you. Second case in point:

Mom: "Honey, why didn't you call me to tell me you'd be running late?"
Dad: "Because yeah."

Dad: "Honey, why did you put more scrapbook supplies on the credit card?"
Mom: "Because yeah."

So you see, Coley, you're cleverly developing your own, unique vernacular, and if you ever need to know why we love you so insanely, we'll just smile, and say, "Because yeah."

Same holds true if you're ever grounded...

materials Helvetica Neue font (Adobe Systems)

Cathy nimbly plays the Verbatim Game on many of her pages. Her journaling incorporates the actual words of family members for a slice-of-life reality that merges easily and honestly with her design sense.

Her objectives: 1) Use a repeated phrase in dialogue as the framework for journaling; 2) Make a point concisely and vividly instead of watering it down by explaining it in your own words—in this case how all the members of a family put a simple phrase to multiple uses; 3) Offer a subtle, humorous twist for a conclusion.

Why it Works: The captured dialogue is particularly effective on "because yeah" for its brevity, repetition and sly wit. The reader is treated to three examples on the left-hand side of the page in which a three-year-old employs a stock response to answer all kinds of questions—from the concrete to the abstract. The response—terse, illogical and none too finely considered—is the very sort of cop-out that will disappear by adulthood, right? Hah! As you see on the right-side dialog, mom and dad are equally adept at using the phrase to gloss over issues.

With just a few snippets of dialogue, Cathy's pinned down with concrete examples our universal tendency to be comfortable and lazy when communicating with loved ones. They, after all, know what we mean, don't they? And for the masterstroke, reread her last line, replete with gently scolding good humor. Parents still hold the supreme prerogative to inflict these responses on their children! —MZ

Treating Words and Photos as Partners

Scrapbookers generally don't journal their soul onto cardstock and then neglect to look for suitable photographs. Nor do they select their best shots for a page, skip the journaling, and call it a layout well done. The exercise would seem incomplete.

It's important to remember that images function best—most times, anyway—when accompanied by good writing. Lengthy or brief, profound or silly, journalistic or poetic, words are fitting partners for photos. Here are a few happy pairings.

File'em under phylum

Anna: I wanted to create a humorous layout highlighting how grumpy this little guy can get—because, honestly, seeing the humor in Micah's moods is the only way I can cope. I wrote the journaling as if I was composing a sixth-grade science report on my favorite dinosaur. I thought the vaguely Latin-sounding silliness of my names for the classification system would add the right touch. (For Verae Crankae, for instance, I simply supplied Latin suffixes to "very cranky.")

Applying the concept: Just for fun, create a layout about your favorite human subject, with you as the devious wildlife biologist, and write your own fantastical description.

The creature profiled in Anna's layout is one whose existence has been recognized for thousands of years. She notes its remarkable adaptation to all habitable areas of our planet, its dietary habits, its biological responses to disturbances in its environment and, most critically, those periods when this animal poses the greatest threat to our security.

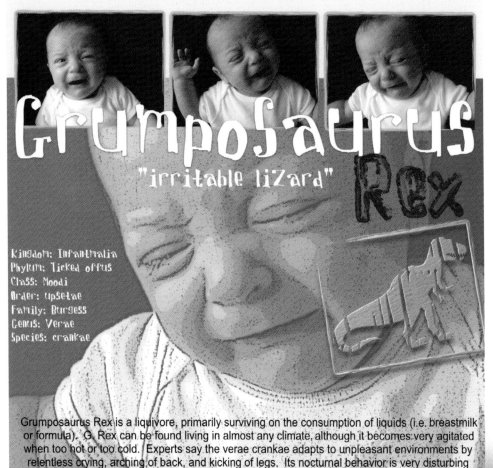

Kingdom: Infantralia
Phylum: Ticked offus
Class: Moodi
Order: upsetae
Family: Burgess
Genus: Verae
Species: crankae

Grumposaurus Rex is a liquivore, primarily surviving on the consumption of liquids (i.e. breastmilk or formula). G. Rex can be found living in almost any climate, although it becomes very agitated when too hot or too cold. Experts say the verae crankae adapts to unpleasant environments by relentless crying, arching of back, and kicking of legs. Its nocturnal behavior is very disturbing to others in its habitat, and therefore its irritability is very contagious.

materials MicrosoftPhotoDraw 2000 (Microsoft) • *digital page by Anna Burgess*

The essential role of a parent: prepare your children as best you can, and then let go. Below, one mother projects ahead to the mission that awaits her, while on the next page another mom reflects back on her task accomplished.

The Future is Now

Judith: When I saw the photo, I was captivated by the expression on Nate's face. His faraway glance seemed to focus on the future, so I decided that my journaling should too.

Applying the concept: Search for photographs that work as metaphors to inspire your own predictive and hopeful prose. Judith chose a door to symbolize the many "passing through" phases she expects her child to navigate as he walks, runs, bikes and motors his way from toddler to manhood. Dare to foretell what might be in your child's life, and what role you'll play.

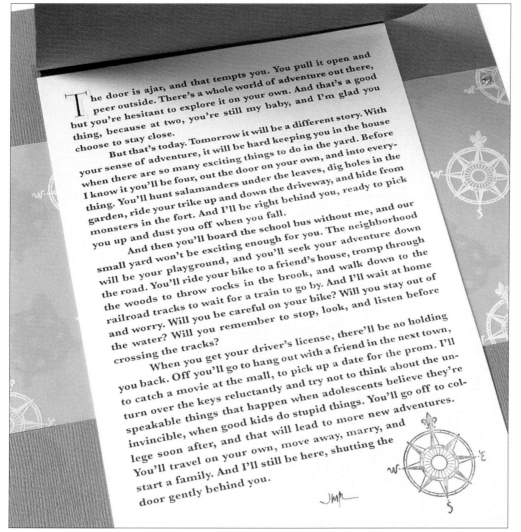

The door is ajar, and that tempts you. You pull it open and peer outside. There's a whole world of adventure out there, but you're hesitant to explore it on your own. And that's a good thing, because at two, you're still my baby, and I'm glad you choose to stay close.

But that's today. Tomorrow it will be a different story. With your sense of adventure, it will be hard keeping you in the house when there are so many exciting things to do in the yard. Before I know it you'll be four, out the door on your own, and into everything. You'll hunt salamanders under the leaves, dig holes in the garden, ride your trike up and down the driveway, and hide from monsters in the fort. And I'll be right behind you, ready to pick you up and dust you off when you fall.

And then you'll board the school bus without me, and our small yard won't be exciting enough for you. The neighborhood will be your playground, and you'll seek your adventure down the road. You'll ride your bike to a friend's house, tromp through the woods to throw rocks in the brook, and walk down to the railroad tracks to wait for a train to go by. And I'll wait at home and worry. Will you be careful on your bike? Will you stay out of the water? Will you remember to stop, look, and listen before crossing the tracks?

When you get your driver's license, there'll be no holding you back. Off you'll go to hang out with a friend in the next town, to catch a movie at the mall, to pick up a date for the prom. I'll turn over the keys reluctantly and try not to think about the unspeakable things that happen when adolescents believe they're invincible, when good kids do stupid things. You'll go off to college soon after, and that will lead to more new adventures. You'll travel on your own, move away, marry, and start a family. And I'll still be here, shutting the door gently behind you.

materials patterned paper (EK Success) • vellum • compass stamp (Stampabilities) • ribbon • bottle cap (Li'l Davis Designs) • brads (Making Memories) • letter sticker (me & my BIG ideas) • Baskerville font (Linotype) • *page by Judith Mara*

The Heart Aches—and the Hand Writes

Barbara: I worked on this layout the day after my son left to study in London for a semester. I journaled before I even thought about pictures, not my usual method at all. Writing this down helped me to realize that although I truly was happy for his adventure, it was okay to acknowledge my "other" feelings.

Applying the concept: Use short, declarative sentences in a second-person narrative that demonstrates the universality of raising children. When you get to the specific incident that's depicted in the photograph, switch to first-person. In so doing, Barbara makes the universal experiences more particular, and reminds the reader—and herself—that the necessary parental letting-go is not always easy.

God gives you this miracle, this gift. You are entranced. Soon life revolves around diapers, meals and sleep. Gradually, you realize this little being actually IS a being and begins to have his own unique personality. As changes happen, you change. You go with the flow. The baby disappears and you find a toddler in his place. Some days drag, others fly. Days are filled with needs, activity and lots of love. As busy as you are, once in a while you think that this is all going to come to an end. You realize that your true job is to prepare this treasured boy to go out into the world without you to hold that little hand. It is a fleeting thought. Who has time to think of that? Off to preschool. Off to kindergarten. Sports, friends, sleepovers. Every little thing is another step, preparing him, readying him to go out into the world. Off to middle school. Off to high school. The days have flown by so quickly that they are a whirl. You cherish every possible moment. The reality of the leaving is getting closer and closer. It is no longer a fleeting thought. Off to college. And yesterday, off to London. Now I am in this place. My miracle, my gift is a half a world away from me. He no longer needs my hand to hold. He is smart, strong and focused. He is everything I dreamt he would be, prayed he would be and so much more. My pride has no bounds. And as happy as I am for him, my heart is aching for that little hand in mine.   01.27.04

Matthew Scott Carroll

London

SECURITY CHECKPOINT

Letting Go

Life

materials patterned paper (Karen Foster design) • Scriptorama-Hostess title font (Jukebox Type) • Times New Roman journaling and "London" font (Internet) • zipper pull (All My Memories) • square punch (EK Success) • watch face • *page by Barbara Carroll*

Mark My Words

To remember is, in large part, to honor. Do it with words as well as photos.

Why it Works: Grandfathers offer children the best of both worlds. They're adults, of course, able to offer supervision and wise counsel. But in retirement, they remember some of the merriment and foolishness that busy fathers seem to forget. Leave disciplining to the dads—grandpas are just plain cool to hang with!

Rachel honors her deceased grandfather through her detailed and heartfelt journaling. We see him picking up the kids at school and repairing roller skates; we smell his scent of newly mown grass; we hear him laughing and cursing along the Maryland shoreline; we meet a generous and gently cantankerous man who left indelible impressions on an 11-year-old girl.

Is there any better tribute to those who have left us than to recall with bracing clarity what they did with us while they were alive? To remember where we were when we heard the news of their passing? Evoke all the senses. Let out all the stops. Your writing, done well, has the power to bridge generations. –MZ, Associate Editor

"I put off making this layout for six months," says Rachel. "I didn't want to start it unless it was going to convey exactly how I felt. I wanted those who saw the page—strangers as well as family—to remember the wonderful bond that can exist between child and grandparent, the love and memories shared, as well as the heartache of losing a grandparent."

materials patterned paper (Miss Elizabeth's) • chalk and scrabble letters (EK Success) • metal plaque • brads • Footlight MT Light font (AGFA Monotype Library) • Typo Upright BT font (Bitstream) • vellum • stamps • embroidery floss • *page by Rachel Critchfield*

Men Matter Too

MEN. THEY SUBTLY RAISE AN EYEBROW when we walk in with yet another bag of goodies from the scrapbook store. They grumble and groan when they get the bank statement with all those online charges. But maybe, deep down, the disgruntlement comes from not being invited to contribute to our pages. Maybe they need a way to connect with us—and with this incredible hobby.

Having a male perspective on our layouts can be a great resource and, believe it or not, provide the perfect emotion we want for a particular page. Whether it's a heartfelt message that addresses the people who share his existence, or a humorous autobiographical admission (below), a journal entry from the man in your life serves as a lasting record of his participation in the extraordinary moments of your shared lives.

There's no reason to assume men don't devote just as much time as women do to self-reflection. Perhaps they just need a forum for sharing. Since my husband, Dino, was a little disheartened about turning 30, I challenged him to record light-hearted facts about his personality or past experiences.

MATERIALS sticker frame and accents (Magenta) • letter stickers (Frances Meyer) • decorative letters (FoofaLa) • *Page by Shannon Watt*

More than just a legacy for posterity, men's entries can strengthen existing relationships by allowing them to express their thoughts in a meaningful way. How to encourage the process? Try these approaches.

Writing to a Loved One

Some men might find it easier to express themselves by creating a poem or writing a letter to a loved one. Tara Whitney's husband, Jeff, was so touched by this photo of their daughter, that—once prompted to write about it—he filled a page with poetry about the bond he shares with McKenna.

Tara cut clocks from the patterned paper to use as accents on the left page. She enlarged a favorite photo of McKenna on her computer and printed it herself.

MATERIALS clockwork patterned paper (Colors By Design) • green and yellow handmade paper (Artistic Scrapper) • Garamouche font (P22 Type Foundry) • Sonnets small clock sticker (Creative Imaginations) • *Page by Tara Whitney*

Go with the Flow

Encourage him to use photos, songs and other elements in his environment for inspiration. Recently, my husband was listening to a song on the radio that triggered emotions he felt as a young father. I encouraged him to go home and write while the feelings were still fresh. He came up with a list of questions that conveyed the quirks of living with his bubbly daughters and the uncertainties of fatherhood. By taking the time to write this, Dino shared his perspective of fatherhood, something I could never have given our children.

MATERIALS Encino Caps font (Internet) • Zig Writer pen (EK Success) • handmade paper • *Page by Shannon Watt*

write from the heart

The Next Level

Given the opportunity, I think most men would admit that the relationship they have with their partners is life-sustaining. Granted, we tend to see only grudging admissions of such, but hey, if we gave them a scrapbook-safe opportunity to tell us what we mean to them, we might be surprised at the results.

Matthew Lincoln crafted prose to tell his wife, Erin, how his universe was radically altered by her presence.

A Youthful Perspective

Maybe the trick is to engage a male's viewpoint while he's still young and more open to honest expression. Scrapbooker Barbara Carroll was delighted by the tribute her 21-year-old son, Matthew, wrote to his father. ⑤

THE NUDGE TO DIVULGE

With Father's Day and graduation approaching, here are a few journaling ideas to encourage fathers, husbands and sons to grace your pages with their valued insight.

Fathers
- Write a letter to your newborn about the day he/she was born.
- How has fatherhood changed you?
- What do you wish for your child on his/her birthday?

Husbands
- Write about your courtship/proposal.
- What traits have you "inherited" from your spouse?
- How is marriage different than you expected?

Sons
- Agree to a "Where will you be in 10 years?" interview
- What's your earliest memory as a child?
- Describe the highlights of your teenage years.

Grandfathers
- How do parenting and grandparenting differ? Describe the differences.
- Tell the grandchildren stories about your children. Kids love hearing about what kind of children their parents were.
- Describe what life was like before the technological innovations of today.

MATERIALS Fresh Cuts font (EK Success) • Chemistry font (Creating Keepsakes) • Think Small and Sleigh Ride fonts (twopeasinabucket.com) • eyelets • ink • twine • brads • *Page by Erin Lincoln*

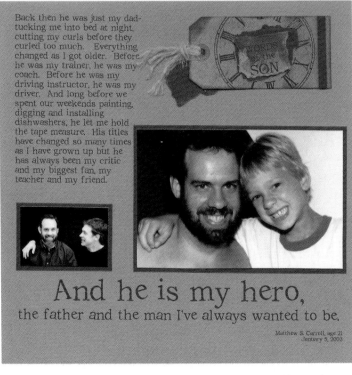

MATERIALS CK Newsprint font (Creating Keepsakes) • tag (Making Memories) • rubber stamp (Stampers Anonymous) • black stamping ink • twine • *Page by Barbara Carroll*

moments

THE WORLD WILL NEVER STARVE

FOR WANT OF WONDERS,

BUT FOR WANT OF WONDER.

....

G. K. CHESTERTON

What new supplies should you buy? How do you use what you have? In this section, you'll learn to get the most out of your scrapbook supplies, from alphabet stamps to polka dots to ribbon.

Use

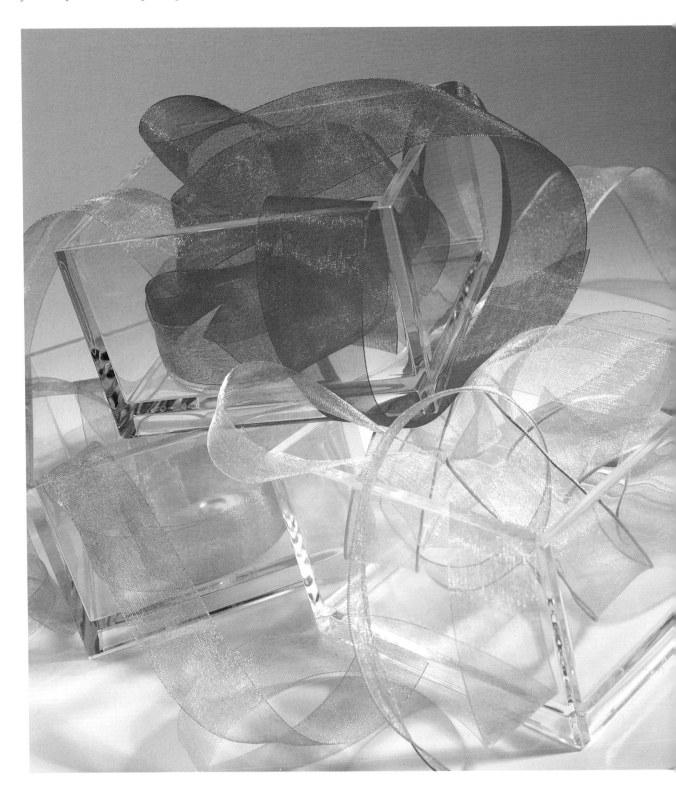

Creative
SPACE

COLORED
PENCILS

Lisa Adams Photography

Do you long for a space of your very own? Are you a kitchen table scrapper who spends precious creative time packing and unpacking supplies from a crammed box or closet, and looking for things you know you have but can't seem to find? If this sounds all too familiar to you, help is on the way! By investing a little space and money, your very own scrapping sanctuary can become a reality.

by Donna Downey

Personally, nothing makes me happier than a well-organized and attractive workspace that allows me to see and access my scrapbooking supplies. When I'm organized, I'm happy. I also love to see how other scrappers organize their spaces, and I've noticed something interesting; we tend to make our creative spaces functional, but not always attractive. So, I decided to design something that a space-challenged scrapper could easily assimilate into any room. And it had to be both an efficient workspace and an inviting place of inspiration. By working through the following steps, I hatched a fool-proof plan:

Define your space Whether it's a nook in your kitchen or a wall in your bedroom, define your space by taking measurements. Knowing the exact dimensions will allow you to plan how to use it best. Draw a sketch of your space to take with you when you shop. It's easier than trying to explain it to someone at your local hardware store. If you like, take along a photo of the room and color swatches to help you coordinate your new space with the rest of the room.

Make a list What supplies do you need to store? How much room do you have to devote to workspace? Listing these things can help you identify the size and type of furniture and accessories you need. Decide where the items will fit and how much space you'll allot for them. Add the larger items (desk, shelves, etc.) to your sketch.

Create a budget Consult your list—and your bank account balance—and decide how much you can spend on furnishings. Decide which items you're willing to spend more money on and where you're willing to skimp. Look around the house to see what you already have; you may be able to recycle items from other areas. (For example, an old tackle box or makeup case could be used to store embellishments and small tools, freeing up money for larger purchases.) Allow yourself time to search for the best deals on higher-ticket items like desks and shelving.

I started with four feet of wall space and made my sketch. Then I made a list of eight things I definitely needed to buy for my space, and worked out a budget of $500. Plan in hand, I headed out the door.

WORK SURFACE

Optimize your workspace by choosing the largest work surface you can afford that will fit into your area.

COMPUTER DESK

$250

This whitewashed 4- x 2-foot desk has more of a furniture feel. The built-in side shelf (not shown) and drawers provide storage space, and the neutral color works with a variety of decors.
pier1.com

Do it for less

FOLDING TABLE
$18-$60
The Lifetime Accents folding tables, available at membership warehouse stores, provide an inexpensive and functional work surface. They come in many sizes and styles to fit most needs.

More Options

Yard and garage sales are the perfect places to find tables and desks that can be refinished or painted and placed into small spaces.

TOOL/ADHESIVE STORAGE

Choose a system that allows you the most efficiency. Easy access to your tools and adhesives is a must.

SHELVING

Optimize your vertical space by adding a shelf or shelves above your workspace.

6-SHELF CUBIT & DRAWERS
$99.75 (1 cube and 4 drawers @$9.95each)
These drawers are ideal for storing all the "little things" like adhesives, small tools, scissors, rubber stamps, punches, etc. scrapncube.com

Do it for less

PLASTIC STORAGE CADDY WITH HANDLE
$2-$10
Commonly sold as utensil carriers or cleaning supply totes, plastic caddies are available at craft, grocery and discount stores. They're easy to transport and stow away when not in use.

SHELF KIT
$18.94
This Lewis Hyman 48 x 8 shelf kit comes with hardware to install. Other sizes are available. lowes.com

Do it for less

UNFINISHED SHELVES
$9-$15
Craft stores, home improvement centers and unfinished furniture stores offer pre-assembled, unfinished shelves that can be painted, stained, stamped, etc., to match any décor.

More Options

Go to your local hardware store, ask them to cut a board to the size you need, and then pick up some inexpensive fittings for attaching it to the wall.

PAPER STORAGE

Choose something sturdy and convenient that keeps your paper and cardstock accessible. If possible, store all your paper where you can see it.

IDEA STORAGE

This tool should definitely be mobile. When making a trip to your local scrapbook store, this goes with you.

6-SHELF CUBIT
$59.95
These shallow 12 x 12 shelves can accommodate approximately 300 sheets of paper per shelf. The unit can be positioned horizontally or vertically.
scrapncube.com

Do it for less

STACKABLE PAPER TRAYS
$48.99 each
Each box of Perfect Paper Stackable Paper Trays comes with 10 plastic trays perfect for 12 x 12 paper and cardstock.
scrapbook.com

More Options

Plastic stacking crates are affordable and hold standard legal-size file folders, which are large enough to store 12 x 12 cardstock.

STORAGE CLIPBOARD
$13.86
Fasten your notes and lists to the top of this Eldon Durable clipboard and put swatches, photos, etc. inside. Your next trip to the scrapbook store will be a huge success.
officedepot.com

Do it for less

HARDBOARD CLIPBOARD
$1
Use a traditional clipboard as your portable desktop to keep your notes secure.

PHOTO STORAGE

Develop a system for organizing your photos. Choose one that works best for the way you like to scrapbook.

EMBELLISHMENT STORAGE

Maybe it's time to re-think this one. We spend a lot of time and money on these colorful little things and then we hide them in a drawer…Why?

PEN STORAGE

Keep your pens and pencils nearby as you work.

PHOTO BOX
$3-$5

Photo boxes are an inexpensive and effective way to organize photos. Available at craft, photo, and discount stores, they come in a variety of fun colors, styles and designs.

Do it for less

MINI PHOTO ALBUMS
$.50-$1.00 each

These inexpensive photo albums hold up to 100 4 x 6 photos. Simply label the cover or inside pocket with a list of photo contents for easy reference.

GLASS JARS
$.75-$2 each

Glass jars are a fun way to display your treasures. They look great, and you can see what you have on hand. bottles.com

Do it for less

RECYCLED GLASS JARS
Free

Recycle empty mayonnaise, jelly, baby food, and other jars. Just wash them, peel off the labels, paint the caps, and decorate as you wish.

METAL TIN
$1.50

Inexpensive metal tins from craft stores are a fun way to store and display your markers and pens. Use them as is or paint them. Add dried beans to steady the pens.

Do it for less

USED COFFEE CAN
Free

To create the same storage, simply rinse out an empty coffee can and paint or decoupage it.

THE BOTTOM LINE
Total cost: $505.84

Ummm… can someone lend me $5.84? The bottom line is that creating the perfect workspace is all about what makes you happy. Create a space that you want to be in, one that inspires you to be creative. Add a scented candle, turn on your favorite music, and break out your favorite scrapping snack. Make sure you have a coaster for your favorite drink and a comfy chair, and let the scrapping begin!

Crammed for space? Look up! We'll show you three ways to gain vertical storage space in your scrapbooking area. Go ahead, put those scrapbook supplies on display...or hide them in your closet. It's up to you! Our budget-friendly solutions will show you how.

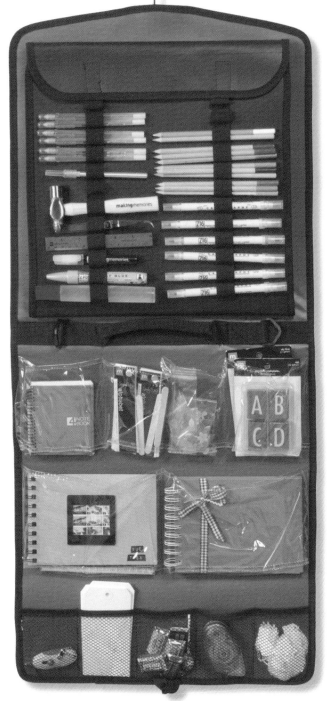

◄ What you need:
Jokari Scrapbook Organizer
jokari.com

Why: Need a portable, compact place to store scissors, punches, pens and other tools? This handy closet bag has lots of secret compartments, and the whole thing folds into a briefcase-sized carrier complete with shoulder strap. Stash all your tools in your closet or behind your door when not in use, then easily haul it all to your kitchen table or a scrapbooking session away from home.

What you need: ►
Generic expandable rack and jump rings available at major discount chains

Why: Hang tools, reference cards, packaged items and other things from the convenient hooks of an expandable rack, placed just above your scrapbooking desk or table. This leaves your workstation clear of extra pen, scissor and tool containers, and you can grab whatever you need in an instant. Since they expand and contract (and come in many sizes), you can even find one to fit inside a cupboard or closet

▼ What you need:

Generic wooden shelf, penholders and other containers. Our see-thru containers are from The Container Store, containerstore.com

Why: Scrapbook supplies are colorful and fun. If you've got space on the wall above your scrapbooking desk, in a craft room, or even in a laundry room, put all your stackables and storables on display in convenient clear containers. When you scrapbook, grab just what you need from your shelf and leave the rest stored safely out of reach of your little ones. Shelves are inexpensive, easy to install, and you can place them at whatever height you choose.

PHOTO BY CHERYL SHRADER

"LIFE BEGINS AS A QUEST OF THE CHILD

FOR THE MAN AND ENDS AS A JOURNEY

BY THE MAN TO REDISCOVER THE CHILD."

———

LAURENS VAN DER POST

From Shoebox to Showtime!

BY MICHELLE HOBBINS

Getting through your year-end backlog of photographs

I HAVE A PROBLEM.

I have twelve magnetic, acidic albums full of wedding and baby pictures. I have more than 375 rolls of developed film stored in envelopes. As "family historian," I hold in my possession two boxes of memorabilia dating back to 1830. And, to top it all off, I'm looking at a stack of holiday photographs that's been on my desk since last December! You've probably guessed my problem. I have a serious scrapbook backlog.

I've done the math. At a rate of two pages per hour, it would take me 157 consecutive days of uninterrupted crop time to catch up. And I continue to take photos faster than I can crop them. The backlog is growing.

Believe it or not, after years of soul-searching, I've found several helpful ways to deal with my backlog. It's easy. Just Get a Grip, Get Organized, and then Get Going.

GET A GRIP

Manage your fears, your priorities, your expectations

Think Positively

REALIZE that you will never, never, NEVER be done. You will keep taking pictures faster than you can scrapbook them, you will never have 157 consecutive days to dedicate to scrapbooking, and not all of your "Christmas 2003" photos will find their way into an album. We inherited boxes from our grandparents, and guess what? Our grandchildren will inherit boxes too.

Once you accept this fact, you can move on and deal with the problem. In fact, you may even start thinking of your backlog as an asset, a stockpile of options rather than an obligation.

Do What's Most Important

YOUR scrapbook backlog is evidence of a rich, full life and detailed history. From it, choose the projects that are most important to *you*, not to your friends, your mother or favorite page designers.

Don't trap yourself into thinking you have to scrapbook chronologically. In fact, it's ultimately more satisfying to start with the things that are most important to you now. For instance, while exploring my family history, I came across some original documents that are on the verge of decay, which makes a heritage book my priority. My friend has a son who started college this fall, so her priority is a book of memories for him.

Here's a glimpse of what's important right now to a few scrapbookers I know of all ages:

"Life from when we were babies, and pages of sports for my brother, because he's a huge sports kinda guy."
– Gretchen, 11 years old, Iowa

"Seasonal pages… they're less intimidating for me, and I want to capture special holiday memories for my children."
– Judy, 41 years old, Ohio

"'Whoppers'— a scrapbook of great fishing spots and tech-niques, including how to clean and fry pan fish. My grandkids need to know these things!"
– Gene, 62 years old, Wisconsin

Break the Rules

MANY scrapbookers believe that every page must be perfect, and must include a title, journaling and embellishments. Not true! If creating titles takes too much time, make only one title page for the entire album. If you hate journaling, just label your photographs, substitute an itinerary, or create one journaling box for the entire album. Forget the embellishments and opt for a photo collage—which is also a great way to use lots of photographs. Remember, there are no MUSTS!

In the end, the trick isn't to get rid of the backlog; it's to appreciate it. It represents you, and you have a wealth of memories and experiences to draw upon. With so much material, you'll never be at a loss to tell your story, and you'll never be bored scrapbooking!

GET ORGANIZED
Prioritize and categorize your files

Box It Up

NOW that you realize you can't do it all and that you should start with the memories that matter most to you, you need a way to organize your photos. To make sure you use your limited scrapbooking time efficiently and stay focused on your favorites, organize your photos into an A-B-C filing system, as follows:

A **IMPORTANT**
These are photos you love that need a scrapbook home ASAP.

B **SOMEDAY**
These photos belong in a scrapbook eventually, and they would likely be just fine slipped into archival, pocket-style photo albums.

C **NEVER**
These photos are outtakes and extra pictures from events that have already found homes in albums.

Start all your new projects with photos from the "A" file. When you're done with a particular event, move extra or duplicate photos to the "C" file.

The "B" files, to be used someday,

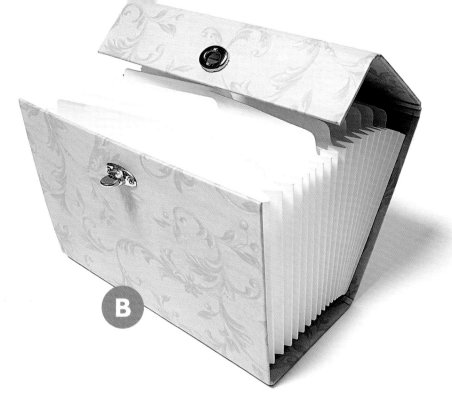

need special storage consideration. If you don't have a lot of scrapbooking time, this is where most of your incoming photos should be. Label and save them until you run short on "A" photos, until you need material for a long cropping retreat, or until you retire.

Now for that tricky "C" file. Those extra photos and poor-quality shots may really belong

in the trash, but if throwing away pictures seems just too final, save them in a "C" file. Every now and then, clean out your file, just like you clean out your closet. When you're done, you will feel much more organized and efficient. I know. After scrapbooking a recent trip to Ireland, I threw away the extra photos in my "C" file. It felt so good!

Save to Disk

JUST knowing you have memorabilia that should be moved out of old, unsafe albums can make you feel guilty. But finding the time to redo them is a challenge. Wouldn't it be great to copy those pages in color, or place them on digital media, such as CDs or DVDs? If you don't have the means or the time, call in the experts.

Have your magnetic albums scanned and placed on a CD or DVD for as little as $1 per page. Or have them scanned and reprinted on archival-quality paper for a few dollars. Just send the pages to a duplication service, and they do the work for you. Not only have you preserved precious heirlooms, you also get to keep the original "as is" for as long as it lasts.

Or, if you just want a few pictures out of an old magnetic album, use a self-service copy machine or photo kiosk to do it yourself. I've even used the copy shop to duplicate full pages from magnetic albums onto my own acid- and lignin-free paper. Since magnetic albums are usually 8.5 x 11, they fit nicely on a color copier; for best results, lift off the clear album page overlay when photocopying.

Digital archiving A great way to store photos

Check your local copy store or the Internet for scrapbook duplication and CD services. Here are a few to get you started:

Digital Scanning Services will scan and restore photographs, documents, old magnetic albums, even objects and slides. **digitalscanningservices.com**
My Scrapbook CD scans old and new albums, creates online slideshows and high-resolution printable files on CD or DVD, optionally adds text, scans individual photos out of albums, and reprints on archival-quality paper. **myscrapbookcd.com**
Saving Scraps of Life scans old and new scrapbooks and stores them on CD or DVD as online slideshows, e-mail-suit-able images or high-resolution printable images.
savingscraps.com
Kinko's office and print centers offer document imaging services, self-service and full-service color copiers, rental of computers with high-resolution scanners, and digital photo kiosks.
Kodak Picture Maker and **Sony PictureStation** photo kiosks, available at camera stores, scrapbook stores, pharmacies and other retail stores, include a scanner and editing tools. Restore or enhance photographs as large as 8 x 10. Output is printed on photo-quality paper. Kodak and Sony both have store locators on their Web sites.

GET GOING

Scrap faster using coordinated products and Simple Schemes

Coordinated Product

K & Company Amelia patterned paper, right, border stickers, charmers, frames and word tags *kandcompany.com*

NOW that you've changed your attitude about your backlog and found an easy way to organize your photos, it's time to get going on your next scrapbook!

If you'd like to really make a dent in those extensive files of photos, you've got to find a way to scrap faster. If you're a typical scrapbooker, you spend as much time selecting papers and searching for matching embellishments as you do actually creating your pages. Save oodles of time in the planning and design stages by using coordinated products and Simple Schemes.

Reduce the time you spend browsing, deciding, second-guessing and comparing. Choose one product line for a particular album or section of your scrapbook, such as the three pictured on this page. (They're found in most scrapbook stores.) The hard work of matching papers and accents has been done for you, and you won't be overwhelmed by all the product choices out there. Then follow our Simple Schemes to create your title page, table of contents and filler pages, and you'll eliminate the time you usually spend arranging and rearranging each layout.

SEI Mini Memories Rusty patterned paper, cardstock and alphabet stickers *shopsei.com*

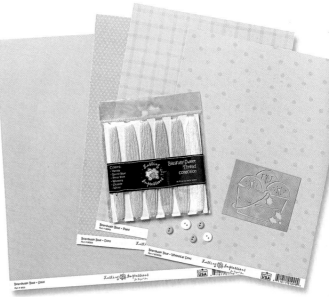

Lasting Impressions Boardwalk Blue patterned paper, above, cardstock, thread, embossing template and buttons *lastingimpressions.com*

title page scheme

table of contents scheme

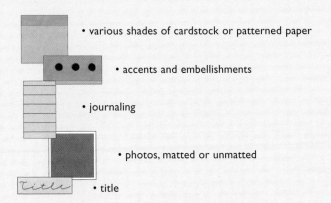

- various shades of cardstock or patterned paper
- accents and embellishments
- journaling
- photos, matted or unmatted
- title

filler page scheme

Simple Schemes

BRENDA BRAUN, of Spokane Valley, Washington, completed all these pages in no time—using a single set of schemes and one of the three coordinated product lines pictured on the previous page. Notice how each page looks unique and individualized, even though the same design guidelines were used.

title page

filler page

LASTING Impressions' Boardwalk Blue coordinating solids, stripes and other patterned papers helped Brenda with her cool winter pages.

title page

filler page

filler page (modified)

K & Company's Amelia line is great for heritage albums. Brenda used dotted, floral and gingham paper and matching 3-D tags to create these ancestor tribute pages.

filler page (modified)

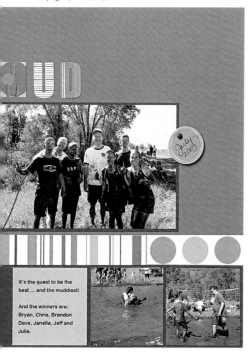

table of contents (modified)

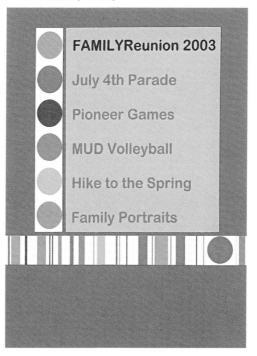

FOR her family reunion layouts, Brenda used SEI Mini Memories coordinated paper and alphabet stickers. Our Simple Schemes made the design fast and easy.

solutions

If you feel overwhelmed

by the size of your photo stack, it's time to take a different approach. You don't need all your photos to save the memory of an experience or an event; you just need one. Then, rely on the combination of the photo and some descriptive journaling to tell the whole story and save the mood of the moment.

This approach has some advantages:

Room to journal. A picture may be worth a thousand words, but your words have worth, too. When you use just one photo on the page, you have plenty of room to tell the story.

Room to play. With a single photo, you have room to add accents that contribute to the story—and still maintain a sense of spaciousness.

Focus on the quality of the content, not the quantity of photos used! Slip remaining photos into protector pages in an album if you like, and put them behind your story page.

BEING A KID

There were some really great shots of you playing up at Chelsea Heights from this roll. For some reason, this photo—one in which you are nowhere to be seen—is by far my favorite. See, with this photo, I close my eyes and see you running like a wild banshee, digging in the dirt, screaming all the way down the winding slide, and going up to any kid you can find in an effort to make a new friend for an hour. Carefully lined up where the concrete meets the sand, this tells me my boy is happy and doing exactly what any four-year-old boy on a summer day should be doing—having the best time ever. Sure, I've got more photographic proof, but I think some things in this life are best left to the imagination. 8.02

SUMMERTIME

A BATH TONIGHT

If you love Cathy Zielske's designs as much as we do, pick up a copy of her book, Clean and Simple Scrapbooking, *from simplescrapbooksmag.com**

materials staples (Making Memories) • Dynamoe Hard and Futura fonts (Internet) *page by Cathy Zielske*

Boost your Workspace

A mini-magnet board on your desk means you can see your sketch, scheme or inspiration while you work! The more creative you get with your workspace, the more creative you'll feel in it!

magnet board by Pressed Petals
pressedpetals.com

clips by Umbra
umbra.com

circle magnets by iPop
madisonparkgreetings.com

Preserving Newsprint

Scrapbookers have a love/hate relationship with the newspaper: We love to save clippings for our albums, but we hate how quickly they yellow, fade and eventually deteriorate. Here are two solutions for keeping the scrapbook/newspaper union more permanent:

• Coat newsprint with Archival Mist, a spray that neutralizes acid while depositing an alkaline buffer to protect against future damage.

• Color-copy the article onto acid-free cardstock. Colored ink gives the copy a realistic look, while cardstock is more stable than newsprint. Photo-copying the article also allows you to reduce or enlarge the text as necessary.

More Fun Than a Card

These fun mini-albums by Stacey Sattler are easy to make, so you can keep one for yourself and give others away as gifts. Best of all, they're cheap! Make these for about $3—less than the cost of some store-bought cards.

Brag Book on a Chain

Carry this album made of luggage tags in your purse and show off your favorite photos. ❶ Trim patterned paper to fit into the tag openings. ❷ Trim photos and adhere to the paper. ❸ Add accents and slip finished "pages" into the tag openings. Tags also come with plastic ties, which attach easily to backpacks, purses or key rings.

materials Scotch luggage tags (3M) • patterned paper (Daisy D's Paper Co. and Anna Griffin) • alphabet stamps (Hero Arts) • rub-ons, safety pin and eyelet letter (Making Memories) • flower charm (KI Memories) • ribbon

A Little Bit of Autumn

Make this tiny album from a page of slide holders. ❶ Trim the page into strips. ❷ Fold one or more strips accordian-style, and punch small holes on one side to make the binding. ❸ With the book open, cut cardstock slightly larger than the pages to make the cover. ❹ Punch holes that line up with the binding holes and attach cover to page binding with ribbon. ❺ Decorate the cover and add a title.

materials slide holder (Deluxe Designs) • alphabet stamps (Hero Arts) • plastic slide protectors • ribbon • ink

Carter's Favorite Things

Make this scrapbook from tags that are already attached at the back. ❶ Cut blocks of cardstock to fit on the tags. ❷ Ink the edges of the tags and blocks with an ink pad. ❸ Trim drawings and labels to fit, and ink the edges. ❹ Adhere the blocks to the tags and embellish tags with ribbon.

materials gang tag (Impress Rubber Stamps) • ribbon • brown ink pad

The Wheels on the Bus

This scrapbook is a great way to hold a collection of school photos inside a large die-cut shape. ❶ Cut apart individual photo album sleeves from an album page. ❷ Stack the pages between two die cuts. ❸ Attach all layers at the top with colored brads. ❹ Label and add accents.

materials patterned paper and letter stickers (Doodlebug Design, Inc.) • bus die cut (Ellison) • photo album pages (Pulp Paper Products) • brads

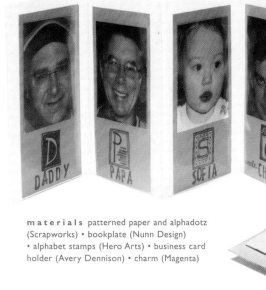

materials patterned paper and alphadotz (Scrapworks) • bookplate (Nunn Design) • alphabet stamps (Hero Arts) • business card holder (Avery Dennison) • charm (Magenta)

We Are Family

This tiny family scrapbook fits into a business card holder! ❶ Cut apart a page of business card holders vertically. ❷ Insert cut cardstock blocks to fit into the holders. ❸ Attach photos and stamp or accent the blocks. ❹ Slip finished blocks into holders. ❺ Place album into holder and add accents.

Go Topless

Here's a way to stretch your scrapbooking dollar and your creativity. It's what we call a "two-fer," two albums for the price of one! The front and back cover of most post-bound albums can each be used as the base for one ribbon-bound "topless" version. Your title page doubles as a cover and coordinates with your binding material for a quick-and-easy decorative album to display!

materials post-bound album and protectors (Making Memories) • Sharon Ann patterned paper (C-Thru Ruler Co.) • mesh paper (Magenta) • vellum title (Pixie Press) • charms • ribbon • markers • brad • jute • chalk • *samples by Kris Parkin*

Simple Steps

Step 1: Gather your tools and supplies.

Here's what you'll need:
• drill and block of wood
• post-bound album and protectors
• trim, such as ribbon, twine or jute

Step 2: Drill holes

Fold the spine twice, once over the covered flap and again onto the album back. Drill holes through the whole spine, using the existing set on top as a guide.

Step 3: Tie album together

From the back of the cover, thread ribbon, twine, or jute through holes. Thread page protectors onto the cover, and then push ribbon through the holes in the spine. Fold spine over protectors and tie tightly.

Original Artwork

"I was inspired to create this page when my daughter Emily wanted to color one day," says reader Amanda Goodwin. "Instead of giving her a coloring book or a sheet of computer paper, I handed her a 12 x 12 sheet of cardstock. While she was creating her masterpiece, I snapped some photos. By the time she finished, I had everything I needed to create a layout. Just as Emily brings color to her artwork, she brings color to our lives."

you color
my world

Emily, not only do you bring color to your beautiful works of art, but you bring color into the lives of everyone you come in contact with! Your smile is enough to brighten someone's day, and your genuine, "I love you!" is enough to melt their heart.

materials
stickers (SEI)
• Garamouche font
(P22 Type Foundry)
• eyelets • *page by Amanda Goodwin*

A CHILD'S CREATIVITY + A PHOTO + A MOTHER'S PERSPECTIVE = A TRUE PIECE OF ART.

scrapbooking made easy • use   **121**

Fast and Fabulous Pages

Simple Scrapbooks contributing editor Donna Downey uses this stress-busting, 3-step page-building process to create fast, fabulous layouts when she's in catch-up mode. Try it. You'll save time and money, and free your creative energy to focus on showcasing your favorite photographs. It can really be this easy!

1. SELECT A SINGLE COLOR of cardstock for your background.

2. TIGHTLY TRIM SNAPSHOTS and build a photo collage.

3. LIMIT PRODUCT USAGE. Not every page needs an accent. Introducing one additional color of cardstock for a title or journaling will add variety while keeping your design very simple.

materials Simply Stated rub-on word (Making Memories) • Marydale font (Internet) • *page by Donna Downey*

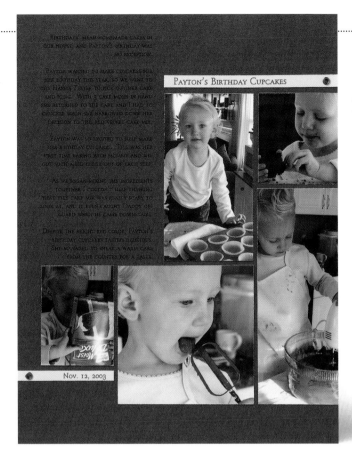

PAYTON'S BIRTHDAY CUPCAKES

Nov. 12, 2003

Scrapbook pages don't have to be complicated and time-consuming to look great!

materials Schindler small caps font (Internet) • eyelets • *page by Donna Downey*

Whiteners'
sunflowers
09.03

Flowers
... are a proud
assertion
that a ray of
beauty
outvalues all
the utilities
of the world.

Ralph Waldo Emerson

materials Moms Typewriter font (Internet) *page by Donna Downey*

Get Oriented

What size are you? 12 x 12? 8 x 8? 8 1/2 x 11? 11 x 8 1/2? Scrapbooks come in all shapes and sizes. And sometimes, they come in a standard size with a new orientation, like the new 11 x 8 1/2 albums. This new landscape orientation gives you more designing options for both your "paper and paste" and digital projects. Ask your local scrapbook store about this new size, currently available from the following companies:

SEI
shopsei.com
800.333.3279

Century Photo Products
centuryphoto.com
800.767.0777

materials Nostalgiques letter stickers (EK Success) • Garamond font (Adobe Systems) • ribbon • *page by Cathy Zielske*

Saving on Supplies

If you're like me, you hate to waste paper. It costs money—money that you could use to buy more scrapbooking supplies. Instead of matting a photo to a block of cardstock, cut a frame to place over the photo and save the middle for other projects.

Get your
patterned paper
out of your files and
onto your layouts.
Strategies for
combining patterns
are key!

patterns
for success

by Amy Sorensen

I've got a dilemma: I'm obsessively fond of patterned paper. Orange patterned paper, to be precise. Splashed in fruity hues or stippled in pumpkin tones, an orange pattern is impossible for me to resist. But if you glanced through my scrapbooks, you'd find precious few layouts accented with any patterned paper, let alone orange. Why? Patterned paper seems intimidating. Maybe it will overpower the pictures; the colors might clash, the patterns jar. So I've stuck to using timid bits of patterned paper as accents and kept most of my stash filed away.

I bet you face the same problem, because buying patterned paper is easy; actually using it is a little scary. The solution?

A bold step: combine patterned papers. Work with more than one pattern on a layout and your pages will be unique and colorful. They'll have an emotional appeal. And you'll be using your stash of precious paper rather than letting it languish. Read on to discover guidelines and strategies to help you unlock the secrets of patterned paper combinations.

Illustration by Traci O'Very Covey

general guidelines

Creating contrast is the key to successful pattern combinations. The resulting tension adds energy, emotion, and visual appeal. First, choose a paper with themes, colors, and proportions that support your pictures. Then add other patterns, keeping these basics in mind: establish variety in size and design; pair big patterns with small; and combine soft, flowing, or organic lines with the regularity of stripes or plaids.

1 Emphasize one paper over the others to create cohesion. Low contrast or neutral patterns are good for large areas, while bold, bright, or graphic patterns work best in smaller spots.

2 Use compatible styles. For example, you wouldn't match vintage florals with contemporary geometrics, because the two styles don't feel the same.

3 Choose closely related color schemes. Since the differences in pattern create the contrast, use colors with similar values, intensities or temperatures.

A gradient of stripes, florals, and tone-on-tone patterns establishes contrast that creates a unified design.

keep shining

Stacey Sattler | Toledo, OH

keep shining my bright And shining star of a son

materials patterned paper (Sweetwater) • alphabet stamps (PSX and Hero Arts) • ink (Ranger Industries, Inc.) • antique pearl buttons • brass frames • paper flowers

specific strategies

Once you understand the general guidelines, you'll use these specific strategies for creating combinations with confidence.

- ◼ Use coordinated paper lines. They're designed to work together.

- ◼ Combine organic designs (like florals) with linear patterns (like stripes or checks), and vary the pattern sizes.

- ◼ Use unequal amounts of paper.

four generations of family

Marnie Flores | Madison, WI

A color characteristic that unifies several different papers —here, it's the tan background in each pattern— creates an evocative whole.

title page

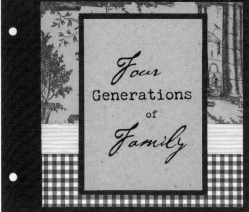

dedication page

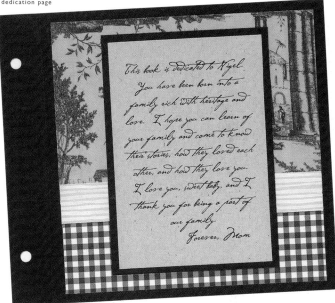

filler page

filler page

materials patterned paper (KMA, Magenta and K & Company) • book screws (Tsukineko)

STRATEGY ONE:
coordinated paper lines

Thin stripes, fat stripes, and squiggly lines create variety; a full piece of horizontally-striped paper emphasizes the focal-point photo, journaling, and pattern all at once.

girlfriends

Marnie Flores | Madison, WI

materials patterned paper and Alphadotz (Scrapworks) • Doodle Dash font (Inspire Graphics) • metal-rimmed tags (Avery Dennison)

Create a soft, subtle combination by pairing variety in line structure—both straight and curly. The monochromatic color scheme lets it shine.

blue sky

Pam Talluto | Rochester Hills, MI

"I never get tired of the blue sky"
.... Vincent von Gogh

Sara and Marc caught on the roof
June 2000

materials patterned paper (Close To My Heart) • Cezanne title and Splendid 66 journaling fonts (Internet) • vellum • staples

sisters, soulmates

MaryRuth Francks | Spokane, WA

m a t e r i a l s patterned paper, letter stickers and buttons (Doodlebug Design, Inc.) • Tempus Sans font (Microsoft Word) • Beautiful font (twopeasinabucket.com)

The placement of round buttons on the vertical pattern both reinforces the circular design and heightens the visual contrast.

grandma knows best

Stacey Sattler | Toledo, OH

m a t e r i a l s patterned paper (Design Originals) • ink (Ranger Industries, Inc.) • CAC Pinafore font (Internet) • buttons

Repeated in each paper is the feel of an antique sewing pattern, which helps create a style that mirrors the subject's era.

Color connections—tan and celery in the floral and stripe, powder blue in all three—help the combination click.

brothers

Stacey Sattler | Toledo, OH

materials patterned paper (Magenta, Chatterbox, Inc., and All My Memories) • rub-ons (Making Memories) • tokens (Doodlebug Design, Inc.) • bookplate (twopeasinabucket.com) • ribbon

girl power

Pam Talluto | Rochester Hills, MI

The large block of floral print emphasizes femininity, while the bold stripes suggest strength, resulting in visual and emotional energy.

materials patterned paper (NRN Designs, Lasting Impressions and Scrapbook Wizard) • Codex and Typist fonts (Internet) • colored pencils

STRATEGY THREE:
plaid + stripe + tone-on-tone

3

hilary harker

Marnie Flores | Madison, WI

The organic swirls of the tonal yellow paper in the tag add a softness to the more rigid patterns of stripes and plaids, tying the layout together.

materials patterned paper (Paper Garden, Doodlebug Designs, Inc. and All My Memories) • letter stickers (SEI) • square metal-rimmed tag (Making Memories)

one of the highlights of Matthias and Emma's visit to Washington was the afternoon we spent in Riverfront Park.

Some of the highlights of our day in the park:

- Lunch on the beautiful lawns
- Feeding the Ducks
- The Red Radio Flyer wagon
- The Train Ride around the park
- The Carousel Ride
- "Running" with the Bloomsday runners

riverfront park

MaryRuth Francks | Spokane, WA

An equal amount of stripes and tone-on-tone pattern, accented with strips of plaid made with moss and periwinkle colors, creates a balanced combination.

materials patterned paper (Paper Fever, Cross My Heart and Making Memories) • Unforgettable title font (twopeasinabucket.com) • CK Handprint journaling font (Creating Keepsakes) • buttons

White Hot!

9 IDEAS FOR WHITE SCRAPBOOK PAGES

Close your eyes for a minute and think about the color white: clean white linens, soft white portrait backgrounds, crisp white shirts. There's just something about white that's fresh and new and invigorating. And that goes for white scrapbook pages, too.

So what's so great about white pages? White is fast and easy. Just add your photos, journaling and a few touches of color. There's no need for a lot of extra effort or materials. White is versatile. It works well for a page loaded with photos, or it can be perfect for showcasing just one. White is universal. It goes with any color and provides a strong contrast for your photos, helping even those that aren't matted to stand out.

At the same time, there are some challenges to scrapbooking on a white page. The brightness of the white can reflect other colors, making your photos look washed out. Too much white may be overpowering and make your eyes tired. And an album filled with white pages risks looking tedious and uninspired.

But armed with a little knowledge and a few design tips, you can turn out page after white page that simply sparkles and shines! Check out these ideas and tips, and soon you'll be creating "white hot" pages, too!

BY GAYLE HUMPHERYS

trlly love a child....

SILLY

encourage

Brandon - May 2002

Supplies *Eyelets:* The Stamp Studio; *Stamping ink:* ColorBox, Clearsnap, Inc.; *Letter stickers:* Karen Foster Design; *Pen:* Zig Millennium, EK Success; *Idea to note:* Renee created the "swirls" using a long-bristled stencil brush dabbed on an inkpad.

"Encourage Silly"

by Renee Camacho
Nashville, TN

WHY IT WORKS

White can be just the right choice for showcasing a black-and-white photo. The bright colors of Renee's ink swirls reflect the playful mood of the photo, and layering the ink on white ensures that the "true" pigment comes through. Renee also introduced a pleasing contrast of line in her layout through the rectangular photo and circular swirls.

DESIGN TIP

Using stamping ink is a safe and easy way to add texture and color without having to layer additional elements on the page.

YOU CAN DO THIS

Say Cheese.......
Daddy was going outside to work on the pond and put a bandanna on his head. Since you were tagging along to help, he decided that you also needed a bandanna!

June 2, 2002

Page by Christy Branham. **Supplies** *Patterned papers:* My Mind's Eye (red), source unknown (navy); *Buttons:* Dress-It-Up, Cut-It-Up; *Embroidery floss:* DMC; *Computer font:* Kristin, downloaded from the Internet.

Strap-hinge albums commonly come pre-loaded with white scrapbook pages. Since strap-hinge album pages are designed to hold photos on both the front and back of the same page, it can be difficult to use page embellishments such as eyelets or sewn-on items that might go through the entire page. Christy Branham found an easy way to get around this problem: place the embellishment on patterned paper first! Follow these three easy steps:

1. Cut a piece of patterned paper or cardstock to go underneath the eyelet, brad, button or other fastener-type accent. It might be part of a photo mat or simply a small square or strip.
2. Attach or sew the accent to the cut piece of paper or cardstock.
3. Adhere the accented piece to your scrapbook page with adhesive.

"Finkle Shore's Park"

by Leslie Lightfoot
Stirling, ON, Canada

WHY IT WORKS

Leslie's layout is a terrific example of using white for "positive" and "negative" space. She created positive space with the square detail photos on top—the closeness of the photos and the equal spacing between them gives a smooth path for the eye to follow. Notice how Leslie positioned two visual triangles within this top section—one using photos of the green field and one using close-ups of her son in his red hat.

The large white border around the bottom photo functions as negative space. It permits the eye to rest from the detail on the top, and helps the large photo stand out. Creating a "flip-up" area under the large photo gave Leslie extra room for journaling and additional photos without affecting this margin space.

LIFT HERE

Supplies *Square punch:* Marvy Uchida; *Computer font:* Daniel, downloaded from the Internet

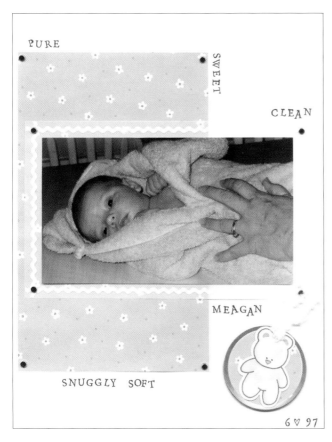

PURE

SWEET

CLEAN

MEAGAN

SNUGGLY SOFT

6 ♥ 97

Supplies *Patterned paper, rickrack sticker and die cut:* Doodlebug Design; *Tag and brads:* American Pin & Fastener; *Rubber stamps:* Hero Arts; *Stamping ink:* Stewart Superior Corp.; *Fibers:* Adornaments

"Meagan"

by Wendy Anderson
Heber City, UT

WHY IT WORKS

The repetition of white in various page elements brings unity to this layout. The small white flowers in the patterned paper reflect the theme of the layout. Patterned paper with white designs is a good choice to use with a white background. Wendy also incorporated white through the rickrack sticker border and tag fibers, further integrating the white background into the layout and promoting a harmonious arrangement.

"Bahsoo!"

by Polly Lund
Providence, UT

WHY IT WORKS

Layering the photos on top of each other not only enhances the "peek-a-boo" theme of Polly's layout, it also gives focal-point status to each photo. The white background provides a great contrast for the sepia photos, as well as for the layered vellum. The muted accent colors complement the photos without distracting from them, and their placement in opposite corners provides a sense of balance.

DESIGN TIP

Notice how all of the page elements have an "imperfect," playful feel—the ripped hearts, the hand-drawn border and the casual font.

Supplies *Computer font:* Scrap Twiggy, "Lettering Delights Deluxe" CD, Inspire Graphics; *Pen:* Zig Writer, EK Success; *Vellum:* Paper Adventures; *Pop dots:* All Night Media; *Embroidery floss:* DMC

After an entire weekend of vigorous playing, these two exhausted little cousins took a much-needed break to watch some TV.

May 2002

"Television Break"

by Pascale Michaud Finucan
Carleton Place, ON, Canada

WHY IT WORKS

The white text on top of the photos and blue strip helps integrate the white background into the overall layout, so it doesn't look like an afterthought. Placing the photos close together with equal spacing between them gives the eye a smooth path to follow. Pascale's sleek font choice also reinforces the clean, organized feel of the lines and spacing in the layout (notice how the width of the letters matches the spacing between the photos).

Supplies *Computer font:* Futura, Microsoft Word
Note: Pascale hand cut her letters. To save time, you can use stickers.

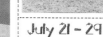

WHIRLWIND

WASHINGTON

July 21 – 29

During our visit to Maryland, we spent several HOT days exploring Washington, D.C. Great Aunt Mary was in the hospital, but Aunt Paula was able to accompany us to the National Air and Space Museum, the Washington Monument, the Vietnam War Memorial, the National Museum of American History, and the Lincoln Memorial.

On our own, we also went to Frederick, Maryland to the Museum of Civil War Medicine. Zane really enjoyed that and the gift shop yielded some great books and Civil War soldiers.

Supplies *Star die cuts:* Sticky Die Cuts, Provo Craft; *Computer fonts:* Stars & Stripes (title and date), "The Art of Creative Lettering" CD, Creating Keepsakes; Arial (journaling), Microsoft Word; *Pen:* Zig Millennium, EK Success; *Memorabilia:* Pilot "wings" from United Airlines, small banner cut from museum brochure, and a postcard from Vietnam War Memorial

"Washington Whirlwind"

by Harriet Miller
Lake Oswego, OR

WHY IT WORKS

Harriet's layout is a great example of how well a white background can work as a "clean canvas" for displaying a lot of photos with little embellishment. The photos are laid out in a grid-type fashion, accentuated by pen stitch marks. Simple accents complete the page and balance the layout (notice the visual triangle of stars through the two stickers and the pilot wings).

White Is White … Right? Wrong!

Take time to carefully select which variation of the color white you want for your layouts. Because white often has "warm" or "cool" undertones, you may significantly alter the way your photos feel on the page. For example, the warmth in older sepia photos would be lost if placed on a cool, ultra-white background. A colonial white, however, lends the appropriate luster to those images.

"Floating Skyward"

by Kim Morgan
Pleasant Grove, UT

WHY IT WORKS

White is the perfect background choice for this layout featuring colorful photos. By placing the top photos close together and lining up all the margins, Kim created a strong line that directs the eye through the layout. A limited color palette helps keep the viewer focused on the photos. Kim chose toned-down values for the mats and accents. The positioning and grouping of the photos provides one central area for both the title and journaling, so the eye doesn't jump around too much.

DESIGN TIP

White is a strong contrast to bright and dark colors. When working with a white background, introduce new colors one at a time and try working with analogous colors (three or four colors next to each other on the color wheel) to minimize color contrasts that can dominate photographs.

FLOATING
SKYWARD

Each year that we visit the Freedom Festival balloon launch, you enjoy it more — as long as we don't stand too close to the noisy flames. 7/4/02

Supplies *Pen:* Zig Writer, EK Success; *Eyelets:* Doodlebug Design; *Embroidery floss:* DMC

"White is not a mere absence of color; it is a shining and affirmative thing, as fierce as red, as definite as black. God paints in many colors; but He never paints so gorgeously, I had almost said so gaudily, as when He paints in white."

—*Gilbert K. Chesterton*

White background paper repeated in thin photo mat

Low contrast colors pulled from photos

Photos overlapped and in contrasting shapes

Horizontal lines add direction, and stability, and echo shirt pattern

Page by Jenny Jackson. **Supplies** *Letter stickers:* Wedge Outline Sherbet Alphabet Letters, Provo Craft; *Computer font:* PC Block Italic, "For Fonts Sake" HugWare CD, Provo Craft.

When using a white background, keep these seven design guidelines in mind to get the best results. Remember, you don't have to use each element in every layout. Concentrate on two or three.

1 Margins and Spacing. Experiment with the negative space around and between your photos and other elements to find the combination that is the most pleasing. Often, using the same amount of space between photos (especially those that are close together), or lining everything up along the margins, creates a good line for your eye to follow.

2 Repetition of White. Look for ways to repeat white throughout your layout, such as in patterned paper or text placed on a colored accent or photo. This helps integrate the white background into the overall composition.

3 Visual Triangles. Help create balance and direct eye flow by placing items of the same color or shape at the points of a "visual triangle."

4 Color Contrast. Since white contrasts with almost any color, try to select accent colors that are analogous (close on the color wheel). These colors have a low contrast between them, which helps reduce the overall color contrast on the pages. Try to select colors that enhance your photos. Strong contrasting colors (those farther apart on the color wheel) should be used sparingly and with visually strong photos.

5 Photo Placement. Group your photos so they create balance and direction. Don't be afraid to overlap, create small clusters, and use contrasting shapes. Try cropping small detail photos to help your focal-point photo stand out.

6 Use of Lines. Consider using horizontal or vertical strips of paper on your layout. Lines add color, provide eye direction, and give a clean, graphic look. Lines also help connect or separate different elements on your page.

7 Leftover Space. Don't feel as though you have to fill up every inch of white space. Blank space lets your eye rest and helps you place emphasis on other areas or groups of photos on the page. If you feel you have too much white space left over, add more journaling, memorabilia or small page accents.

COOL IN THE POOL

STEPHANIE
JULY 2002
ALMOST 2

Supplies *Cardstock:* White Leather, Memory Lane; *Computer font:* RennieMacintosh, source unknown; *Square punch:* Marvy Uchida

"Cool in the Pool"

by Barbara Carroll
Tuscon, AZ

WHY IT WORKS

The white background gives this simple page a contemporary, graphic feel. The focal-point photo is positioned off-center, yet the title and small photos are centered to provide some balance. The lower photos (cropped with a square punch) narrow in on the details, and their smaller size helps keep the eye focused on the main photo. By printing the colored text and line right on the page and not matting her photos, Barbara ended up with a quick and easy layout!

DESIGN TIP

Jenny helped define the edge of the ripped center strip by sponging the torn edge with the same ink pad she used to stamp the background.

"Climb High, Climb Far"

by Jenny Jackson
Gilbert, AZ

WHY IT WORKS

Jenny used rubber stamps to give the white background a quick and easy texture. The ripped diagonal strip helps break up the stamped background and bring the eye to the center of the layout. The neutral colors of the ink and mat add interest to the layout but don't compete with the photos for your attention. Rubber stamps are a great solution for titles and quotes.

Supplies *Rubber stamps:* Close To My Heart (background), PSX Design (alphabet); *Stamping ink:* Close To My Heart

Accent Builder 101

By Stacy Julian

How to Sort, Store and Use your Stuff

Paperclips, bookplates, hinges, T-pins and twine. If you've walked the aisles of a scrapbook store recently, you may be like me—downright afraid of the huge variety of little embellishments that you can buy. Frankly, it's overwhelming, even if you're a seasoned scrapbooker. Accent Builder 101 to the rescue! This quick course is *Simple Scrapbooks'* solution for making sense of it all. We'll help you categorize and store your purchases, give you simple equations for combining and using them effectively, and provide lots of examples of easy accents you can make to enhance your pages.

Instead of efficiently trying to store 72 different types of embellishments, you'll be able to quickly classify everything you bring home into one of four categories and then easily find and work with what you have. The most exciting part is the creative confidence and freedom you'll discover by simply looking at all this stuff in a whole new way—as building blocks to custom accents.

Sort & Store

To get you started, we suggest investing in four stackable storage drawers, labeled with the following four categories:

1. Tags
2. Attachments
3. Trim
4. Tuck-ins

Sort your current stash of stuff into the four categories (examples follow on the next four pages), then simply drop new purchases in the right drawer when you bring them home.

Is it a tag? Throw it in your tag drawer. Is it ribbon or twine? You've got a spot for that, too. What about those tiny attachments? Use mini-containers like film canisters or zipper bags to separate brads from safety pins, but store them all in the same drawer.

As you begin sorting, you'll likely discover a personal preference for one category over another. This is perfectly okay and will actually help you settle on inspiration and ideas you can really use.

If you don't currently have any tuck-ins, purchase a few and see how they add to your creative potential.

Oh, and don't worry too much about the categories. Is a button an attachment or an extra? Well, it can be either one, depending entirely on how you use it.

Trust me, four labeled drawers will make it much easier to store and use all this fun and inspiring stuff.

Tint Stacking Drawers, available in sizes extra small through large: The Container Store **containerstore.com**

Building custom accents is easy when you know how to sort and store your embellishment purchases. Here, I combined a tuck-in frame with some ribbon, a tag and buttons! **m a t e r i a l s** patterned paper (KI Memories) • Inspirables frame and Zig Writer black pen (EK Success) • ribbon • buttons • tag

1 Tags

Tags come in all shapes, sizes and colors, but they always have a hole at the top so they can be attached to something else. Tags are wonderful for recording dates, short photo captions or even extensive journaling. They also work well to ground and unify smaller decorative elements. The versatility of tags makes them a must-have for scrapbookers of all levels.

1. Wish in the Wind 2. Kangaroo and Joey 3. Paper Reflections 4. Making Memories 5. Pebbles, Inc. 6. Avery Dennison 7. Westrim

2 Attachments

An attachment is anything that holds one or more things together. Eyelets, brads, buckles, jump-rings, paper and spiral clips, photo anchors, hinges, and any kind of pin are all attachments. Adhesive is no longer the only way to "attach" something to your page!

1. Making Memories 2. K & Company 3. The Happy Hammer 4. Paper Pizazz 5. Doodlebug Design, Inc.

Borrowed from the textile industry, trim is anything you tie, glue or stitch onto a page or another accent to add that "gotta touch it" texture to your pages. Choose from colorful ribbon and fibers to twine, jute, thread, lace, yarn and more. From the youthful feel of ric-rac to the elegance of organdy or velvet, these multi-purpose products can be used in simple ways to add a particular style to your pages.

Trim³

1. The Scrapbook Wizard   2. Trimtex   3. Little Black Dress Designs   4. Fiber Scraps   5. My Homemade Memories
6. Li'l Davis Designs   7. The Weathered Door   8. Making Memories   9. Twill Expressions

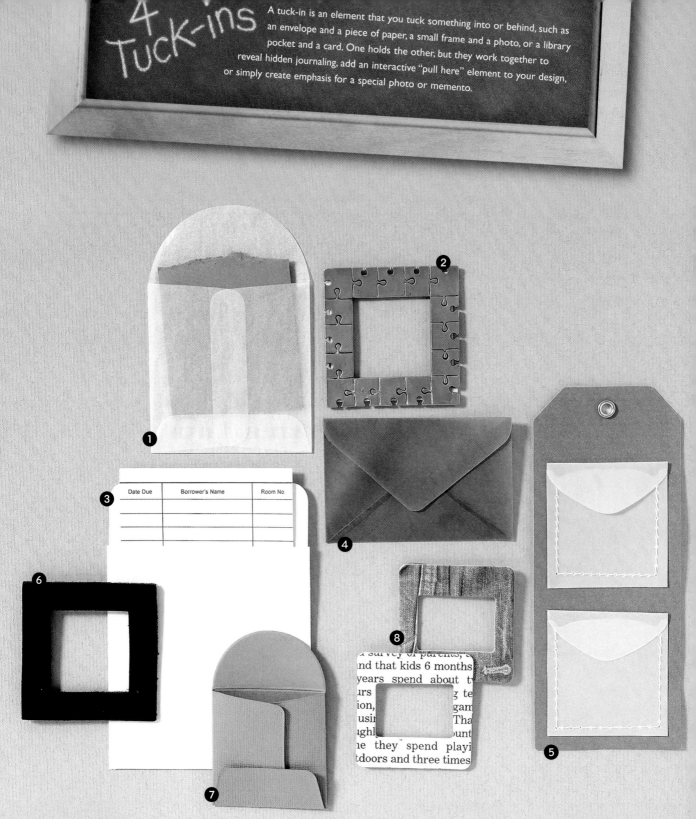

4 Tuck-ins

A tuck-in is an element that you tuck something into or behind, such as an envelope and a piece of paper, a small frame and a photo, or a library pocket and a card. One holds the other, but they work together to reveal hidden journaling, add an interactive "pull here" element to your design, or simply create emphasis for a special photo or memento.

Date Due	Borrower's Name	Room No

a survey of parents, ...
...nd that kids 6 months...
...years spend about t...
...urs ...g te...
...ion, ...gam...
...usi... ...Tha...
...ugh... ...unt...
...e they spend playi...
...tdoors and three times...

Extra! Extra!

Now, what about everything else? They're extras. From Christmas stickers to birthday charms, extras include seasonal elements like silk flowers and leaves, 3D alphabet letters, words or phrases, vintage bottle caps, fabric labels, and anything with a theme (baby, school, sports, holidays, vacation, relationships, etc.). You'll use these items to finish off any of the accents you build. Store them in a fifth stackable drawer, or in any other way you like.

1. Impress Rubber Stamps 2. Provo Craft 3. Boxer Scrapbook Productions 4. EK Success 5. Colorbök 6. Making Memories 7. embellish IT! 8. Deluxe Designs

Easy Equations

Once you've set up your drawers and sorted your stash, mix and match to create limitless accents. Try simple equations like these:

Tuck-in + Tag = hidden journaling

Trim + Attachment = a quick and easy border

Study the ideas on the next four pages for more easy equations. And remember, at *Simple Scrapbooks* we take an "easy on the accents" approach that helps you design clean pages. Very often, one accent on a page is all you need! Whether you combine elements from two drawers or all four, you'll be amazed at the endless possibilities you have to create something unique for your photos and story.

Try using a photo as the foundation for your accenting! A little trim and an attachment creates emphasis to help set this photo apart as my focal point.

christmas '02

Never forget: Chanda's excitement at introducing her new husband to the traditions of her childhood • The way Trey is mesmerized by every detail of Grandma's Christmas village • Dancing to the oldies • Seeing the 2nd generation of Hall cousins sing together on Christmas Eve • The $10 dollar bills tied to Grandma Addie's tree • Hearing mom read *A Cup of Christmas Tea* • The smell of roast pork and rolls baking in the oven • Falling asleep by the fire • How proud Dad is of their new house and all that Mom has done to make it magical • The "I got what I wanted" look on a little boy's face • Grandpa reading the Christmas story from the second chapter of Luke • The wonderful feeling of coming home

materials cardstock (Close To My Heart) • ribbon (Impress Rubber Stamps) • T-pin (Making Memories) • word stickers (Pebbles, Inc) • hemp • charms

Mix & Match

1 Tag + Trim + Extras

2 Tuck-in + Attachment + Extras

Rea[s]ons **2** LOVE ME!

3 Tag + Tuck-in + Trim

n irresisti svl that's my girl ... th adore with

5 Tuck-in + Extras

charming

4 Tuck-in + Tag + Trim + Attachment + Extra

Moments

6 Tuck-in + Trim + Attachment

holidays

materials 1. heart ribbon sliders (Sarah Heidt) • tag (Little Black Dress Designs) 2. mini brown paper bag (Impress Rubber Stamps) • lil' clips (American Traditional Designs) • letter stamps (PSX) • word sticker (Pebbles, Inc.) 3. leather frame and ribbon (Making Memories) • patterned paper • transparency 4. book pocket (Boxer Scrapbook Productions) • moments frame (Melissa Frances) • decorative clip (EK Success) • sticker (K & Company) • tags • ribbon 5. envelope (Paper Source) • mesh (Magic Mesh) • label (me & my BIG ideas) 6. envelope (Paper Source) • patterned paper (Anna Griffin) • clip (Nunn Designs) • printed ribbon (Making Memories)

① Tag + Trim + Extras

TRUlove

② Tuck-in + Trim + Extras

It's Party Time

③ Tuck-in + Attachments + Extras

⑤ Tag + Tuck-in + Trim + Attachment + Extra

⑥ Tuck-in + Trim + Extra

Red Jimmies Marathon Book Nike T-shirt

Womens Conference

Sisters

Smile

03

GIFT LIST christmas

④ Tuck-in + Tag + Extras

play

⑦ Tag + Trim + Attachment + Extra

materials 1. tag and rub-ons (Making Memories) • twist ties (Pebbles, Inc.) • ribbon 2. Qwikit pocket (Provo Craft) • stickers (Close To My Heart) • fiber 3. slide mount (Hot Off The Press) • stickers (Creative Imaginations) • mini clothespins 4. library pocket (Ideal School Supply) • tag (Avery Dennison) • letter stamps (Hero Arts) • mini tag (Making Memories) • buttons • stamping ink • thread 5. tag • mini envelope (Impress Rubber Stamps) • flower eyelet and brads (The Happy Hammer) • color clips (Scrapworks) • jewelry tag (Avery Dennison) • ribbon 6. envelope (embellish IT!) • patterned paper (Daisy D's) • ribbon (Lavish Lines) • charm (Pebbles, Inc.) 7. tags, ribbons and rub-ons (Making Memories) • charms (K & Company)

More Ideas

① Tuck-in + Attachment + Extras

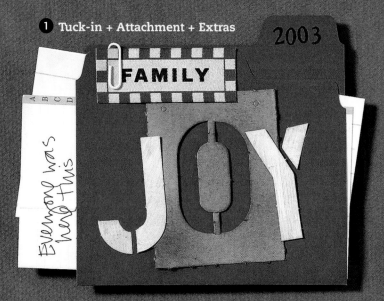

2003

FAMILY

JOY

Everyone was here this

○ N L I N E

Visit our Web site to see how four of the custom
accents shown in this article have been used on actual
pages **simplescrapbooksmag.com/magazine**

under

our tree

② Tuck-in + Trim + Extras

③ Trim • Tag • Extras

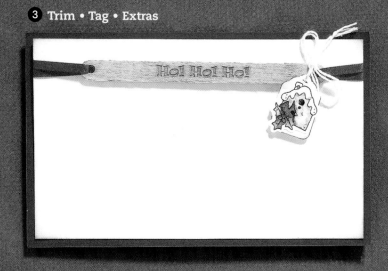

Ho! Ho! Ho!

love

④ Tag + Trim + Extra

materials 1. file folder (FoofaLa) • patterned paper (Making Memories) • stencils (Avery Dennison) • label (me & my BIG ideas) • number stamps (PSX)
• paper clip 2. book pocket (Boxer Scrapbook Productions) • sticker (Kopp Design) • letter stickers (Li'l Davis Designs) • jewelry tag • ribbon 3. QuoteStix
(Everlasting Keepsakes) • sticker (Provo Craft) • tag (Avery Dennison) • ribbon 4. tag (Westrim) • metal heart (Making Memories) • letter stamps (PSX) • ribbon

1 Tag + Trim + Extras

4 Tuck-in + Extras

2 Tag + Extra

5 Tuck-in+ Attachment + Extras

3 Tag + Trim + Extras

7 Tag + Trim + Extras

6 Tuck-ins + Trim

materials 1. tag (Tumblebeasts) • snowflake transparency (Artistic Impressions) • abc's letter tiles (Doodlebug Design, Inc.) • twist ties (Pebbles, Inc.) • ribbon 2. patterned paper (Making Memories) • label (me & my BIG ideas) • tag 3. tag (Deluxe Designs) • rub-on (Making Memories) • metal word (Die Cuts with a View) • ribbon 4. frame (Li'l Davis Designs) • metal charm (Westrim) • word sticker (K & Company) 5. fabric frame (Li'l Davis Designs) • flower (Making Memories) • ribbon • brad 6. mini envelope (Paper Adventures) • frame charm (Pebbles, Inc.) • ribbon 7. tag (Paper Reflections) • unbuttons and paper ribbon (Little Black Dress Designs) • rub-on letters (Making Memories)

I love your enthusiasm. I love that you pretend not to get cold. I love that you can spend time with Dad on the slopes. I love that you give it everything and sleep til 10:00 the day after. I love that you want to describe every move, slide jump and fall to me when you get home. I love to see you so in love. ♡mom

one cool kid

CLARK LOVES SNOW

Lay out your photos, add your journaling and then go to your accent drawers. This will ensure that the decorative accents support, but don't overwhelm, your design. **materials** Flavia patterned paper (Colorbök) • textured cardstock (Paper Loft) • Real Life stickers (Pebbles, Inc) • large alphabet stamps (Performance Art Stamps) • small alphabet stamps (PSX) • Staz-On ink (Tsukineko) • slide mount (Hot Off The Press) • metal word and blue ribbon (Making Memories) • Alphadotz letters (Scrapworks) • square brads (The Happy Hammer) • snowflake brad (Carolee's Creations) • gingham ribbon (Close To My Heart)

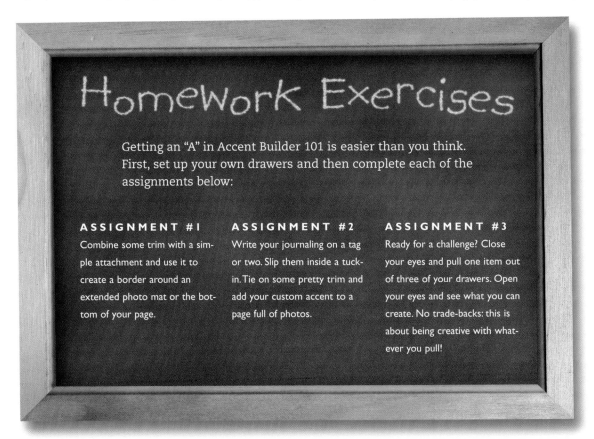

Homework Exercises

Getting an "A" in Accent Builder 101 is easier than you think. First, set up your own drawers and then complete each of the assignments below:

ASSIGNMENT #1
Combine some trim with a simple attachment and use it to create a border around an extended photo mat or the bottom of your page.

ASSIGNMENT #2
Write your journaling on a tag or two. Slip them inside a tuck-in. Tie on some pretty trim and add your custom accent to a page full of photos.

ASSIGNMENT #3
Ready for a challenge? Close your eyes and pull one item out of three of your drawers. Open your eyes and see what you can create. No trade-backs: this is about being creative with whatever you pull!

Stick To It!

BY KERRY JENSEN

Scrapbooking is *quicker* with a sticker

I must confess—when it comes to designing scrapbook pages, stickers are near the top of my "essential supplies" list. Their current good standing on my layouts stems from pleasant schoolgirl memories of trading stickers with my friends at recess. But those childish trading days are over.

Now on each trip to the scrapbook store, I am amazed at the variety of stickers available to fit my many design moods and themes. Just knowing there's such a wide selection lifts my spirits. Naturally, I pick up a sheet or two of economical and downright easy-to-apply stickers that "a-peel" to my pages!

The truth is, with a few basic guidelines, stickers will liven up your scrapbook pages *and* save you time. Here are four techniques and lots of expert tips that will make a believer out of you. Scrapbooking is quicker with a sticker, and these pages prove it! →

Figure 1. Anchoring stickers on contrasting boxes frames the images, creating an eye-catching page accent. For a unified look, select patterned paper that complements the look and feel of your stickers. *Pages by Jennifer Blackham.* **Supplies** *Stickers and patterned paper:* Debbie Mumm, Creative Imaginations; *Computer font:* Emmascript, Adobe.

TECHNIQUE #1 ANCHOR AWAY

Stickers floating alone on a scrapbook page can look haphazard, creating a "sticker sneeze" effect. Instead, anchor them to something. Mounting a sticker on cardstock will emphasize the sticker and give your page a more polished look. Journaling boxes are another great place to anchor stickers (Figure 1). For variety, try placing them directly on other page elements, like ribbon or vellum envelopes (Figure 2).

CLICK AND STICK — Access these handy stickers online or in your local scrapbook store

The acid-free stickers accompanying the layouts in this article are those our designers used for inspiration. This way, you'll know exactly what to look for at your local scrapbook store. Perhaps you'll find they're indispensable to your pages, too. Check the web sites at right for more information:

Another online source for stickers is www.simplystickers.com. This user-friendly site shows off the sticker "lines" of numerous manufacturers with just one click.

- www.debbiemumm.com (Figures 1 and 2)
- www.colorbok.com (Figure 2)
- www.provocraft.com (Figures 3, 7 and 8)
- www.meandmybigideas.com (Figures 4, 5 and A)
- www.nrndesigns.com (Figure B)
- www.makingmemories.com (Figure B)
- www.karenfosterdesign.com (Figure C)
- www.eksuccess.com (Figure 7)
- www.mrsgrossmans.com (Figure D)
- www.scrapbookmania.com (Figure D)
- www.inspiremescrapbooks.com (Figure D)

DON'T GET STUCK!

The following tips will keep you from getting into a sticky situation when working with stickers:

• Cut stickers apart while they're still on the sheet; this way, you can move them around the page until you decide where to place them.

• Before committing stickers to the page, lightly place them so they can be easily removed if necessary.

• When using letter stickers, try jumbling the letters instead of placing them in a straight line. This casual look is easy to create—no ruler necessary!

• Use Un-du adhesive remover (pictured at right) to remove a sticker already adhered to a surface.

Un-du adhesive remover can "do" just about anything when it comes to fixing a sticky situation! Make sure to read the directions carefully before using.

Figure 2. Anchor stickers in unique places, such as on ribbon or vellum pockets. *Note:* Lana created vellum pockets by dividing the length of the vellum into thirds. Then she cut a slit partway down the center of each third and adhered the edges back to create the look of a pocket. *Pages by Lana Rickabaugh.* **Supplies** *Floral Stickers:* Debbie Mumm, Creative Imaginations; *Sticker letters:* David Walker, Colorbök; *Patterned paper:* Colors By Design; *Vellum:* K & Company; *Computer font:* DJ Sketched "Fantastic! 2" CD, DJ Inkers; *Ribbon:* Offray.

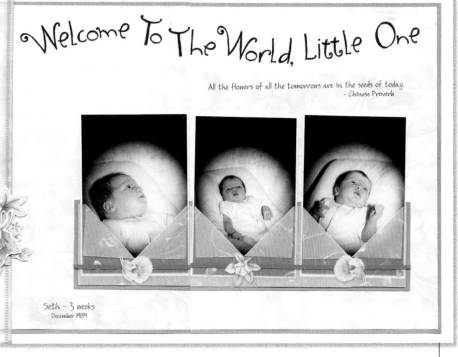

TECHNIQUE #2

THINK "TRIANGLES"

To give your pages a balanced look, create a visual triangle. Use this basic design technique once—or multiple times—when positioning stickers, photos or journaling boxes on the page (Figures 3 and 4). The imaginary triangle needn't be exact; a general approximation will do. This tried-and-true rule is a simple way to design consistently eye-pleasing scrapbook pages.

Figure 3. Use stickers to create a visual triangle that frames your photo subject. *Page by Jennifer Blackham.* **Supplies** *Stickers:* Build-a-Series, Provo Craft; *Patterned paper:* Colorwheel Collection, Provo Craft; *Computer font:* Scrap Rhapsody, "Lettering Delights" CD Vol. 2, Inspire Graphics; *Deacidification spray:* Archival Mist.

Figure 4. Notice how Vivian has placed sticker flowers of the same hue at the points of a visual triangle. Design tip: Minimize color contrast by using colored cardstock. The muted effect helps to emphasize photos. *Pages by Vivian Smith.* **Supplies** *Stickers:* me & my BIG ideas; *Patterned paper:* Scrap-Ease; *Computer font:* Yippy, downloaded from the Internet; *Chalks:* Craf-T Products; *Eyelets:* Impress Rubber Stamps; *Pen:* Pigma Micron.

Figure 5. Playing in the sun looks even more fun with these quick and simple daisy borders as accents. *Page by Renée Senchyna.* **Supplies** *Border stickers and title:* me & my BIG ideas; *Bumblebee, floral and butterfly stickers:* Colorbök; *Vellum:* Keeping Memories Alive: *Patterned paper:* Daisy D's Paper Co.; *Computer font:* CK Handprint, "The Best of Creative Lettering" CD Combo, *Creating Keepsakes;* *Pen:* Zig Writer, EK Success.

TECHNIQUE #3 ORDER AT THE BORDER

With stickers, borders have never been easier. And with so many sticker styles to choose from, the design possibilities are practically endless (see the "Click and Stick" sidebar on page 154). A bonus? There's little measuring or cutting involved. Many stickers are made specifically for use as borders, such as the daisy border in Figure 5. Why not combine multiple stickers to create your own borders? (See Figure 6.) Whether they're used as subtle accents or as frames for photos or entire pages, border stickers are versatile page enhancers.

Figure 6. Combine smaller stickers to create an interesting border. Need help? Mount the stickers on cardstock first, trim and then adhere to your page. *Page by Shannon Watt.* **Supplies** *Stickers:* Kathy Davis, Colorbök; *Computer fonts:* Annifont and Encino Caps, downloaded from the Internet.

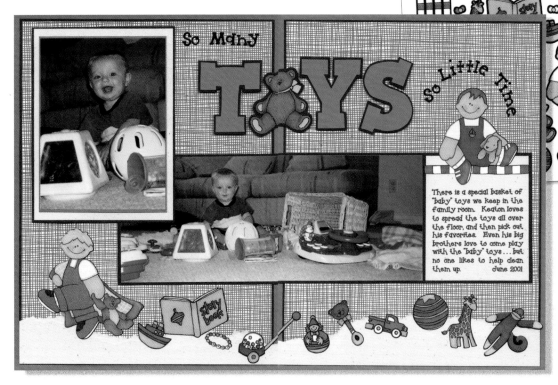

Figure 7. These toy stickers look like they were pulled right out of the photographs! Notice the creative ways in which the stickers are anchored. *Page by Jennifer Blackham.* **Supplies** *Stickers:* Stickerkins, EK Success; *Letter stickers:* Provo Craft; *Lettering template:* ScrapPagerz.com; *Patterned paper:* Northern Spy; *Computer font:* PC Whimsey, "For Font Sakes" HugWare CD, Provo Craft.

TECHNIQUE #4 MAKE A SCENE!

Use stickers to create a scene on your page that invites interaction with your photos. The layout in Figure 7 might look like it took hours to put together, but it's really a snap to group stickers with photos to create the scene you envision. Many sticker manufacturers design stickers expressly for that purpose.

Once you get going, you'll be surprised how far one sheet of stickers will take you. Also, you'll never need to worry about wasting the leftovers, because you'll find that there are countless uses for them: handmade cards, gift tags and boxes, envelope seals, children's foreheads. And you know that headboard in your bedroom that has been looking a little drab lately? Have at it, because these days a little adhesive remover will fix just about anything! ⑤

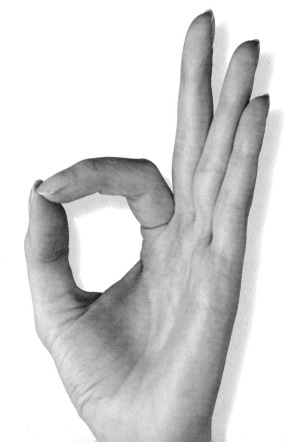

MOMENTS

IT'S NOT WHAT YOU

LOOK AT THAT MATTERS,

IT'S WHAT YOU SEE.

————

HENRY DAVID THOREAU

SIMPLE STAMPING

By Donna Downey

Rubber stamping started out as a separate craft, but it has made the leap to scrapbook pages in a big way. The reason? Rubber stamps are easy to use, versatile and affordable, and archival inks are plentiful.

Even if you're just starting out, or you have limited time and money to invest in scrapbooking, you can still have fun with rubber stamps. Pick up one of the sets on the following pages, a couple of ink pads, and you're off! When you're ready to branch out, share the wealth by stamping with friends. You'll expand your possibilities by sharing stamps and ink, and it's a great excuse to spend time together.

Here's what you need to know to get started, and to get the most out of the stamping supplies you collect. We'll explain the basic stamp types, unearth the most popular stamps, get tips and recommendations from designers, and explore the number of ways to use a stamp to get the most out of your purchase.

Stamping Basics

Rubber stamps come in so many styles, sizes and shapes that it may seem overwhelming to know just where to start. (I sometimes find myself aimlessly wandering the stamp aisles of my local stores, just trying to take it all in.) But if you keep in mind the basics in the chart below, you'll find a few stamps that will serve you well.

When buying stamp pads, remember there are two types of ink: **Dye inks** dry quickly on paper surfaces, but tend to bleed a bit on porous surfaces; and **Pigment inks** take slightly longer to dry, but will leave crisp clear lines. Most stamp pads contain acid-free ink, but you'll want to read the information provided with the product to make sure.

The six basic styles

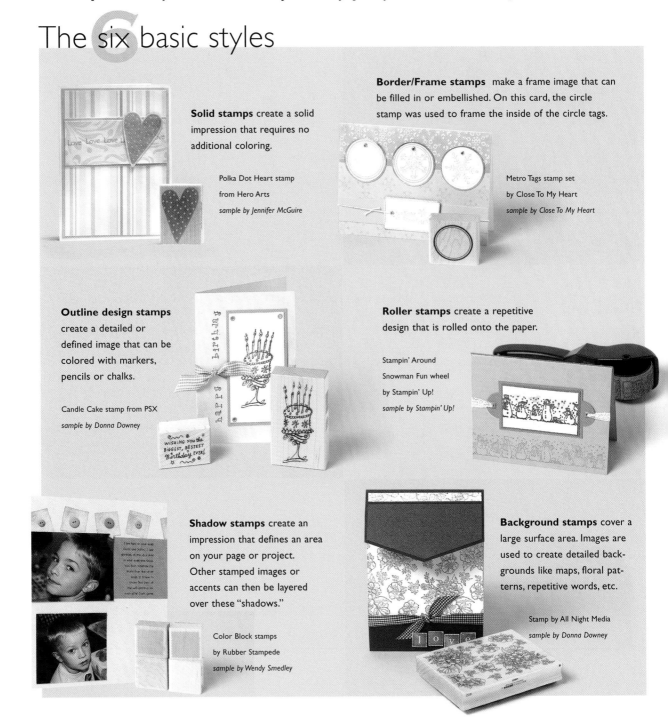

Solid stamps create a solid impression that requires no additional coloring.

Polka Dot Heart stamp
from Hero Arts
sample by Jennifer McGuire

Border/Frame stamps make a frame image that can be filled in or embellished. On this card, the circle stamp was used to frame the inside of the circle tags.

Metro Tags stamp set
by Close To My Heart
sample by Close To My Heart

Outline design stamps create a detailed or defined image that can be colored with markers, pencils or chalks.

Candle Cake stamp from PSX
sample by Donna Downey

Roller stamps create a repetitive design that is rolled onto the paper.

Stampin' Around
Snowman Fun wheel
by Stampin' Up!
sample by Stampin' Up!

Shadow stamps create an impression that defines an area on your page or project. Other stamped images or accents can then be layered over these "shadows."

Color Block stamps
by Rubber Stampede
sample by Wendy Smedley

Background stamps cover a large surface area. Images are used to create detailed backgrounds like maps, floral patterns, repetitive words, etc.

Stamp by All Night Media
sample by Donna Downey

1

brandley

Marnie Flores | Madison, WI

"Stamps can create the perfect backdrop for a page. With their subdued colors, stamps that mimic antique wall paper are a superb way to accent a vintage page."

materials stamp (PSX) • inks (Ranger, Colorbox) • stamp, chalk and ribbon (Stampin'Up!) • Cloisonne embossing powder (Stampa Rosa) • letters, photo corners and metal chain (Making Memories) • Shrinky Dinks Shrink Film (Spinmaster Toys) • copper leafing pen (Krylon)

6

WHY USE RUBBER STAMPS?

Six top designers explain why they enjoy using rubber stamps on their pages.

2

grin

Joy Uzarraga | Hinsdale, IL

"Rubber stamps are extremely versatile. You can change the look of one stamp by simply mixing and matching it with others. I enjoy knowing I can use stamps to make other paper projects—in so doing, I always feel like I'm getting more for my money!"

materials Zig writer pen (EK Success) • shadows, letters and peach flower stamps and ink (Hero Arts) • purple and blue flower stamps (Penny Black, Inc.) • ink (Ranger Industries and Clearsnap, Inc.) • mesh (Avant Card)

freedom

Kim Heffington | Avondale, AZ

"Stamps are great and you can customize them to your needs. The possibilities are endless! If you pick basic shapes and designs, you really can use them for years. This is a money saver in the long run."

materials flower stamp (Close To My Heart) • ink (Stampin' Up!) • photo corners and Simply Stated Rub-ons (Making Memories) • ZIG Millennium pen (EK Success)

bubble bath baby

Jenny Jackson | Gilbert, AZ

"The best part about using stamps in your scrapbooks is that you get to choose the colors. With a little creativity, you can change colors and create an entirely different layout using exactly the same stamps."

"There are so many great stamps that are often overlooked in the decorating aisle of your craft store. I found the perfect stamps for this layout and for several more layouts I am working on. They were so inexpensive and easy to use, I bought them all!"

materials duck and bubble stamps (Rubber Stampede) • ink (Marvy Uchida) • pen (Tombow) • patterned paper (Pebbles, Inc.) • eyelets (Making Memories) • ribbon • CK Teacher's Pet font (Creating Keepsakes)

Bubble Bath Baby!
Dayna just loves to be in the bath. She often sits in her little blue bath chair for a few minutes while I straighten up the bathroom & get myself ready. She is perfectly content splashing in the water & playing in the bubbles. On this day, she has just turned one & has discovered that the bubbles disappear in your mouth...but they sure make you look cute while they are dangling off your chin! You are the cutest bubble-bearded baby!

little one

title page   contents page   "Feel of Cape Cod" section opener

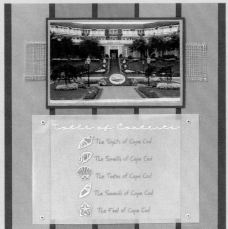

getting a sense of cape cod

Kathleen Samuelson | Weston, FL

"I have a section in my scrapbooking notebook that I designate for stamps. As I add to my stamp collection, I stamp the image in black ink. I write the manufacturer's name under the image for easy reference."
DONNA DOWNEY

"I really like the versatility and subtle feel that the different stamp techniques give my pages. By only needing a few products and supplies to complete this entire album, I was able to travel, scrap, and stamp easily. I usually make the framework for a vacation album before we leave, and then I take the album and minimal supplies on the road. *(Note: Kathleen uses a small HP Photo printer to print her photos while traveling.)* Stamping makes it easy to produce multiple albums economically. Most years, I make a small Cape Cod album for my parents and siblings, and one stamp goes a long way."

materials shell stamp set, texture stamp and embossing powder (Close To My Heart) • ink (Hero Arts) • Versamark Watermark ink (Tsukineko) • Zig Writer pen (EK Success) • eyelets, vellum tags, metal tag & Twistel (Making Memories) • mesh (Magic Scraps) • CK Artisan & CK Cursive fonts (Creating Keepsakes)

Aidan discovers that the best **popcicles** are made by **Mother Nature**.

- after the big snow, Christmas 2002

popcicle

Lisa Russo | Oswego, IL

"I used this small, inexpensive stamp and Versamark inks to make a wintery, watermarked pattern on my paper."

"I've become addicted to using rubber stamps in my scrapbooking! I love using a single stamp to create backgrounds and accents in any color or texture I want. It's even fun to stamp several images together to create a customized collage or background pattern."

materials snowflake stamp (Stampabilities) • Versamark ink (Tsukineko) • snaps and circle tag (Making Memories) • Chestnuts & Sleigh Ride fonts (twopeasinabucket.com)

shabby cover

Donna Downey | Huntersville, NC

"Nothing makes me happier than getting the most for my money. Stamps allow me to create some of my favorite images over and over again and stretch my creative comfort zone, and they're a great way to add texture and depth to my pages. I love layering stamped images."

materials background word stamp (Hero Arts) • large alphabet stamp on tag (Stamper's Anonymous) • definitions stamp on tag (Junque) • date stamp (Making Memories) • watch stamp (Rubber Stampede) • ink (Stampin' Up!) • 12 X 12 album (DMD Industries, Inc.) • Marydale font (Internet) • fiber • envelope • tags • ribbon • vintage key

In a Bind

Which album is right for you?

YOU'VE HEARD THE TERMS TIME AND TIME AGAIN: spiral, strap, post, ring. No, we aren't talking about the latest "get skinny quick" attire sold on QVC; we're talking about common types of album binding. If you've ever been in a bind over what type of album to purchase, read on.

While albums are constructed using similar materials, a key difference that you should be aware of is the album binding. Each type of binding has features that make it better for some types of scrapbooks than others, and knowing about those features will help you choose an album that is compatible with the result you have in mind.

Ask yourself these questions: How often will this album be viewed? Where will it be when not in use? How many photos do you want to fit into it? Who is looking at this most often? Are page protectors a must? →

ONLINE

Finding an Album

Are you having a hard time finding an album with the type of binding you want in the size you need? We want to make it easier for you to find what you're looking for. Just visit our web site, _simplescrapbooksmag.com_, and click on the Album Locator for a list of album types and information about suppliers.

Assembling a Post-Bound Album

1 Begin by folding the side tabs (where the holes are located) of the cover and back of the album toward the white inside of the album.

2 Insert the posts through the holes in the side tab of the front cover so that the head of each post is next to the white inside of the album. The album cover is the piece without the Close To My Heart logo (if assembling a Lasting Legacy Album).

3 Place the Memory Protectors on the posts. The logo on the page protector should be placed face down so that it touches the side tab of the cover.

4 Slide the back cover over the posts so your album lies open and the logo is visible. Insert one screw into each post and twist until tight.

5 Add the spine to the album by inserting one long edge of the spine into the groove on the edge of the front of the album. Insert the remaining long edge of the spine into the groove on the back of the album.

Assembling a Strap-Hinge Album

1 If your album has a covered spine, slide the spine cover off.

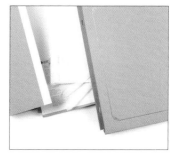

2 Unthread the back cover and cover holder and remove them.

3 Add pages by slipping the album straps through the wire stitches. Replace the cover holder in the same manner.

4 Replace the back cover and re-thread the straps through the cover holder.

5 To tighten, position the back cover at a 90-degree angle to the pages and hold the cover holder down while gently pulling the strap up until the spine is secure.

	DESCRIPTION	KEY FEATURES

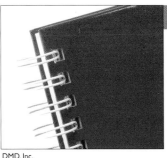

DMD, Inc.

SPIRAL BINDING

What is it about the funky metal binding that's so appealing? Page turning is pleasing with this binding system, and pages lie flat when opened for easy viewing. You can remove pages from a spiral-bound album, but you can't add or rearrange pages, so sketch out your album prior to starting it.

- Great for theme album
- Pages can be removed permanently, but not added
- Perfect for gift albums

Sew Be It

THREE-RING BINDING

Metal rings in the center allow for easy expansion and rearrangement of pages. Traditional yet timeless, a three-ring binder is easy to operate. Look for strong, thick rings.

- Easy to find
- Each inch of binding gives you approximately 20 pages
- Easy to add, remove and rearrange pages

Close To My Heart

POST BINDING

Covers are joined by metal posts that can be extended to add additional pages. Pages lie nice and flat, and look connected when open, not divided by rings.

- Pages lie flat and look connected when open
- Top-loading sheet protectors allow easy reorganization of album
- Extender posts are available to easily expand the album

Creative Memories

STRAP BINDING

Flexible plastic straps in the cover run through wire loops embedded in each page. This sturdy binding is good for albums that will be viewed often, and for kids' albums. Binding is expandable.

- Protectors cover pages on three exposed sides, keeping dust and dirt away from pictures
- Once the album is assembled, pages stay tight and safe
- Pages lie flat when open at any point in the album

BOOK BINDING

A more formal album bound just like a book. Pages can't be expanded, but are extremely durable and classic. This binding look lends itself nicely to sitting on a bookcase in a more formal setting. It's a nice look for heritage albums.

- Pages bound permanently into the album
- Pages cannot be removed or added
- Book "feel" is comfortable

©PHOTODISC

"LIFE IS A GREAT BUNDLE

OF LITTLE THINGS."

————

OLIVER WENDELL HOLMES

Shop Class

OK, I ADMIT IT. I'm a scrapbook product junkie. Which is funny, because normally I don't like to shop. I run into a store, grab what I need, and get out. Not true when it comes to shopping for scrapbooking products. I can wander forever, through store aisles, catalog pages and Web sites, losing track of time completely as I imagine the great projects I could do with everything I see.

The good news is that, whether you've just discovered scrapbooking or you're an avid fan like me, there are lots of ways to get your fix.

You can visit a local scrapbook store to amass a stockpile of materials, or find a personal consultant to provide for your every need. You can peruse a catalog or go online in the middle of the night. Read on to learn about the benefits of these four fantastic shopping options, so you can shop around and feel confident that you're getting all of your goodies at the best price.

Unfortunately, I can't tell you how to explain these "essential" purchases to your partner—or how to get the part-time job you'll need to pay off the credit card!

SS Creative Editor, multi-media maven and savvy shopper, Wendy Smedley

illustrations by Brenda Braun

Your Local Scrapbook Store

Scenario
You're a touch-and-feel shopper, hesitant to buy things you haven't personally examined.

Benefits
In a scrapbook specialty store, you see everything firsthand and talk with knowledgeable people.

- Handpick paper, stickers and accents to coordinate with your photos.
- Walk out of the store with product in hand.
- Try out scrapbook tools to discover what you can't live without.
- Get ideas and inspiration from in-store product displays.
- Educate yourself by attending in-store demos and classes.

Wendy's favorites

Memories 18 locations across the country
800.929.7324
memories.com

Archivers 16 locations across the country
archiversonline.com

Recollections two stores with more planned
recollectionsonline.com

Catalog Shopping

Scenario
You're always on the go and can't find time to shop during business hours.

Benefits
Using catalogs to buy your scrapbook supplies is the ultimate in convenience. Shop while lying in bed or sitting on the sidelines at your next sporting event.

- Take all the time you need to select purchases.
- Get the product delivered directly to you.
- Compare various catalogs for the best price/value.
- Shop anywhere, anytime.
- Read detailed product descriptions.

Wendy's favorites

Creative Xpress
800.563.8679
creativexpress.com

Keeping Memories Alive
800.419.4949
scrapbooks.com

Times to Cherish
877.665.4458
timestocherish.com

On the Web

Personal Consultant

Scenario

The nearest scrapbooking store is two hours away, or you want to see what all your choices are without driving from store to store.

Benefits

If you've got an Internet connection, you can quickly shop at one or more sites without leaving your desk.

- Swiftly search for specific items from among thousands of offerings.
- Purchases delivered to your doorstep in a matter of days.
- View the site's latest products by clicking on "New Products" button.
- Keep track of purchases in your "shopping cart."
- Delete selections easily before checkout.
- Create and save a wish list for future reference.

Wendy's favorites

- Gonescrappin.com
- Scrapbookthis.com
- Scrappiness.com
- Twopeasinabucket.com

Scenario

You don't know how to get started, and you'd like someone to help you.

Benefits

A consultant will keep you from getting overwhelmed by teaching you how to get started, keeping you informed and motivated, and coaching you on your product selections.

- Get personalized help.
- Schedule your consultant visits around your schedule.
- Learn about scrapbooking among friends in a casual environment.
- Select from a core of time-tested products
- Choose from exclusive product collections that are not available in stores.
- Attend motivating crops and informative classes hosted by your consultant.

Wendy's favorites

Close To My Heart
888.655.6552
closetomyheart.com

Scrap In A Snap
866.462.7627
scrapinasnap.com

Creative Memories
800.341.5275
creativememories.com

Stampin' Up!
800.stampup
stampinup.com

If you're pressed for time and would like instant results, follow one of our proven formulas for success—you'll have a project done in no time. You can do this.

Do

Flexible Summer Scrapbooking

The school year is winding down, and that means your routine (which took nine months to get used to!) is about to dissolve into the crazy, unpredictable daze of summer. With four kids at home, I've had to adopt a flexible scrapbooking style. Some days I have time to create detailed layouts; other days, my layouts are quite simple. It's nice to know my pages can be beautiful regardless of how much time I have to spend on them.

When you look at the three sample pages of Lizzie and Sarah, you'll notice that the emotion and memory evoked doesn't change from Step 1 to Step 3. The feeling of the pages is not dependent on the embellishments that are added.

So, whether you've got a half-hour to spare or a day of leisure ahead of you, you can create a scrapbook page that captures special memories. In the layouts on the next three pages, I'll show you how you can adapt your design in just a few easy steps. Simply choose the level that fits your summer schedule!

Choose a look that fits your schedule

Figure 1. Beautifully simple pages are easy to create—all you need are great photos, thoughtful journaling and cardstock. *Pages by Robin Johnson.* **Supplies** *Patterned paper:* Mara-Mi; *Pen:* Zig Writer, EK Success; *Computer fonts:* CK Script, "The Best of Creative Lettering" CD Vol. 1 and CK Primary, "The Art of Creative Lettering" CD, *Creating Keepsakes.*

Option 1: Essentials.

A simple layout may require more thinking time than actual creating time. Start by asking yourself these questions: What is the essence of my page? Which photo is most engaging? What simple words will best capture the message I'm trying to convey? Once you make these decisions, putting your page together is easy.

In Figure 1, I used floral background paper to highlight the wildflowers in my photos. I accentuated my focal-point photo with a torn white mat. Using my computer, I printed my journaling on yellow cardstock and centered it on the right-hand page. Then I simply added supporting photos above and below it.

Supplies Checklist
- 1 sheet 8½" x 11" patterned paper
- 1 sheet 8½" x 11" white cardstock
- 2 sheets 8½" x 11" yellow cardstock
- Black pen
- Paper trimmer
- Adhesive

Figure 2. "Step up" your design with extras like photo corners and tags. *Pages by Robin Johnson.* **Supplies** *Patterned paper:* Mara-Mi; *Pen:* Zig Writer, EK Success; *Computer fonts:* CK Script, "The Best of Creative Lettering" CD Vol. I and CK Primary, "The Art of Creative Lettering" CD, *Creating Keepsakes; Tags:* American Tag; *Photo corners:* Boston International.

Option 2:
Add Product

To step up my design, I added a yellow mat and photo corners to the focal-point photo (Figure 2). I also trimmed the individual girls' photos to make room for tags with their names and ages recorded on them.

To provide a sense of balance, I used strips of the floral background paper to create a border along the outside edges of each page.

Supplies Checklist

In addition to the items listed in Step I, you'll need:

- 1 additional sheet of yellow cardstock
- 4 white photo corners
- 2 small white tags
- 1 colored marker

Figure 3. Final touches, like the blue mats and punched daisies here, make a layout simply beautiful. *Pages by Robin Johnson.* **Supplies** *Patterned paper:* Mara-Mi; *Pen:* Zig Writer, EK Success; *Computer fonts:* CK Script, "The Best of Creative Lettering" CD Vol. 1 and CK Primary, "The Art of Creative Lettering" CD, *Creating Keepsakes; Tags:* American Tag; *Photo corners:* Boston International; *Daisy punch:* Marvy Uchida; Brass fasteners, Hy-Glo.

Option 3: Add Time and Technique

In Figure 3, I added a thin blue mat to each of the photos and tags. I also added a torn white strip to the floral border. I replaced the string on the tags with a more natural-looking twine and added a shadow to my title with a powder-blue pen. Finally, I created a fun flower accent by overlapping two punched daisies and secured them to my page with small brass fasteners. It's the perfect spot for "hanging" the tags.

Supplies Checklist

In addition to the items listed in Step 2, you'll need:

- Small daisy punch
- 5 small brass fasteners
- Natural-looking thread
- Light-blue pen

Friends may come and friends may go, but finding
someone you call your "best friend" is a wonderful thing. One day I managed to get 11-year-olds Kyle and Lucas to stand still long enough to snap a few telling photographs.

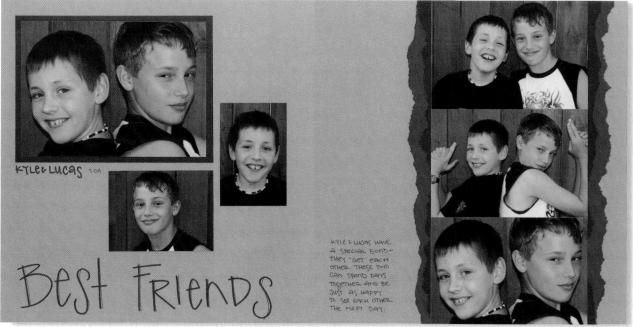

materials cardstock • black pen

Option 1: Essentials

To make the photos stand out, I chose a background cardstock color that complements the background in the photographs. Black photo matting emphasizes the boys' hair and clothing. The only thing left: the journaling. How quick and easy is that?

• 2 sheets 12 x 12 bronze cardstock
• 1 sheet 12 x 12 black cardstock
• black pen
• archival adhesive
• paper trimmer

Boy /boi/ n. A youthful male child. An immature or inexperienced man, especially a young man. A son.

(gig-əl) v. To laugh with short catches of the breath in voice; to laugh in a light, affected, or silly manner; to titter with childish levity.

kyle

lucas

BEST FRIENDS

THROUGH THICK & THIN, KYLE & LUCAS ARE ALWAYS THERE FOR EACH OTHER. FROM COMMON BOY LANGUAGE—"POOP!" & "DUDE"— TO SHARED SECRETS, IT'S GREAT TO HAVE A BEST FRIEND. JULY 2004

(mis'che-vəs) adj. Tending to cause trouble or annoyance; playfully irresponsible.

additional materials Empire Classic Upper die cut letters (QuicKutz) • definition stickers (EK Success) • rub-on letters (Scrapworks) • black corrugated paper

Option 2: Add Product

With this step I wanted to include a little more of the boys' personalities. The definition stickers were a simple, tongue-in-cheek addition. I also created roughhouse "male" texture with the black corrugated paper. The expanded journaling, including some of their favorite expressions, gave me a page that sketches the boys in more detail.

In addition to the materials listed in Option 1, you will need:
• 1 sheet 12 x 12 black corrugated paper
• rub-on letters
• die-cut letters
• 3 definitions stickers

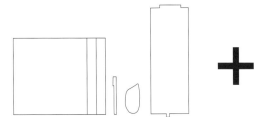 +

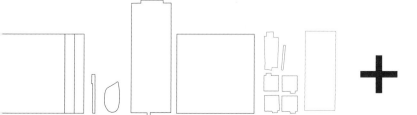

additional materials white cardstock (Bazzil Bassics Paper) • Paper Accents craft tags (Accent Designs) • twine

Option 3: Add Time & Technique

I needed a more masculine feel to my page, and I had a little more time to work on this one. Torn white cardstock on the left-hand page makes the title pop—and balances the white rub-on names on the right side. I also anchored two of the definition stickers on tags, and added twine to the tags and title to give the layout a grittier appeal.

In addition to the materials listed in Option 2, you will need:

- 1 sheet 8 1/2 x 11 white cardstock
- twine
- 2 tags

I Love This Place!

Monterey california
february 2004

While living in San Francisco, Monterey was a nice escape from the city. This hike along the coast is called 17 mile drive... It is one of my favorite places on earth!

sky
ocean
waves
rocks
sand

Ty was 11 months old

materials cardstock • black pen

Option 1: A Favorite Place

The bright blue ocean, my husband's light blue shirt, and my son's purple fleece jacket led me to choose an analogous color scheme for my page. I used white cardstock for my background and three shades of blue for accents and photo mats. I matted the father-and-son photos and cut strips of cardstock to stack alongside the picture of my son and myself. Then I added a title and journaling. Who said making a layout of my favorite place had to be hard!

essentials:

- 1 sheet of 8 1/2 x 11 light blue cardstock
- 1 sheet of 8 1/2 x 11 dark blue cardstock
- 1 sheet of 8 1/2 x 11 medium blue cardstock
- 2 sheets 8 1/2 x 11 white cardstock
- archival adhesive
- black journaling pen
- black archival marker
- paper trimmer

additional materials CK Flourish font (Creating Keepsakes)

Option 2:
A New
Perspective

I wanted to include more photos, so I cropped them into small squares and rectangles. The shots I added were about our toddler discovering nature, so I changed my title to "Discover Monterey" and made my journaling more descriptive. I added color to the page with blue cardstock and patterned paper mats on the journaling and title blocks. Photo corners, tiny purple flowers and a tag provide the finishing touches.

+ product:

In addition to the materials listed in Option 1, you will need:

- 1 sheet light blue patterned paper
- 2 packages pre-made decorative flowers
- 4 photo corners
- purple fibers
- 1 white tag

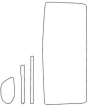 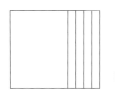  

additional materials Modern 20 font (Internet)

Option 3: Discovery

What Ty discovered that day was texture—the feel of water, sand and rock. For texture's sake, I wrinkled and sanded blue cardstock for my title block and a few paper strips, and I printed the word "discover" on torn vellum. I created a visual triangle of sensory words, tucking them in chalked photo corners and tacking them down with brads. For added flair in the lower right-hand corner, I cut the center from an additional tag and added patterned paper and a flower.

+ time and technique:

In addition to the materials listed in Option 2, you will need:

- vellum
- brads
- small tag
- X-ACTO knife
- sandpaper
- chalks

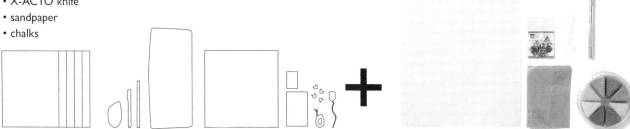

I Am Thankful

materials Pigma Micron pen (Sakura)

Option 1: Basic Blessings

At this time of year, I often reflect on the gifts in my life. For this seasonal Thanksgiving layout, I chose the seven things I am most thankful for and created a simple two-page spread. My pictures and some handwritten journaling are enough to describe my feelings, so the only materials I needed were two sheets of light brown cardstock and a black pen. I left the photos their original size, attached them to the cardstock and recorded my thoughts. I had these meaningful pages completed in no time.

essentials:

- 2 sheets 12 x 12 light brown cardstock
- black pen
- adhesive

additional materials patterned paper (Chatterbox, Inc.) • Beautiful font (twopeasinabucket.com) • Century Gothic font (Internet) • brads

Option 2: Simple Joys

To add interest to my layout, I included a few accents, trimmed some of my photos and typed my journaling. For my title, I opened a new Microsoft Word document, set it to landscape orientation, typed my title, and printed it on medium brown cardstock. I trimmed the cardstock to 2 x 10 $\frac{1}{2}$, mounted it on patterned paper, and set it with two copper-colored brads. For my left-hand page, I trimmed my photos and mounted them together as a unified image, then typed and printed a journaling block to run the length of the photos.

+ product:

In addition to the materials listed in Option 1, you will need:

- 1 sheet 12 x 12 patterned paper
- 1 sheet 12 x 12 med. brown cardstock
- paper trimmer
- brads

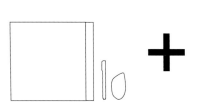

+

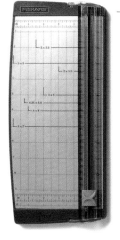

additional materials tags (Avery Dennison) • ribbon (SEI)

Option 3: Life's Abundance

Taking it a few steps further, I trimmed my light brown background cardstock $1/2$ inch and mounted both pages on darker cardstock. On the right-hand page, I converted my patterned paper border to a pocket by stitching around the sides and bottom and adding a strip of cardstock and two brads to the top. I printed individual paragraphs of journaling onto both sides of three tags and included a colorful ribbon to visually connect each tag to the corresponding photos. Finally, I crinkled and stitched my title, and chalked the page edges for a finished look.

+ time and technique:

In addition to the materials listed in Option 2, you will need:

- 3 sheets 12 x 12 dark brown cardstock
- tags for journaling
- ribbon
- handheld hole punch
- chalks
- sewing machine

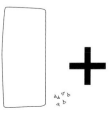

+

by Elisha Snow

A milestone anniversary is a wonderful time to celebrate family and loved ones. It's a time for children to honor their parents, reflect on past memories, and share in the commitment to create new memories together. Christine Wallace made a gift album for her parents' 40th wedding anniversary that accomplishes all three of these goals at once.

The title of Christine's album, "Child of My Child," perfectly describes the link between parents, children and grandchildren, and it shows off the enduring legacy of forty years of marriage. Each two-page spread is dedicated to one grandchild, and each includes information, quotes and photos that reflect the child's personality.

If you're looking for a way to create your own gift album for an upcoming special occasion, simply follow Christine's formula for success:

TITLE PAGE

❶ Use coordinated patterned paper to unify the album and allow the colors to flow from page to page.

❷ Pre-determine which size photos to use, and which quotes, poems, or other journaling will work best for each page.

❸ Choose embellishments that will ground the pages and complete the album.

But don't stop at anniversaries. A wedding, birthday, graduation or any other special achievement offers a great excuse to make a meaningful gift album for someone you love.

FILLER PAGES

FILLER PAGES

FILLER PAGES

To read the steps Christine followed to create this gift album, see her filled-out Formula Worksheet on the following page. Then use the enclosed blank worksheet to try this fast and easy process yourself!

CLOSING PAGE

Christine's Worksheet

Purpose: I'm creating this album as a gift for my parents' 40th wedding anniversary. It showcases their ten beautiful grandchildren.

Format: A 12 x 12, post-bound album

Organizational System: Each grandchild is featured on individual two-page spreads, arranged from oldest to youngest.

Framework: A title page, a dedication page, filler pages and a closing page.

Color Scheme: Chatterbox patterned paper with matching cardstock throughout. Additional tags, titles, and other accents coordinate with the paper.

Decorative Accents: Homemade quote tags on each page; distressed and torn patterned paper; buttons, brads, and other metal accents.

Design Scheme: Each spread features one 5 x 7 and two 4 x 6 photos of each child. The full name of each child, plus their initials and date of birth, is used on his or her page. The title page features all 10 grandchildren, pictured by family (four families in all). Next to each photo is the name of the parent from the Morrissette family. The dedication section is a small bookplate on the inside back cover. The closing page also features photos of all 10 grandchildren accompanied by a quote.

Preparations: I need to find a quote for each child that reflects individual personalities. I also need to take black and white pictures of each grandchild and size them accordingly.

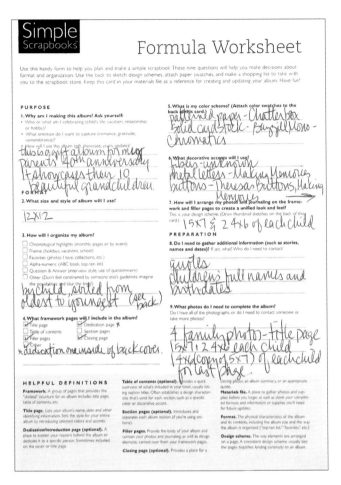

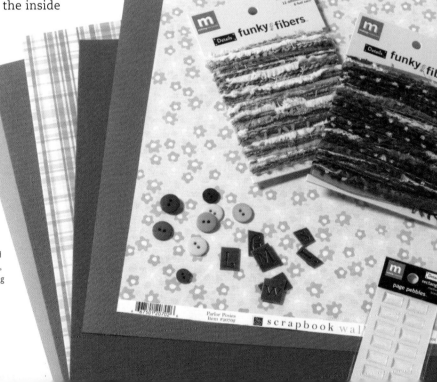

materials 12 x 12 album • patterned paper (Chatterbox, Inc.) • Page Pebbles, brads, metal letters and buttons (Making Memories) • stamping ink • embossing powder • fibers

Formula Worksheet

Use this handy form to help you plan and make a simple scrapbook. These nine questions will help you make decisions about format and organization. Use the back to sketch design schemes, attach paper swatches, and make a shopping list to take with you to the scrapbook store. Keep this page in your materials file as a reference for creating and updating your album. Have fun!

PURPOSE

1. Why am I making this album? Ask yourself:
- Who or what am I celebrating (child's life, vacation, relationship or hobby)?
- What emotion do I want to capture (romance, gratitude, remembrance)?
- How will I use this album (gift, showcase, yearly update)?

_____

_____

FORMAT

2. What size and style of album will I use?

_____

_____

3. How will I organize my album?

- ☐ Chronological highlights (monthly pages or by event)
- ☐ Theme (holidays, vacations, school)
- ☐ Favorites (photos I love, collections, etc.)
- ☐ Alpha-numeric (ABC book, top-ten list)
- ☐ Question & Answer (interview style, use of questionnaire)
- ☐ Other (Don't feel constrained by someone else's guidelines; imagine the possibilities and blur the lines!)

_____

_____

4. What framework pages will I include in the album?

☐ Title page	☐ Dedication page
☐ Table of contents	☐ Section pages
☐ Filler pages	☐ Closing page
☐ Other	

_____

_____

5. What is my color scheme? (Attach color swatches to the back of this card.)

_____

_____

_____

6. What decorative accents will I use?

_____

_____

_____

7. How will I arrange my photos and journaling on the framework and filler pages to create a unified look and feel?
This is your design scheme. (Draw thumbnail sketches on the back of this card.)

PREPARATION

8. Do I need to gather additional information (such as stories, names and dates)? If yes, what? Who do I need to contact?

_____

_____

_____

9. What photos do I need to complete the album?
Do I have all of the photographs, or do I need to contact someone or take more photos?

_____

_____

_____

HELPFUL DEFINITIONS

Framework. A group of pages that provides the "skeletal" structure for an album. Includes title page, table of contents, etc.

Title page. Lists your album's name, date and other identifying information. Sets the style for your entire album by introducing selected colors and accents.

Dedication/Introduction page (optional). A place to explain your reasons behind the album or dedicate it to a specific person. Sometimes included on the cover or title page.

Table of contents (optional). Provides a quick overview of what's included in your book, usually listing section titles. Often establishes a design characteristic that's used for each section, such as a specific color or decorative accent.

Section pages (optional). Introduces and separates each album section (if you're using sections).

Filler pages. Provide the body of your album and contain your photos and journaling, as well as design elements carried over from your framework pages.

Closing page (optional). Provides a place for a closing photo, an album summary, or an appropriate quote.

Materials file. A place to gather photos and supplies before you begin, as well as store your completed formula and information or supplies you'll need for future updates.

Format. The physical characteristics of the album and its contents, including the album size and the way the album is organized ("top-ten list," "favorites," etc.).

Design scheme. The way elements are arranged on a page. A consistent design scheme visually ties the pages together, lending continuity to an album.

fast, friendly formula | by Wendi Speciale

materials album (DF Albums, Ltd., My Album Digital line)

IT'S 3 A.M. AND I CAN'T SLEEP.
My mind is in overdrive. What if I never make another scrapbook page again? I sit here wide-awake, trying to force creativity that is blocked. I realize that what I need is a good dose of "reminders" for forging onward.

I need a scrapbook to remind me why I pursue this hobby (and profession)—not how, not when, not where, but *why* I love this marriage of digital photos, journaling and design. Often, it's easy for me to get caught up in the *Will they like it?* rut, or the *Oh, I want to do this, but I read it's so out of style now!* trap.

The truth? I don't really care. If I like a particular style, I do it. My solution? The album of digital images you see here. Every time insecurity sets in, creativity is stymied, or discouragement stops me cold, I will have this album to remind and inspire me. I'm always making books for everyone else; now it's time to make a book for me, to remind me!

Purpose Inspiration! When enthusiasm wanes, this book will remind me why I scrapbook.

Format I'll use an album from DF Albums, Ltd., especially designed for digital scrapbooking.

Organizational System With each page "reminder" as to why I scrapbook, I'll place a picture that comes to mind—only one picture per page.

Framework Pages Title page, table of contents and filler pages.

Color Scheme Brown (for eternal), blue (for my son), yellow (for inspiration), and green (my favorite color). The one-reminder-per-page design feature will appear in blue, as will any descriptive text.

DEDICATION PAGE

CONTENTS PAGE

FILLER PAGES

Decorative Accents (including computer fonts) One font, Ariel, used throughout. The reminders will be bold, lowercase and larger than any other text on the page. As accents fit the page, I will add them. (Note the computer-generated tag on the "inspired" page.)

Design Scheme: One-page layout per reminder, using the color scheme. Every page will be designed similarly yet have interesting perks.

Preparation The hardest work involves finding a picture that complements the reminder. I'll also take care with my journaling to describe why the reminder is important to me.

Photographs One small photo per page. Eye-catching journaling is really of primary importance here, and the picture is secondary.

Closing Page Definitely FINISH the RACE! A picture of my hero—my mother—will grace the closing page. This is the strongest reminder of all for why I scrapbook. As I add pages, I will keep this one as the last page of the book—my anchoring inspiration.

fast, friendly formula | by Tara Whitney

WE ALL KNOW HOW IMPORTANT A SPECIAL BLANKET CAN BE TO A CHILD, but I never realized how important my daughter Anna's blankets would be to me!

I'm so touched by the time and effort my family and friends dedicated to creating these keepsakes for my daughter—I realize that this album is also very much a tribute to them. These people mean the world to Anna and me.

Purpose I'm creating this album as a keepsake for my daughter Anna. I want her to know who these designing women were, and what they hoped for her as they made these special blankets that will surely become treasures.

Format A 7 x 7 strap-hinge album.

Organizational System The album will feature two pages for each woman who created blankets for us. I will take a photo of Anna with each person, and ask her to write a letter explaining how and why her blanket came about.

Framework Pages A title page, a table of contents page, eight filler pages, and a dedication page that comes at the end. I am also leaving two blank

materials 7 x 7 album (Creative Memories) • Sew Crafty Mini sewing machine (Provo Craft) • Threads woven labels (me & my BIG ideas) • Metal Words "priceless" (Making Memories) • letter stickers (SEI) • Garamouche journaling font (P22 Type Foundry) • antique brads • buttons • ink

pages so I can add photos of some of the favorite blankets that I purchased during my pregnancy and in Anna's first year of life.

Color Scheme Two shades of purple and two shades of green (with a little bit of pink). I'll take my colors from the blankets.

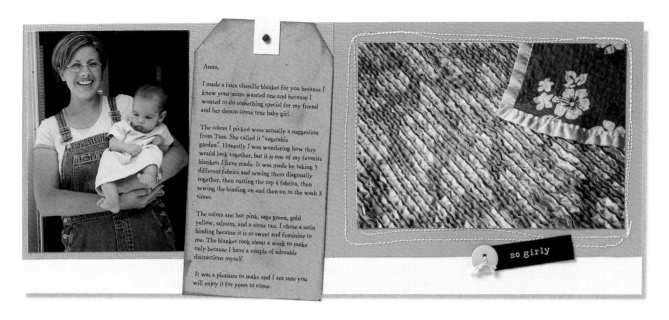

Anna,

I made a faux chenille blanket for you because I knew your mom wanted one and because I wanted to do something special for my friend and her dream come true baby girl.

The colors I picked were actually a suggestion from Tara. She called it "vegetable garden". Honestly I was wondering how they would look together, but it is one of my favorite blankets I have made. It was made by taking 5 different fabrics and sewing them diagonally together, then cutting the top 4 fabrics, then sewing the binding on and then on to the wash 3 times.

The colors are: hot pink, sage green, gold yellow, salmon, and a stone tan. I chose a satin binding because it is so sweet and feminine to me. The blanket took about a week to make only because I have a couple of adorable distractions myself.

It was a pleasure to make and I am sure you will enjoy it for years to come.

so girly

To my sweet baby granddaughter Anna Morgan.

Your arrival is such a blessing in our lives. Mimi wanted to make you a blanket. Pretty, soft, and PINK. Your momma said she saw a lovely soft and golden brown yarn she wanted. It was to match your golden complexion and big brown eyes. How she knew that was exactly how you would turn out I'll never know. But she was so right! A beauty you are... to be wrapped up in my blanket with all its flaws and imperfections. Just always remember, my love for you is flawless and there could never be, a more perfect love than that.

Bundle of Joy

Decorative Accents Brads, buttons, tags, stitching, and woven word labels.

Design Scheme Each filler page will include a photo of Anna with the person who made the blanket and also a photo of the blanket itself. It will also include their letter to her printed on a large tag. I will use cardstock that complements the colors in each blanket. Sewing-type embellishments will support the handmade theme, but they'll be used sparingly. The title page will include each color used in the album, and I would like to use a large photo on the opening page.

Preparation I need to take a close-up photo of each blanket being showcased, and one shot of each of us posing individually with Anna. We'll also write Anna a letter explaining our motivations.

fast, friendly formula | by April Peterson

THE FLOWER PICTURES BEGAN SIMPLY
ENOUGH. I had just bought a new digital camera—
the first "real" camera in my life—and I could
hardly wait to begin using it. With no children,
pets or events immediately available for me to
document, I decided to simply take a walk and see
what struck me.

Spring flowers were beginning to bloom, and their
bright colors caught my attention. That was the
first of many walks for me, and I have a great many
pictures to show for it. All I had to do was decide
the best way to share them with others. I used the
Simple Scrapbooks Formula Worksheet to plan my
album.

materials $8^{1}/_{2}$ x 11 album (Dalee Book Co.) • metal frame (Making Memories) • ribbon • Cool font (scrapvillage.com)

Purpose To showcase my photography and to have
my favorite flower pictures organized in one place
so that others can enjoy them.

Format An $8^{1}/_{2}$ x 11 post-bound album by Dalee.

Organizational System Nothing specific regarding
the pictures. Pages will be placed according to
background colors (alternating).

Framework Pages The book will consist essentially
of "filler" pages. To set a tone, I'll choose a special
picture and quote for the first page. The number of
pages will be limited only by the relevant quotes I
am able to find.

Color Scheme I'll mount the pictures on either black
or white paper, depending on what looks best with
the picture. The pictures mounted with white will
be placed on dark gray cardstock. The pictures
mounted with black will be placed on white or pale
gray cardstock. I chose these colors because I didn't
want anything to distract from or compete with the
vibrant colors in the pictures.

Decorative Accents I'll use the same font throughout, but no other accents.

Design Scheme One photo (approximately 5 x 7)
per page. Each page will have a quote relating to
flowers. The word "flower" or the specific name of
the flower will be in a larger size font to highlight it.

Preparation The only things that I need to gather
to prepare for this project are quotations. The
sites I'll use most are gardendigest.com and quote-
garden.com

Photographs I'll use all my own photos. I just need
to get them printed to the appropriate size.

Can we conceive
what humanity would be
if it did not know the
flowers?
– Maurice Maeterlinck

title page

Filler pages

The earth laughs in **flowers.**

- Ralph Waldo Emerson

Each **flower**

is a soul opening out to nature.

- Gerard de Nerval

Filler pages

Flowers are happy things.

- P.G. Wodehouse

Flowers have spoken to me more than I can tell in written words. They are the hieroglyphics of angels, loved by all men for the beauty of the character, though few can decipher even fragments of their meaning. - Lydia M. Child

fast, friendly formula | by Marnie Flores

materials Life's Journey accordion album (K & Company) • patterned paper (SEI) • letter stickers (Creative Imaginations) • cellophane envelopes (Zinggzoo Ink) • token (Doodlebug Design) • watercolor markers (Tombow) • eyelets • ribbon • jute • buttons • chalk

note Marnie made her own tags by tracing standard office-store versions.

CINNAMON BUNS BAKING IN THE OVEN ON A COLD WINTRY DAY. The anticipation of raisin pudding for Sunday dessert. The comfort of warm tuna casserole on Tuesdays before piano lessons. Many of my childhood memories are inextricably linked to the foods and aromas of my mother's kitchen. This simple accordion theme album gave me the chance to display my favorite childhood recipes—and the recollections that go with them—in one place. I was surprised at all the memories that came flooding back as I spent time recalling the tastes and smells of my childhood.

Purpose: The purpose of this album is twofold. First, I want to bring together my favorite childhood recipes. Second, I want to record the memories attached to these foods as a reminder of my family and my home.

Format: A four-page, 7 x 7 accordion album.

Organization System: The recipes will be divided into three sections: breakfast, supper and dessert.

Each recipe will be printed on a tag so it can be removed from the album and used. I'll start with just four recipes per section. The accompanying memories will be recorded on the reverse of each tag.

Framework: The album will feature the cover as its title page, followed by a dedication page and three filler pages, one for each category.

Color Scheme: The papers will be pinks and whites, my favorites. The patterned paper will be selected from a coordinated set. The tags will be embellished with eyelets, ribbons and chalks, in hues that mimic the secondary colors in the patterned paper.

Decorative Accents: Fonts, fonts, fonts. Ribbons and thread. Eyelets, tags, buttons, and a doodlebug token.

Design Scheme: Each page will feature pink paper matted on white. The filler pages will each have a cellophane envelope to hold the recipe tags. Each tag will be one of three shapes and one of four colors. The tags will feature printed recipes on the front

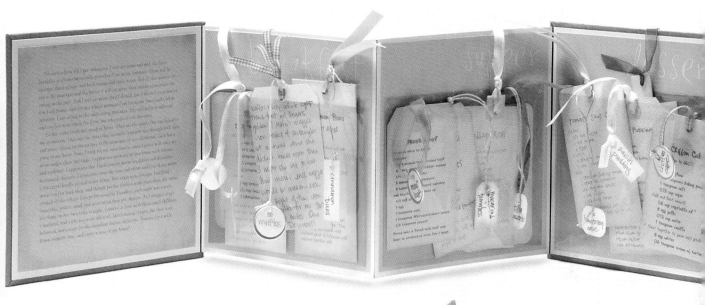

and handwritten memories on the reverse. Each tag will be chalked, with a small circle tag at the end of the ribbon for easy reference. The filler pages will be labeled by category in the top right-hand corner.

Preparation: I need to collect all the recipes and ask my mom if she has done anything in particular to personalize the recipes over the years. I need to spend a few minutes with each food to remember all the good things that make me smile, and then I need to jot down my thoughts.

fast, friendly formula | by Cori Dahmen

SPORTS—ESPECIALLY BEING PART OF A TEAM—has benefits that aren't always apparent in the layouts I make about the events themselves. We've all developed new skills and improved old ones through our participation in sports. Naturally, I want to preserve these memories, but I also want to remember the valuable lessons we've learned. This album serves as a simple reminder that we benefit in many ways when we get in there and play the game.

Purpose: I'm creating this coffee table album as a visual reminder for my kids that sports are about more than winning. The lessons we learn from sports are tools that will serve us well throughout our lives.

Format: a 6 x 6, 2-ring binder by Provo Craft.

Organizational System: Each two-page layout includes one or more photos about a specific sport as well as journaling that highlights the lesson learned. This album will be updated as our family pursues new experiences.

A title page, a dedication page, a table of contents, filler pages and a closing page.

Color Scheme:
Because of the variety of colors in the photos, I'll use neutral colors: black and white paper; black, white and tan sports stickers; and silver eyelet accents. This minimalist approach helps keep the focus on the photos and the journaling.

materials 6 x 6 album (Provo Craft) • tag template (AccuCut) • sports stickers (SRM Press, Inc.) • metal sports charms (Making Memories) • Katie upper and Sonja lower die cut letters (QuicKutz) • Graphite Light font (Internet) • Zig Writer pen (EK Success) • eyelets

Dedication and table of contents

Games, exercise, activities and organized sports all work together to develop our minds and bodies. It is easy to join in the fun, play hard and smile when we are done. But it is the lessons we learn from sports about life, about who we are and about what matters most that can make the biggest impact. If we walk away from a game or a sporting event with increased knowledge of how to play the game we've gotten our money's worth. If we walk away having learned a lesson on how to live our lives or how to treat others, then we won the game.

Table of Contents

Filler pages

Support of the sport is a sport itself. You can get as much, or more, exercise and joy by being on the sidelines as you can by being on the field.

cheer

foot·ball (foot'bôl'), *n.* 1. any of several games played with an inflated leather ball on a rectangular field having two goalposts at each end by two teams whose object is to get the ball over a goal line.

Fall 2003

Filler pages

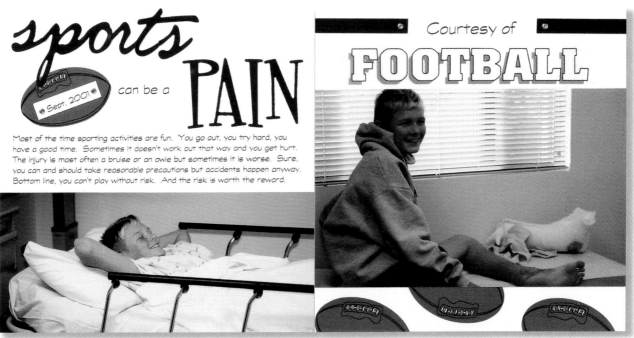

sports

can be a PAIN

Sept. 2001

Most of the time sporting activities are fun. You go out, you try hard, you have a good time. Sometimes it doesn't work out that way and you get hurt. The injury is most often a bruise or an owie but sometimes it is worse. Sure, you can and should take reasonable precautions but accidents happen anyway. Bottom line, you can't play without risk. And the risk is worth the reward.

Courtesy of

FOOTBALL

Decorative Accents: The stickers themselves, along with an occasional die cut tag and eyelet, are the only embellishments.

Design Scheme: The sports stickers are the basis of each design and are used to enhance the mood reflected in the photos and the lessons the photos represent. A simple, bold and graphic look, with clean cuts and lines, unify the book.

Preparations: I need to make copies of pertinent photos so they can be used in the kids' event albums as well as in this one.

fast, friendly formula | by Robin Johnson

A

AS A YOUNG MOTHER WITH THREE KIDS UNDER THE AGE OF FIVE and a husband with a demanding career, I struggled just to get through the day—let alone do something for me! One desperate day, I started a "Journal of Joy." Before going to bed each night, I recorded three things that happened that day that I was grateful for. That journal made a huge difference in my life—my perspective changed, and I learned how wonderful each day could be if I simply took the time to look for the good.

Wondering how you can remember life's little joys? Try this variation on a "Journal of Joy." This is one simple scrapbook you'll be grateful for!

Purpose: Documenting what I enjoy about life will help me recognize my blessings. This album will also help my family learn about me and see what I enjoyed about my role as a mother.

Format: I selected a spiral-bound album (Canson) with 20 pages. I can put 5–6 "Things I Am Grateful For" on a page, and fit 100 items in the album (Figure A).

Organizational System: A numbering system that keeps track of the things I'm grateful for. My journaling entries will be placed in random order throughout the book (Figure B).

Framework Pages: I'll decorate the album cover (Figure A) and make a title page (Figure C).

Color Scheme: I'll use deep earth tones that complement the album's kraft-colored paper (Figure D).

Decorative Accents: A variety of accents—from charms and beads to Band-aid wrappers—that complement the things I'm grateful for (Figure E).

Design Scheme: Because the book contains a lot of text, I'll limit the number of elements on each page. To save time, I'll print all of the titles at the same time and use rubber stamps to add numbers to the title blocks (Figure F). I'll add a subtle accent by rubbing gold ink along the torn edge of the word strips, and vary the look of my handwriting on each entry to add variety and clarity (Figure G).

materials Album (Canson) • Patterned paper (Scrap-Ease) • Button (Dress-It-Up, Cut-It-Up) • Ribbon (MSI) • Fabric squares: Craftmart • Rubber stamps (PrintWorks, All Night Media) • Stamping ink (Stampa Rosa) • Brads (Prym Dritz and Magic Scraps) • Fibers and Embroidery floss (DMC) • Copperplate and Lucida Calligraphy fonts (Microsoft Word) • Charms (Halcraft) • Beads (Designs by Pamela, Blue Moone Beads) • Stickers (SEI, Inc.) • *Album by Robin Johnson*

Preparation: Create a list of things I'm grateful for. I'll consider talents, special moments or memories, events, perspectives, feelings, hopes and beliefs. I'll also consider items inside my home and the world, and items about my family and me.

Photographs: I'll need to locate photos that complement the journaling. (Note: If you're missing specific photos, make a list and take pictures of those things. And keep your eyes peeled for photos that inspire new entries. You may be surprised at what you find when you sort through your photos with an attitude of gratitude!)

C

B

1 THE FIRST SIGNS OF SPRING

EVEN THOUGH OUR WINTER MONTHS ARE FILLED WITH SNOW FUN, I CAN'T HELP BUT TO CHEER INSIDE AT EVERY HINT OF SPRING. I LOVE TO WATCH AS THE EARTH'S BEAUTY AWAKENS.

2 A NEW BABY

I can't think of anything more precious than the gift of a newborn baby. I love their soft skin, their "fresh" smell, their tiny fingers and toes, their newness. I thank God for the four times that a new baby has entered our home and brought us closer to heaven.

3 SUNRISE

There is something absolutely majestic about the first burst of heaven's light in my day. It fills me with energy and hope.

The tranquil and calming setting sun seems to carry with it all the troubles of the day. I love the shimmering "night lights" that follow it.

4 SUNSET

5 CHILDREN'S ARTWORK

One day, Crissy was not feeling well. Sarah disappeared for awhile and came back with this drawing for Crissy. It is of Sarah's favorite dog, "Patch." She was sure it would make Crissy feel better. It worked and whenever I get artwork from my children, it makes me feel better too!!

G

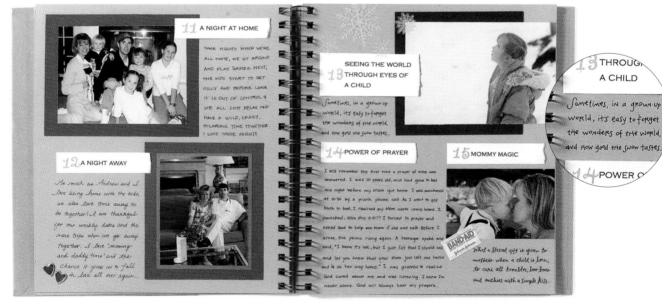

11 A NIGHT AT HOME

SOME NIGHTS WHEN WE'RE ALL HOME, WE SIT AROUND AND PLAY GAMES. NEXT, THE KIDS START TO GET SILLY AND BEFORE LONG IT IS OUT OF CONTROL & WE ALL JUST RELAX AND HAVE A WILD, CRAZY, HILARIOUS TIME TOGETHER. I LOVE THOSE NIGHTS.

12 A NIGHT AWAY

As much as Andrew and I love being home with the kids, we also love time away to be together! I am thankful for our weekly dates and the rare trips when we go away together. I love "mommy and daddy time" and the chance it gives us to fall in love all over again...

13 SEEING THE WORLD THROUGH EYES OF A CHILD

Sometimes, in a grown-up world, it's easy to forget the wonders of the world, and how good the snow tastes...

14 POWER OF PRAYER

I still remember the first time a prayer of mine was answered. I was 10 years old, and had gone to bed one night before my mom got home. I was awakened at 10:30 by a prank phone call. As I went to get back in bed, I realized my Mom never came home. I panicked. Was she O.K.?? I turned to prayer and asked God to help me know if she was safe. Before I arose, the phone rang again. A teenager spoke and said, "I know it's late, but I just felt that I should call and let you know that your mom just left our house and is on her way home." I was grateful to realize God cared about me and was listening. I know I'm never alone. God will always hear my prayers.

15 MOMMY MAGIC

What a blessed gift is given to mothers when a child is born, to cure all troubles, boo-boos and owchies with a simple kiss.

13 THROUGH A CHILD

Sometimes, in a grown-up world, it's easy to forget the wonders of the world, and how good the snow tastes...

14 POWER O

D

F

E

If I had a flower
for every time
I thought of you,
I could walk
forever
in my garden

nature's beauty

Donna Downey | Huntersville, NC

materials corrugated cardstock (DMD Industries, Inc.) • eyelet plaque (Making Memories) ribbon slide (Maya Road) • silk flowers • ribbon

Photo: Special Effects Illustration

what's your passion?

Create a simple page that shares the things you love

by Deanna Lambson

I was just a little girl when my passion for planting flowers began. I remember struggling to climb up on the table, where I sat with my chubby legs outstretched, to help my father plant flower seeds.

We'd fill large gray plastic trays with potting soil. Dad would use a Popsicle stick to make lots of little holes and I'd drop two seeds in each. Then he taught me to cover them with soil and pat it down ever so softly. I still remember the warm, earthy smell of the wet soil.

Perhaps that's why, decades later, you'll still find little pots of budding green sprouts near my warm sunny windows. Whether inside or out, I love to plant. I love to feel the soil. I love the quiet time to think. And I love the promise of what will come.

What's your passion? Reading, running, traveling, doing crossword puzzles? What do you love so much that you'll give up time, money and even sleep to do it? Don't you think something you are so passionate about deserves a page in your scrapbook? That one page could say volumes about who you really are.

Remember, scrapbooking your life is not the same as scrapbooking your pictures. If you don't have time to scrapbook every photo in the box (or boxes), that's OK. Just create one page about the passion that you live and breathe for. Need some ideas? Check out these pages about cats and quilts, fishes and dishes.

Whatever your passion, we give you permission to put it in your scrapbook. And it's even OK if you want to climb up on the table to do it

a passion for...
Uncharted Places
a nomad I will remain

Emily Tyner | Charlotte, NC

Choose one photo that represents your thirst for travel and the excitement of exploring new horizons. Emily enlarged some words in the quote so the viewer can immediately identify the message. A pre-made tag makes it quick and easy.

A **Nomad** I will remain for life: In **Love** with distant and uncharted **Places**

—Isabelle Eberhardt

Travels

materials patterned paper (7 Gypsies) • stickers (me & my BIG ideas) • Rebecca So Nostalgiques tag (EK Success) • Adler font (Internet) • ink • buttons • fibers • circle tag

"It is not length of life,
    but depth of life."

—RALPH WALDO EMERSON

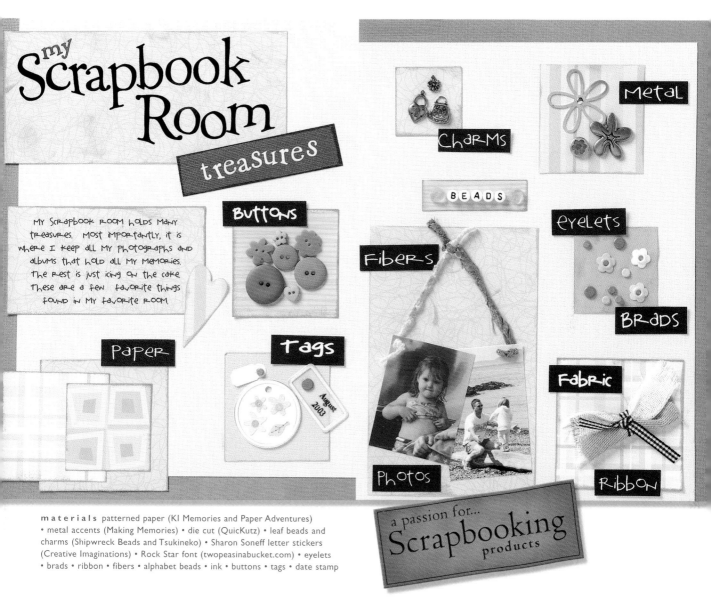

my Scrapbook Room

treasures

My Scrapbook Room holds many treasures. Most importantly, it is where I keep all my photographs and albums that hold all my memories. The rest is just icing on the cake. These are a few favorite things found in my favorite room.

Charms

Metal

BEADS

Buttons

eyelets

Fibers

Brads

Paper

Tags

August 2003

Fabric

Photos

Ribbon

materials patterned paper (KI Memories and Paper Adventures) • metal accents (Making Memories) • die cut (QuicKutz) • leaf beads and charms (Shipwreck Beads and Tsukineko) • Sharon Soneff letter stickers (Creative Imaginations) • Rock Star font (twopeasinabucket.com) • eyelets • brads • ribbon • fibers • alphabet beads • ink • buttons • tags • date stamp

a passion for... Scrapbooking products

Andrea Hautala | Olympia, WA

It's fun to scrapbook, but it's often just as fun to collect all the colorful products. Gather a few treasures from your favorite collections and showcase them on a page. Letter stickers make a quick and eye-catching title. (Besides, they're a pleasure to collect!)

Remember: Scrapbooking your life is not the same as scrapbooking your pictures.

materials patterned paper (Chatterbox, Inc.) • looking glass frame (Scrapworks) • punches (Family Treasures and Marvy Uchida) • JackFrost and Chestnuts fonts (twopeasinabucket.com)

a passion for...
Fishing
fish tremble...

Leslie Pugh | East Wenatchee, WA

Don't hesitate to put photos from several different years on the same page. It shares a powerful message about how much fishing—or *any* passionate pursuit—matters in your life. For a realistic touch, Leslie placed real fishing flies under clear plastic frames.

Fish Tremble When They Hear My Name

It's hard to say exactly why I love fishing so much, especially considering the fact that I have probably been skunked more times that I have been successful. It may just be the thrill of catching fish that does it. However, one part of the lure of fishing might be the fact that I get a break from doing many of the things that I otherwise would be doing such as mowing the lawn, fixing the car, or working! Part of my love for fishing is simply because I have been fishing all my life. As a kid, every summer activity centered itself around fishing. Later, after Leslie and I got married, I got hooked on fly fishing and tying my own flies. I felt like I became the "master deceiver" when I caught my first trout on the first Elk Hair Caddis fly I had tied myself. And at the end of the day, each fishing trip has a special memory.
Some of my favorite memories include:
Digging a misdirected fly out of my leg with a pair of pliers
The day my father-in-law dunked himself in the river
Watching Leslie's line break when she hooked a large misdirected ray.
Landing a 22 inch brown trout under the moonlight
Laughing as a squealing Christian pulls in his 30th bluegill of the day
Seeing my friend Bryan dive into the Green River to retrieve his rod

Yes, there is just something about fishing that definitely has me hooked!
Troy, January 2004

April 2001

July 1998   July 2001   June 2003

Make an Album

There are lots of ways to preserve a passion. Make a simple page within a chronological album, or dedicate a small album to this hobby you love. Mini theme albums like MaryRuth's and Pam's allow you to delve deeper, document more, and really tell your story with passion!

A PASSION FOR FLORAL DESIGN

materials patterned paper (Magenta) • Edwardian Script font (Internet); Century Gothic font (Microsoft Word); CK Cosmopolitan and CK Windsong fonts (Creating Keepsakes) • brads • ink

MaryRuth Francks took a class in college on floral design and has been hooked ever since. This little album shares pictures of all her floral arrangements since then. It is doable in a weekend and easily expanded to include future floral designs. The dedication page is a must. It shares the reason for the album and the passion that inspired it.

materials Sitcom, Commercial Break and Stand Tall fonts (twopeas-inabucket.com); Dear Joe font (Internet) • brads • buttons • vellum • square punch

Jackie Bonette | Taber, AB, Canada

Is your home filled with beautiful hand-made items made by you or a loved one? Take a photo of each one to remember both the intricate handiwork and the love that went into each stitch.

materials stencils (Pebbles, Inc.) • CK Fun font (Creating Keepsakes) • twine • buttons • photo corners

A PASSION FOR BOYD'S BEARS

In 1990, Pam Talluto walked into a Hallmark store and saw Flash McBear. It was love at first sight, and the collection began. This 5 x 7 album explains the significance of each little heirloom. Pam used the pullout formula card provided in each issue of *Simple Scrapbooks* to help her plan the format, colors and design of each page. And she kept her design simple and consistent: a torn red strip at the top and a single photo per page.

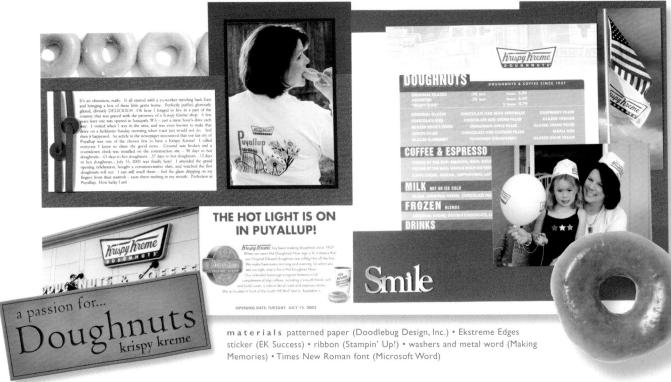

a passion for...
Doughnuts
krispy kreme

materials patterned paper (Doodlebug Design, Inc.) • Ekstreme Edges sticker (EK Success) • ribbon (Stampin' Up!) • washers and metal word (Making Memories) • Times New Roman font (Microsoft Word)

Lisa Cole | Puyallup, WA

Whether it's a favorite restaurant, a flavor of ice cream, or a homemade family recipe, why not preserve your passion for food? Remember that you enjoy eating with all your senses. Tell about the sound of sizzling bacon, the warm smell of fresh bread, and the sweet, melting flavor of a Krispy Kreme donut.

a passion for...
Dishes
dishaholic

Barbara Carroll | Tucson, AZ

Remember the last time you saw something at the store that you "just had to have"? I'll bet you bought it regardless of the price tag. Take pictures of it and record why you love it so much. Make the page fast and easy by printing directly on the background page.

I admit it. I am a dishaholic. Only space issues prevent me from having more. Economic issues should also be a consideration but truthfully, they are not. I have been good for the last few years, only buying too many handmade bowls and a soup tureen. I could easily serve soup to 36 people. As much as I enjoy making homemade soup, this is unlikely to ever be necessary. Then Pottery Barn opened in Tucson. Oh, my. Words were spoken aloud: "the mother ship has landed". The store was open less than a week before I made a visit. It was right before Thanksgiving and I was envisioning a harvest table. There they were. Amber, moss, blanca. How could I resist? I saw them on a Thanksgiving table with a tablecloth of autumn colors. I saw them on red for Christmas. I saw them all together for twelve and separately for just four. The mugs were terrific (cocoa for 12?), the bowls (now I could serve 48!) sublime. I admit it. I am a dishaholic. 11.03

materials Letter Gothic font (Internet)

materials roller coaster page accent (Cock-A-Doodle Design) • stamps (Hero Arts) • Nevermind and Think Small title fonts (twopeasinabucket.com); CK Journaling font (Creating Keepsakes) • bookplate • brads • snaps • ink

a passion for...
Roller Coasters
cedar point

Erin Lincoln | Frederick, MD

What activity gives you a thrill? Is there an outing you repeat year after year? Remember that taking photos of entrance signs helps you avoid "Now, what was that place called?" memory loss after you get home.

"My therapist told me the way to achieve true inner peace is to finish what I start. So far today, I have finished two bags of M and M's and a chocolate cake. I feel better already."

—DAVE BARRY

One *fine* Day

Create a Mini-Album of a Single Event
by Emily Tucker

There are certain days in my life I'll never forget. The day I graduated from high school. My wedding day. The day my children were born. These events were so monumental that I made certain to take pictures to record them.

But there are other days that, while I didn't think to photograph them, are just as precious in my memory: the day I left for college and moved into my first apartment; the day I met my husband; and the day I found out I was pregnant with our first child. If I had it to do over again, I would have snapped some pictures and jotted down a few words for posterity to mark these days as well.

The truth is there are lots of days that deserve special attention. On the pages that follow, see how five *Simple Scrapbooks* readers created mini-albums, each commemorating a single occasion. Some mark incredibly significant events; others document ordinary occurrences that may have otherwise passed unnoticed. All are beautiful reminders of one fine day.

Illustrated by Allen Garnes

title page

One Fine
Day

A day in the life of a figure skater.

dedication page

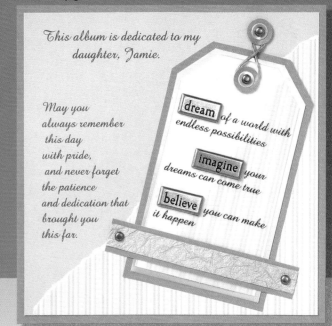

This album is dedicated to my daughter, Jamie.

May you
always remember
this day
with pride,
and never forget
the patience
and dedication that
brought you
this far.

dream *of a world with endless possibilities*

imagine *your dreams can come true*

believe *you can make it happen*

filler pages

Freeskate Program

Your freeskate program was skated to the music from the motion picture, "Rudy." Monica choreographs your programs so that all of your required moves are attempted twice and there is always time at the end of the program to add any moves that you were unable to complete. You skated with more grace and beauty than I had ever seen before. Each required move was executed perfectly and half way through your program you had already performed all of the required elements. The rest was easy; you just had to stay on your feet and look beautiful.

Thoughts from Monica

It's not very often that a coach comes across a student that has the will, drive, and perseverance to stick it out and pass this test. You took the ice with confidence and grace, skating like a swan and mastering every move. I couldn't have been more proud of you that day. I hope that one day I will have a child with as much commitment and strength as you have.

your day to shine

Julie Johnson | Ontario, CA

Julie created an elegant, poignant memento to mark her daughter Jamie's successful completion of a figure skating test. In addition to a play-by-play account of the day, Julie reduced copies of Jamie's score sheets, trimmed them and tucked them into a vellum pocket for easy viewing.

She and Jamie's coach also wrote letters letting Jamie know how proud they both were. Julie notes, "Jamie worked so hard. I wanted her to have something she could look back at and say, 'I did that; I can do anything!'" Can't you just imagine Jamie in the future, coaching another young hopeful and sharing her "I've been there" album?

materials 6 x 6 album, ribbon, stamps and patterned paper (Close To My Heart) • metal frame (K & Company) • metal embellishments (Making Memories) • waxy flax (Scrapworks) • Amazone BT font (Internet)

front

back

LET THE DAY BEGIN
A 24 hour account of real life
Friday, March 19, 2004

8:00 – I am awakened by the girls. Bill has taken the early shift with the
AM kids and I am allowed to sleep in. He leaves for work.

8:15 – wipe down and straighten my bathroom counter as I brush my
teeth...already multi tasking.

8:30 – While Cole is still sleeping, the girls jump in with me as I take my
shower

9:00 – I have managed to get dressed, but the girls are still running
around naked...Cole has woken up, it is his turn for a bath.

9:15 – McKenna & Payton, who are still naked, have been prancing
around the house with their sneakers on their hands pretending
to be...octopuses? OK!?

9:30 – Cole is dressed...and the girls want me to lay out their clothes
so that they can dress themselves

1:40 – unload the car, put away the groceries, and fix grilled cheese
sandwiches for lunch for the girls...McKenna & Payton each
choose a cookie cutter to cut their sandwiches into shapes.
While the girls eat, I change & feed Cole a bottle.

2:00 – With Cole in the stroller, the girls & I go outside to blow bubbles
and play on the swings in the backyard.

3:00 – Payton goes down for a nap while McKenna and I play with her
crayons and markers. Cole is entertained in his bouncy seat.

4:00 – McKenna watches Arthur and Clifford on PBS and I sit at my desk
and scrap. Cole naps.

5:30 – Cole gets a diaper change and McKenna, Cole and I go
downstairs to start dinner.

6:30 – Bill comes home from work and we sit down to eat dinner
Homemade pizza...Even though I hate to cook, I have just been
introduced to Pampered Chef and I love my new cooking stone.

7:00 – with an hour before bedtime, I clean the kitchen and Bill plays
with the girls...Ok really he riles them up and it is the loudest
part of my day.

8:15 – Bedtime is always easy with the girls, they go right to sleep with
hugs and kisses from Mommy and Daddy. "Night, night, sleep
tight, don't let the bed bugs bite."

8:30 – ahh the QUIET. Cole is
talk. We watch a little

10:00 – with Cole in tow, I go
throwing in another lo
before I get comfortab
scrapping time. Cole

1:00 – Cole gets a diaper char
to sleep. I finally go to

3:30 – I am not happy!! Cole
cutting it. We bounce
with him on my lap an
sing...poor thing...I ca
website...at 4:00 AM.

4:30 – finally after snacking or
back to bed.

I sleep soundly because I kno
Cole wakes up again. Cole sle
wakes up with them, feeds th
beginning my day all over aga

24 hours later

Donna Downey | Huntersville, NC

Wouldn't you love to know what your great-grandmother did on a typical day? Provide future generations with a timeline of your daily routine. *Simple Scrapbooks* contributing editor Donna Downey used a notebook and camera to record her real-life adventures as a work-at-home mom. By keeping her design simple—a must for a busy mom of three—

Donna was able to finish this album in under an hour! Note also the honesty with which she records the events of her day. Squabbling children and grocery store ordeals are an integral part of any mom's real world.

materials 6 x 6 Deja Views accordian album (C-Thru Ruler Co.) • metal frame (Making Memories) • Dirty Ego and Zurich Lt BT fonts (Internet)

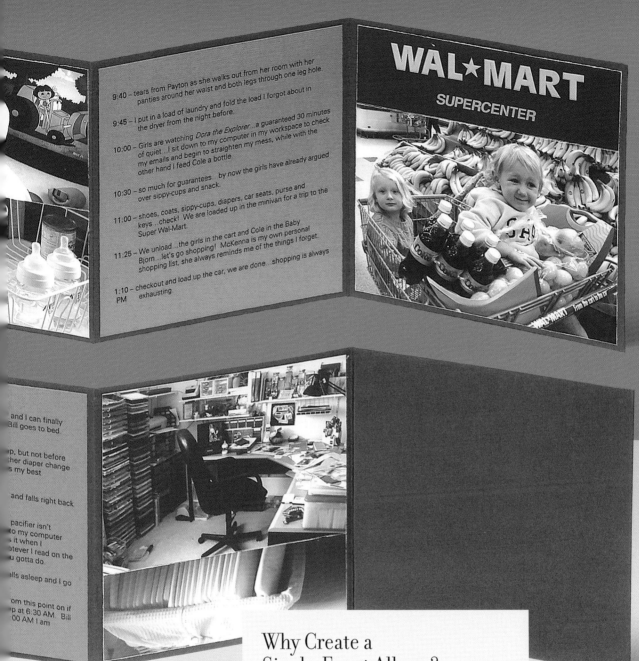

9:40 – tears from Payton as she walks out from her room with her panties around her waist and both legs through one leg hole.

9:45 – I put in a load of laundry and fold the load I forgot about in the dryer from the night before.

10:00 – Girls are watching *Dora the Explorer*...a guaranteed 30 minutes of quiet ...I sit down to my computer in my workspace to check my emails and begin to straighten my mess, while with the other hand I feed Cole a bottle.

10:30 – so much for guarantees ...by now the girls have already argued over sippy-cups and snack.

11:00 – shoes, coats, sippy-cups, diapers, car seats, purse and keys ...check! We are loaded up in the minivan for a trip to the Super Wal-Mart.

11:25 – We unload...the girls in the cart and Cole in the Baby Bjorn...let's go shopping! McKenna is my own personal shopping list, she always reminds me of the things I forget.

1:10 – checkout and load up the car, we are done...shopping is always
PM   exhausting

and I can finally
Bill goes to bed.

p, but not before
ther diaper change
s my best

and falls right back

pacifier isn't
o my computer
it when I
tever I read on the
u gotta do.

lls asleep and I go

om this point on if
p at 6:30 AM. Bill
00 AM I am

Why Create a Single-Event Album?

1. It's a great way to "get your feet wet" as a scrapbooker. Buy just what you need for one fun project and walk away with a great sense of accomplishment.

2. A small album is portable, easy to share with friends and relatives, and fun to display almost anywhere!

3. They make great gifts, especially for the people who shared the event with you.

4. Some topics just don't seem to fit into more traditional, chronological albums. Accept this fact and allow yourself to celebrate your memories in other albums too!

5. Finally, some days are so special they beg for an album all their own.

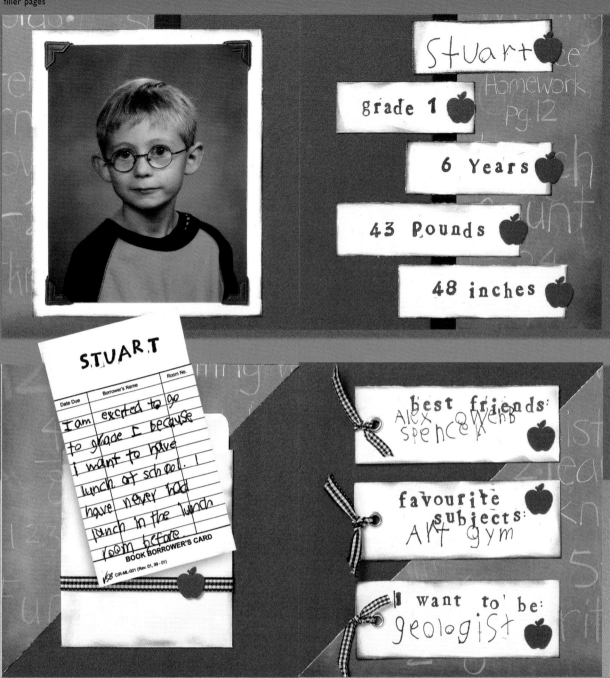

Stuart

grade 1

6 Years

43 Pounds

48 inches

STUART

I am excited to go to grade I because I want to have lunch at school. I have never had lunch in the lunch room before.

BOOK BORROWER'S CARD

best friends: Alex SpenceWebb

favourite subjects: Art gym

I want to be: geologist

title page

BACK TO SCHOOL

2003

first day of school

Jill Beamer | Vancouver, BC, Canada |

The first day of school is full of mixed emotions for both parent and child. Jill captured all the excitement (and butterflies!) in a "Back to School" album. Jill had her children record their best-friends information, favorite subjects, hopes for the coming school year and dreams for the future. Comparing and contrasting the portraits, handwriting and responses of different children on the same day is a telling approach: Imagine what a treasure this album will become if the same questions are asked year after year!

JACQUELINE

Pre-K

4 Years

36 Pounds

42 inches

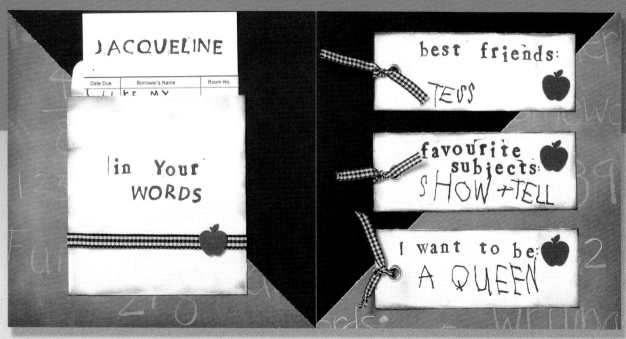

JACQUELINE

Date Due	Borrower's Name	Room No.

in Your WORDS

best friends: TESS

favourite subjects: SHOW + TELL

I want to be: A QUEEN

back to SCHOOL

materials 6 x 6 album (K & Company) • Simply Stated rub-ons (Making Memories) • patterned paper (Karen Foster Design) • photo corners • ribbon (Impress Rubber Stamps) • apple punch (EK Success) • alphabet stamps (Hero Arts) • library cards and pockets • **note** Jill used alphabet stamps for her titles, but there are several typewriter computer fonts available if you don't have time to stamp.

gifts

Details:

I knew for awhile that I wanted to do something really special for Joey's 30th birthday. Talking with his mom we came up with the perfect plan! I bought plane tickets to Utah, she called family and friends, we ordered food and prepared for a great birthday party!
Joey was really surprised and pleased when I gave him plane tickets to Utah for the week of his birthday. But he had no clue about the big surprise party!
On the day of the party things didn't go exactly smooth when John was late getting Joey out of the house! To make matters worse they were over an hour late getting back because they got caught in traffic due to an accident. I had house full of hungry guests waiting for the guest of honor! Once they showed up things went great and we had a wonderful party! Joey seemed really touched that so many people would come to celebrate with us. We had a great week and it was a wonderful way to celebrate his 30th birthday.

Family and Friends who came to celebrate:

Francks
- Mom
- Jimmy
- Jacob
- John

Boone
- Dad
- Mom
- Emma
- David
- Bekah
- Alicia
- Mariah
- Matthias
- Caroline
- Jesse

Wardrip
- Jill
- Bob

Haderlie
- Tim
- Susan
- Samantha

Watton
- Margie
- Moses

Duncan
- Jonathan
- Jamie
- Ethan

30th birthday

MaryRuth Francks | Spokane, WA

A milestone birthday deserves more than just a page or two in your family scrapbook! "My husband's family celebrates everybody's birthday for a week," says MaryRuth, "so when Joey turned 30 I knew had to do something big!" After throwing a once-in-a-lifetime surprise party, MaryRuth created a birthday album recording Joey's big day. She included party pics, a guest roster and even a list of 30 Things We Love About Joey. "And to think, if I'd married the other guy, I could have gotten away with a bakery cake!" MaryRuth adds.

contents page

What: A trip to Utah and a surprise party to celebrate your 30th birthday!

Where: Clearfield, UT

When: March 21–25 2003

Why: Because we love you and you only turn thirty once!

celebration

Thirty

materials 5 x 8 album (Scrapworks) • patterned paper and stickers (Kopp Design)

the interlude | *before the reception*

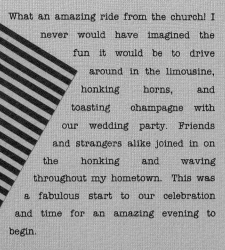

What an amazing ride from the church! I never would have imagined the fun it would be to drive around in the limousine, honking horns, and toasting champagne with our wedding party. Friends and strangers alike joined in on the honking and waving throughout my hometown. This was a fabulous start to our celebration and time for an amazing evening to begin.

my wedding day

Katy Jurasevich | Crown Point, IN

Many brides plan to create an elaborate wedding album "someday." Katy wanted a keepsake to commemorate her recent nuptials, but she didn't want to wait until she found the time to make a full-scale scrapbook. Instead, she selected some of her favorite shots and put them together in a pocketsize wedding album she can tuck in her purse. "This way if I get ticked off at my husband, I can pull it out and remember why I love him so much!" says Katy.

materials 4 x 6 album • patterned paper and photo turns (7gypsies) • letter stickers and wooden frame (Li'l Davis Designs) • ribbon (Making Memories) • American Typewriter and Repress Capitals fonts (Internet) • Play font (lifetimemoments.com) • Times New Roman font (Microsoft Word) • mini brads

Turn a Ho-Hum Photo Album into a Knockout Scrapbook

So, you want to make a cool, classy mini-album, but you don't want to break the bank. Unfortunately, most of the inexpensive albums at your local discount store look… well, inexpensive. But you and your stash of stuff have the power to change that. Here are two album cover makeovers that are sure to impress:

Before

Before

After

After

birthday album

Lisa Sanders | Grain Valley, MO

Lisa brushed this plain red album with white paint for a distressed look. She then glued paper and other decorations directly onto the 4 x 6 album cover.

materials 4 x 6 album (me & my BIG ideas) • patterned paper (Rusty Pickle and K & Company) • Foofabets stickers (Foofala) • TexTiles (Everlasting Keepsakes) • bookplate (Making Memories) • silk flower • button • acrylic paints

travel album

Stacy Julian | Liberty Lake, WA

Stacy cut two 4 x 6 pieces of patterned paper and slid them into the front and back slipcovers of this plastic album. She attached her embellishments to the cover.

materials generic 4 x 6 plastic album • patterned paper (American Crafts) • Memories Made Easy vellum pocket (Colorbök) • Paper Pizzazz accents (Hot Off The Press) • Ting-a-Lings charms (Carolee's Creations)

One *fine* Day

Now it's your turn!

Think Ahead

What special day is marked on your calendar right now? It could be your mother's birthday, a baby shower, a girl's day out or a day trip with your family. What do you want to take away from this event? What will make it special? Plan a mini-album now. When the big day arrives, you'll know what pictures to take, what journaling to capture and what mementos to save.

Pick a Day

Great albums can come from momentous events as well as everyday life. Here are a few not-so-obvious topics for single-event albums:

- The Day You were Born: highlight historical events, world news, pop culture and cost-of-living info for the day you were born—or for the birth date of someone important in your life.

- A Day in the Life: record your daily routine, or that of your partner or a child.

- Moving Day: snap pictures of both your old and new neighborhoods; include the selling price of the houses, your packing list, etc.

- Test Day: include what you ate for breakfast, your feelings before and after the test, some questions or details from the exam, and what you did to unwind or celebrate when it was over.

- Retirement Day: compile notes from co-workers, along with photos of them and your place of employment.

Don't Overlook the Obvious

- Holiday
- Birthday
- Wedding
- Field trip to a farm/zoo
- Visit to a theme park
- Day at the beach
- Sporting event
- Athletic meet

Vision in white

Mrs. Rebekah Martin

June 4, 2001

REMEMBERING

the magic

Your wedding day. You dreamt about it as a young girl. You imagined every detail in your mind—from the beaded wedding dress to the getaway car adorned with shaving cream and tin cans (or in my case, my brother's gym shoes!). The long-awaited day finally came, filled with excitement and romance. But with each passing year the memory of that magical day seems to get further buried beneath work and school papers, active children and car repairs.

I know creating your own wedding album may be at the bottom of your "to-do" list, but whether your wedding was one month ago or 40 years ago, there are some big reasons to make this album a priority. Once you know them, all you need is a step-by-step plan to make it simple. Read on and you'll find that creating a wedding album is as simple as saying "I Do."

Say "I do" to creating a wedding album

by Deanna Lambson

Professional Portrait Album
Album by Kim Morgan. **Supplies** *Album:* Anna Griffin; *Embossed papers:* K & Company (cream and white); *Metallic paper:* Emagination Crafts; *Flower punches:* Paper Shapers, EK Success (small); Fiskars (mini); *Computer font:* Shelley Allegro BT, WordPerfect; *Embroidery floss:* DMC.

Do It for Your Children

Recently, my four-year-old son, Levi, asked for a story as I tucked him into bed. I began with the familiar story of Jack in the Beanstalk when he interrupted me: "Mom, I want to hear a real story about when you and Daddy were little. You know, when you got married." I told him about meeting Don on a ski lift, about falling in love with his voice and laughing as he ate calamari (just to impress me, I'm sure). I shared how I felt at the very moment we committed our lives to each other, and how his daddy's eyes were soft and sparkling.

Levi and I were both silent for a while. Long after he fell asleep, I lay there beside him pondering. There was something in that true-life romance that was comforting to him. And no children's storybook author has written an adventure nearly so fascinating to him as the one his daddy and I have written together.

Do It for Yourself

You know your children will love your story, but what may surprise you is how much fun you'll have reminiscing with your sweetheart. When you were engaged, you couldn't stop thinking about your husband-to-be. You couldn't bear to say good-night at the door. Nothing was as important as being together. And now, years later, few things are as important as that marriage relationship.

When I was married 15 years ago, my mother-in-law gave me a little piece of advice. She said someday Don and I might have a disagreement (impossible!). "When you do," she suggested, "pull out your wedding photos. Look closely at each one and remember all the reasons you fell in love with each other."

When you create a wedding album, that's exactly what will happen … you'll remember. And you may discover something unexpected. The handsome man you married looks incredibly more handsome now. The romance you felt on your wedding day can't compare to the deep love you feel when you look in each other's eyes today.

Creating a Wedding Album

So now you know why it's important to create a wedding album, but how do you actually do it? We have help! I asked three scrapbookers to create wedding albums. Each one has its own unique purpose, content and style. Take a look at their albums and you're sure to fall madly in love!

Professional Portrait Album

Do you have beautiful professional photos of your wedding day? Kim Morgan of Pleasant Grove,

title page

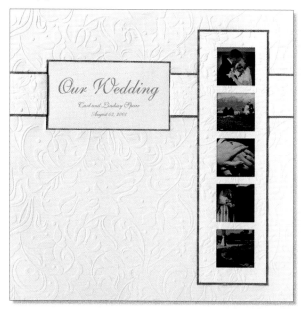

Figure 1. The elegant cream and white embossed papers on the title page set the mood and design for the entire album.

table of contents page

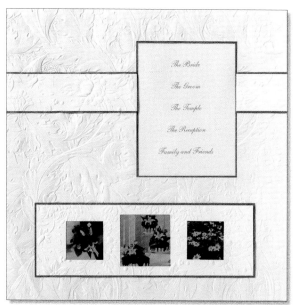

Figure 2. On her table of contents page, Kim introduces the album's five sections.

Utah, decided to create a special keepsake for her dear friend, Lindsay, by creating an album with Lindsay's professional wedding photos.

Kim introduced the album with an elegant title page that establishes the color and design schemes for the entire book (Figure 1). Then, she organized the photos into five sections based on topics that are listed on her table of contents page (Figure 2). Figure 3 shows two of the section pages; each features a small "detail" photo that introduces the section (Figure 3). Kim's filler pages show the wedding photos accented by simple, elegant embellishments (Figure 4).

Using the same pre-embossed cream and white paper on every page simplified the process for Kim (see her completed formula on page 228), while lending a feeling of elegance and consistency to the entire album. Because the album is meant as a display piece, Kim added minimal journaling. The result is a beautiful keepsake that will be treasured for generations to come.

WRITE
now

Making the guest list is one of the most important preparations for the big day. Was there a guest that came to your wedding who was extra special to you? Who was it? Why is he or she so special to you? What is your relationship with this person now?

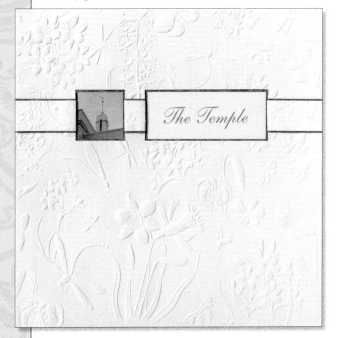 

Figure 3. On each section page, Kim included a small "detail" photo to introduce the section.

KIM'S FORMULA:

Purpose

1. Why am I making this album?
I'm making this album with my friend's wedding photos to display in her home.

Format

2. What size and style of album will I use?
I will use an elegant 12" x 12" post-bound album.

3. What system will I use to organize my album?
I will group the photos by topic, creating a section page for each topic. I'll list the topics on the table of contents page.

4. What framework pages do I want/need in the album?
I will create a title page, table of contents page, section pages and filler pages.

5. What is my color scheme? (Attach color swatches here.)
I will chiefly use cream and white to keep the look of the album clean and classic. I'll accent the colors with gold and lavender.

6. What decorative accents will I use? (Attach samples here.)
I'll add some simple flowers and thin strips of paper tied into knots.

7. How will I arrange my photos and journaling on the framework and filler pages to create a unified look and feel? (Draw thumbnail sketches here.)
The title page, table of contents page and section pages will each have small "detail" photos to give the reader a taste of what's coming up in that section. The filler pages will have accents made of thin, knotted strips of paper.

Preparation

8. Do I need to gather additional information (such as stories)?
No. I will add minimal journaling since the album will be for display.

9. What photos do I need to complete the album?
The photos were done professionally by Scott Hancock Photography.

Figure 4. Notice how each focal-point photo on the filler pages is set behind the page rather than mounted on top of it. In this way, Kim didn't have to trim the photographs.

WRITE
now

Sometimes the smallest details can convey the most powerful emotions. As you recall your wedding, consider the following questions and write as much as you can remember:

- What was the temperature that day? Was it raining? Was it warm and sunny?
- Describe the room you were married in.
- Did you wear jewelry that had special significance?
- Was music a part of the ceremony? What songs have particular meaning to you?
- Are there any smells you associate with your wedding or your first home together, such as your perfume or his cologne, laundry detergent or burnt toast?

He Says, She Says Album

Is your husband's memory of your first date totally different from yours? Why not record your perspectives of your courtship and marriage, like Brenda Cosgrove did in her He Says, She Says album? "Although it was a struggle getting my husband to answer the questions," laughs Brenda, "it was worth it! It was fun for both of us to remember all the good times and to hear the other's point of view." (See Brenda's completed formula on the next page.)

Brenda opens with a title page (Figure 5). Her table of contents page is divided into sections, representing different stages in their relationship—from their first meeting, to their engagement, to happily ever after (Figure 6). The color of each heart on the table of contents corresponds with the color of background paper used in that particular section. Brenda also dedicated the album to her children on a dedication page (Figure 7), sharing with them how much their parents love each other. Each child will eventually receive a copy of the album to keep.

He Says, She Says Album
Album by Brenda Cosgrove. **Supplies** *Album:* Century Craft; *Patterned paper:* Doodlebug Design; *Primitive heart punch:* Paper Shapers, EK Success; *Computer fonts:* CK Bella and CK Journaling, "The Best of Creative Lettering" CDs Vols. 3 and 2, *Creating Keepsakes.*

title page

table of contents page

Figure 5. Brenda's title page introduces the color scheme and basic accents—a white heart punch or eyelet mounted on a cardstock block—for her He Says, She Says album.

Figure 6. Brenda's table of contents is color coded—the color of each heart corresponds with the color used on the section and filler pages in that section.

dedication page

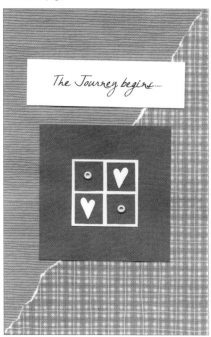

When I was a little girl I dreamed of the many wonderful adventures I would encounter in my life. One of those recurring dreams consisted of a handsome prince sweeping me away on a white stallion to marry him in a castle. That castle and white stallion never came true, however, that prince did come and swept me away to marry him.

I have created this scrapbook and dedicate it to my children to share that love story with them and to celebrate the love that their mother and father have for each other.

Figure 7. On her dedication page, Brenda dedicates the album to her children, with the hope they will celebrate the love their parents share.

section pages

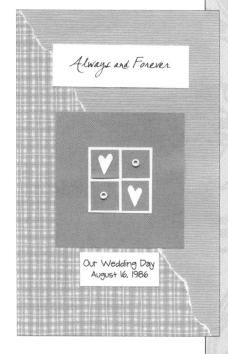

The Journey begins.....

Always and Forever

Our Wedding Day
August 16, 1986

Figure 8. To provide consistency to her album, Brenda used the same design on each section page. The color of each section page corresponds to the color of the heart used in the table of contents.

BRENDA'S FORMULA:

Purpose

1. Why am I making this album?

I'm making this album for my children. My goal is to share the love story I've "written" with my husband. I will copy the album four times so each of my children can have one.

Format

2. What size and style of album will I use?
I will use a white, 6" x 9", three-ring Century Craft memory album with ribbon ties.

3. What system will I use to organize my album?
I will organize my album by subject, from how we met to happily ever after. I will include a different colored heart on each subject on the table of contents page, and use the same color of paper on the background of each section's title and filler pages (Figure 8, above).

4. What framework pages do I want/need in the album?

I will create a title page, dedication page, table of contents page, section pages, filler pages and a closing page. Each filler spread will have at least one page with my perspective, and another with my husband's (Figure 9, page 232).

5. What is my color scheme? (Attach color swatches here.)
I've chosen plaid and striped papers in a variety of bright colors (one color for each section of the book).

6. What decorative accents will I use? (Attach samples here.)
I'll accent my pages with a primitive heart punch from EK Success. If I want to add to the book in the future, I'll have the basic tool I need to create the same embellishment.

7. How will I arrange my photos and journaling on the framework and filler pages to create a unified look and feel? (Draw thumbnail sketches here.)
I will use a different color for each section. Each section and filler page will have striped paper for the background, with a piece plaid paper (torn diagonally) on top. I will use the CK Bella font to create the section titles, and CK Journaling for the title page, dedication page and filler pages. Some of the section pages will include poems or thoughts.

Preparation

8. Do I need to gather additional information (such as stories)?
I need to gather information and stories from my husband (this may be a challenge!).

9. What photos do I need to complete the album?
I will use photos from our courtship and marriage.

How we started Dating
(as told by Craig)

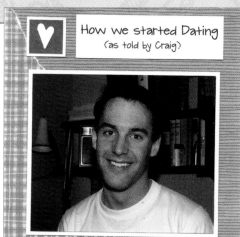

The journey began when my parents asked me to go to a Christmas party they were involved in. I had been away for several years and they wanted me to see some people I hadn't seen in a long time. I did not really want to go but I went anyway. While I was there I visited with many old friends but my attention was on a gap in a folding curtain across the gym where two girls seemed to be looking out and staring at me. I knew one of them as an old friend but I did not recognize the other. I admit I was amused and most of the evening I kept one eye on the curtain to see if they were still there. At the end of the party the old friend that was peeking through the curtain came to say hi. I asked her who the other girl was and she indicated that it was her roommate Brenda Shewchuk. I was truly surprised because that was a girl I had gone to high school with. I remembered her well because in grade 12 she had written in my year book that I had looked good in my basketball uniform and had nice legs. That kind of compliment as a high school kid is not soon forgotten. Brenda's

How we started Dating
(as told by Brenda)

What had started out to be a pretty typical day ended up being the beginning of my journey with Craig. I had worked late and was suppose to go and help in the kitchen for a Christmas party when I got off work. It was a very cold and snowy night and the roads were very bad. By the time I got to the party all my friends were already there helping out. The minute I stepped in the door my roommate Terri told me a boy she knew named Craig Cosgrove was at the party and that he looked great. I remembered Craig from high school and was dying to see what he looked like. It had been 3 1/2 years and I was eager to see if he still looked the same. We could not get a very good view of him as

filler pages

Figure 9. For each subject listed in the table of contents, Brenda included filler spreads—one page relates her perspective, the other shares her husband's.

perspectives

Your wedding album is the perfect place to share the significance of a gown, pin or other item associated with your wedding. Emily Tucker of Matthews, North Carolina, created a lasting tribute to a beautiful wedding dress. The dress, the choice of three brides for their marriage ceremonies in 1967 and 1968, was also the selection of Emily's cousin Megan at her wedding in 2000. Megan also wore the lace from her grandmother's veil that was purchased in France in 1931. "When I put on the veil," Megan whispered, "I could almost feel Gram's support behind me in a physical way."

On each layout, Emily shared each woman's perspective of her wedding day by creating cards that include a photo on the front and that open to reveal journaling and an additional photo. What a wonderful keepsake of a special day in four women's lives!

Share the story of a special wedding keepsake in your wedding album. Pages by Emily Tucker.
Supplies *Colored vellum:* Paper Adventures; *Computer font:* CK Bella, "The Best of Creative Lettering" CD Vol. 3, *Creating Keepsakes*.

Family and Friends Tapestry Album
Album by Lynne Montgomery. **Supplies**
Album: Sew Be It, Timeless Treasures; *Patterned papers:* Anna Griffin; *Ribbon:* Offray; *Beads, Fiber:* Unknown; *Computer fonts:* CK Bella and Pretty; *Rubber stamp:* Hero Arts.

Figure 10. Lynne remembers family and friends by displaying their wedding announcements and photos in her Tapestry Album.

Figure 11. Lynne identified the categories in her table of contents by sorting the wedding announcements she's received according to her relationship with each couple.

Family and Friends Tapestry Album

What do you do with all those wedding announcements from family and friends? Lynne Montgomery of Gilbert, Arizona, just can't part with them. "It would be like throwing away part of my history," says Lynne. "They help me remember friends and family members I rarely get to see."

As a solution, Lynne created an album to display the beautiful wedding announcements she receives and to share the stories behind the relationships (Figure 10). "I call it my Tapestry Album," confides Lynne. "Just as it takes many threads to weave a beautiful tapestry, it takes the many fibers of our lives woven together to create beautiful relationships." See formula on page 235 to note how she compiled her album.

Figure 12. On each section page, Lynne added beautiful ribbons and trims to enhance the wedding theme. The subtle colors lend to the elegance of the design.

YOU CAN DO THIS

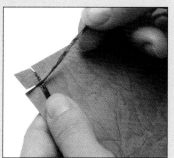

Using gold thread, Lynne created a beautiful border around a heritage wedding photo (inset) with gold thread. You don't have to be a seamstress to achieve this hand-stitched look. Here's how:

1. Cut a mat for your photo from cardstock.
2. Using small scissors, snip slits about $\frac{1}{2}$" long on both sides of each of the four corners (you'll have eight slits).
3. Tie a small knot in the gold thread and pull it through one of the slits, with the knot behind the cardstock.
4. Bringing the thread across the front of the photo mat, tuck it through the slit on the opposite side, bring it across the corner in back, and come up through the other slit on the same corner. Continue wrapping until you've placed the thread on all four sides.
5. Fasten on the back with a small knot or adhesive.

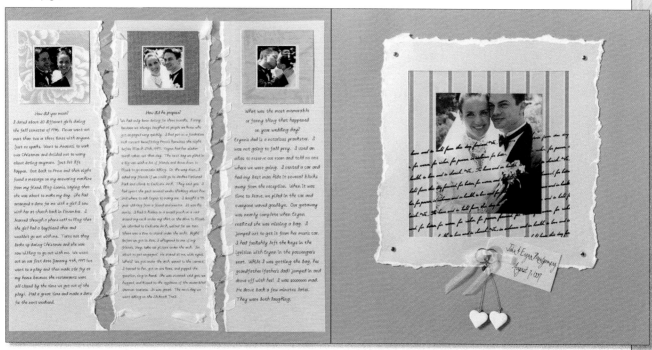

Figure 13. Each filler spread in Lynne's album has a unique design, though the format is the same: questions and answers on the left-hand page, and the photo and announcement on the right-hand page.

LYNNE'S FORMULA:

Purpose

1. Why am I making this album?

For years I've received wedding announcements from family and friends. Every once in a while I get "the box" out and look through them. This album will help me preserve and enjoy these announcements that connect me to so many dear friends and family members.

Format

2. What size and style of album will I use?

The theme for the entire project is "tapestry." Tapestry is complex and rich in design and beauty. It seems to be a good representation of the union of marriage and friendship. I'll use a 12" x 12" album.

3. What system will I use to organize my album?

My album will be organized into four sections: immediate family, extended family, friends, and children of friends (Figure 11, page 233). I will ask each of the couples the same three questions: 1) How did you meet? 2) How did he propose? 3) What was the most memorable or funny thing about your wedding day? I'll include their answers on a spread with their announcement.

4. What framework pages do I want/need in the album?

To start, I will create a title page with a poem about tapestry. Then I'll create a table of contents page and four section pages (Figure 12, page 234). The filler pages will be just as unique as the people represented on them (Figure 13, above). The number of filler pages will grow as I receive more announcements.

5. What is my color scheme? (Attach color swatches here.)

I will use cream, ivory, taupe and sage green.

6. What decorative accents will I use? (Attach samples here.)

I'll use a variety of ribbons and trims that are appropriate to the wedding theme.

7. How will I arrange my photos and journaling on the framework and filler pages to create a unified look and feel?

On the filler pages will be two-page spreads, with the questions/answers on the left side and the photo/announcement on the right side.

Preparation

8. Do I need to gather additional information (such as stories)?

I will gather information from the couples when I receive their announcements.

9. What photos do I need to complete the album?

I will use the photos I receive with the wedding announcements.

TAKING

Baby Steps

MAKING

Huge Strides

Baby albums for time-crunched mothers

by Jeanie Croasmun

My two-year-old son's eyes change a thousand times a day. Sad eyes, happy eyes, crying eyes, eyes wide open with amazement or squinched up in fear. I want to snap a dozen pictures a day because, good or bad, I know tomorrow those eyes will change.

I'm not alone. Boxes of photos and mementos stacked a mile high in closets and under beds attest to the fact that kids are just irresistible. And the things they do in those first years? You want to remember them all.

But remembering everything doesn't mean you have to scrapbook everything. In fact, it's freeing when you don't. When you're creating albums like those of our four designers (a first-time mom; an adoptive mom, an empty-nester presenting her grown son his baby album; and a grandmother acknowledging her grandson), the time you find at any stage in life is painfully scarce. So concentrate on creating memories, pick 15 pages, and scale back your ambitions.

When you do, you'll find that those boxes become a quick task to tackle. Your album gains a unique focus. You keep the memories with time to spare. And with little guys around, it won't be long before they find plenty of ways for you to spend that time, too. With them.

my wish upon a star for you!

Darci Dowdle | Eagle Mountain, UT

> "I want you to know you are a special person who is here to fulfill a special purpose."

Every mother has wishes and dreams for her child. *Simple Scrapbooks* editorial board member, Darci Dowdle decided to put hers into an album for her six-month-old son, Ty.

Time constraints are tough on a new mom, but rather than wait until her son grew up, Darci wanted to get her basic feelings on paper now. To start the process, she compiled an outline of attributes and qualities that she values and that she hopes to pass on to Ty. Each quality, like "love of family and nature," "easy going personality," "courage" and "good health," earns its own page adjacent to a photo that reflects that attribute for Darci.

"I am making this for Ty to let him know how much I love him," says Darci. "It's my hope and wish for him to be happy and grow up to be a good, well-rounded person."

And to add a just-the-facts element to the album, Darci also chose to incorporate some Ty trivia into each page, putting a single fact—like Ty's birth place and the origin of his name, for instance—into a tiny vellum pocket at the bottom of each layout. Star accents complete Darci's wish theme.

filler pages

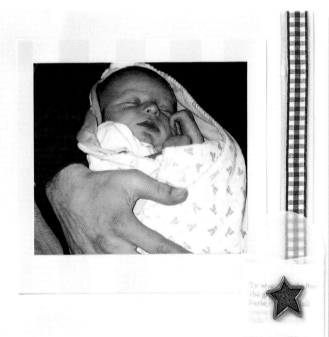

I wish for you to feel secure with yourself. In today's society there are many people and things that make us feel like we are not good enough. I want you to know that you are a special person who is here to fulfill a special purpose. Feel secure in knowing who you are and where you have come from. I wish for you to have a strong testimony that will help you always recognize your talents and abilities. In this picture you obviously feel secure and safe in the arms of your father. Likewise know that your Heavenly Father will always be there for you. I wish for you to always find security in him.

intro pages

I knew that you were a miracle the minute they placed you in my arms. I felt happiness and joy like I had never felt before. Then only seconds after bringing you home I had a whole new set of emotions. I felt fear, a sense of responsibility and inadequacy. I want to be a good parent, and provide for you all that life has to offer. I also want you to understand that I care more about the kind of person you are than anything else. I wish for you so much! I am creating this book so that you will know what qualities and attributes I wished for you to posses when you were just a little baby boy and I was your nervous first time mom.

filler pages

I wish for you to have a deep sense of Patriotism. It is a blessing to be born in this great country. You were born during a time of war, when there were many overseas fighting to protect your freedoms. I hope that you will always respect those who have gone before you while defending this country. When I saw this picture I felt a deep sense of reverence for the flag you are waving. I hoped that you will understand how blessed you are to live in America, and that you will have the courage to defend this country and what you believe in at all times during your life.

materials 6 x 6 album (Close To My Heart) • star snaps, tags, charms and metal frame (Making Memories) • small vellum envelopes • ribbon

katelyn's story

Leanne | Katelyn's Adoptive Mom

"She was the one.
She was mine.
The bond was
instantaneous.
It was amazing."

Leanne had waited, hoped and prayed for years before finally becoming an adoptive mom to daughter Katelyn eight years ago. Since Katelyn asks to hear the story of her adoption again and again, Leanne thought that telling the story in an album just seemed natural.

"I want to ensure that my child understands the gratitude that I feel toward her birth mother," says Leanne, "for having given up a child as an act of love." That meant she would focus on writing down Katelyn's entire story and then choosing the pictures to complement it.

By starting with a 12 x 12 album, Leanne left herself room for comprehensive journaling and plenty of pictures. And by using a coordinated line of pattern paper throughout, Leanne gave her big book a visual boost while still concentrating on the story of her daughter's adoption.

"This album is important to me because it's a beautiful story," says Leanne. "And had not *Simple Scrapbooks* suggested a 15-page format as a way of making manageable what I thought would be something entirely unmanageable, I would never have attempted it. This way, Katelyn can have something tangible now that reaffirms the beauty."

intro pages

filler pages

materials Laura Ashley 12 x 12 album (EK Success) • ribbon, accents and bows (Offray) • raised heart corners, tags and metal letters (Making Memories) • buttons • eyelets

looking back
the early years: 1969-1972

Sue Cross | Oak Park, CA

"...one of the functions of grandparents is to voice the sense of continuity, of family connections through generations. Long memory offers a perspective I certainly didn't have as a young mother."

There's good and bad to waiting 30 years to make a baby album. For Sue Cross, the good was that, as the mother of a grown child, Bryan, who himself is embarking on parenthood, Sue had all the wisdom that age affords a parent plus a flashback view of her son's childhood. The bad? After moving 17 times before Bryan went to college, Sue had a hodgepodge of artifacts: some were gone, some were damaged and others just left her wondering where, when and how.

So Sue relied on what she did have—words, her own, starting with a letter she wrote to Bryan long before he was able to read.

"The text of the letter...is exactly as I wrote it late at night on his father's birthday, when Bryan was six weeks old," Sue says. From there, choosing the elements to include was a matter of deciding what was available and dividing the book into theme-driven sections. Photos, journaling and memorabilia were placed on theme-specific paper. Sue also incorporated "hidden text" features—handwritten notes to her son hidden behind windows and other decorative accents—as a means of expressing her retrospective parental wisdom.

"The best part about the album—besides finally, after 34 years, getting it all down and presentable—was realizing that I had come a long way since those early years. I can see the results of my mothering, and it's a good feeling. Back then, I had no way of knowing how it would all turn out," says Sue.

intro page

November 18, 1969--

Today your father is twenty-nine years old. Not a great age, but so much older than I could ever have imagined when we were married. Those four short years are strangely compressed, I suppose because we were together so little. Now we are again separated. You are in your crib, complaining softly when you move a little, as though life is already hard to bear. Six fast-disappearing weeks ago you were still a part of me, unborn, and no shock, no fear could touch you. Now things to which my ears have hardened make your hands fly up in fright, and the dark of which I must confess I too am afraid makes your eyes wide too.

Why do I love you so? Perhaps I love your innocence, for I find my spirit strangely calmed by your clear blue eyes. There is nothing artificial about you, and whatever you do, you do wholeheartedly. I love you because you are a reminder of the beautiful and unspoiled things I see disappearing around me so rapidly. You make me believe in a future, and the thought is comforting.

I love you because you open my eyes to the good things within myself. I must relinquish so much freedom, must share my husband with you, myself with you; I must give up my comfortable habits and adjust to your presence. I was not sure I could, at first, and I feared your coming. You meant the death of my childhood; it can no longer continue, but must become a lovely haunting memory. I love you because you do not let me dwell on my loss, but make me look forward. You are growing so fast, your spirit and your body, that my mind whirls with it. You are a visible symbol of time passing, and it passes ever more swiftly. I love you because you are a product of love, a gift your father and I gave each other, and to the world.

Some of these reasons make me sad, for they mean our world is not yet perfect, and someday you will no longer be a child. But the duty of a parent is to learn to love without bitterness over what is lost, and I love you because, without intending to, you cause me to perform this duty, and make me glad that I do.

filler pages

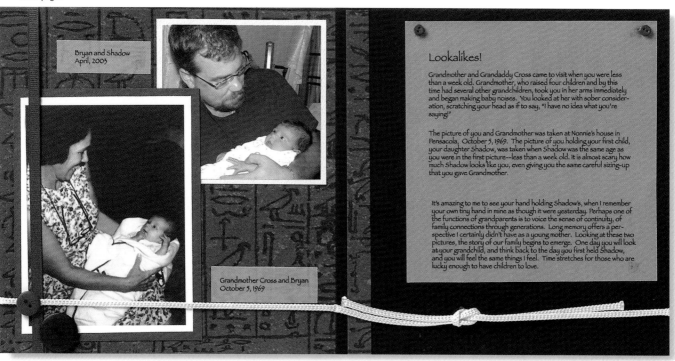

Bryan and Shadow
April, 2003

Grandmother Cross and Bryan
October 5, 1969

Lookalikes!

Grandmother and Grandaddy Cross came to visit when you were less than a week old. Grandmother, who raised four children and by this time had several other grandchildren, took you in her arms immediately and began making baby noises. You looked at her with sober consideration, scratching your head as if to say, "I have no idea what you're saying!"

The picture of you and Grandmother was taken at Nonnie's house in Pensacola, October 5, 1969. The picture of you holding your first child, your daughter Shadow, was taken when Shadow was the same age as you were in the first picture—less than a week old. It is almost scary how much Shadow looks like you, even giving you the same careful sizing-up that you gave Grandmother.

It's amazing to me to see your hand holding Shadow's, when I remember your own tiny hand in mine as though it were yesterday. Perhaps one of the functions of grandparents is to voice the sense of continuity, of family connections through generations. Long memory offers a perspective I certainly didn't have as a young mother. Looking at these two pictures, the story of our family begins to emerge. One day you will look at your grandchild, and think back to the day you first held Shadow, and you will feel the same things I feel. Time stretches for those who are lucky enough to have children to love.

filler pages

Fort Pickens State Park - August 1971

Some of my best memories from my own childhood are of the times I visited this group of old forts. My imagination ran as wild as I did among the old buildings, some restored and some nearly a ruin. When I acted out stories in the old forts, they were still unrestricted, and the "new" fort (from the Spanish-American War) still had some shells in the tracks leading to the elevator to the big disappearing guns. When you saw the forts, the shells were gone and access had been restricted for safety, but you fell in love instantly. You spoke of "olen times" and understood that these buildings were older even than your parents.

By lucky chance, a summer rain had brought out wildflowers in the otherwise barren beach sand. You always asked to stop and smell the flowers, and admire their colors. These are things I love, too, and I rejoiced to see you sharing that love.

You later became an archaeologist, and an avid gardener; the love of old things, history, and growing things has stayed with you. I had no idea, when we stopped to admire the red flowers at new Fort Pickens, in the background, that what I shared with you would be such an influence in your maturity. I think, had I realized this, that I would have shared more of my favorite things—and perhaps less of some, more negative things. A small course change at the beginning of the voyage results in a large difference in the eventual destination.

materials handmade 8 x 8 album (thelittlescrapbookstore.com) • patterned paper and snail stamp (Club Scrap) • Sticko Button Ups (EK Success) • 3D Keepers (C-Thru Ruler Co.) • ladybug sticker (Paper Adventures) • vellum (The Paper Company) • Papyrus font (Internet) • shells and beach glass from the beach • fibers

celebrating you

Kris Parkin | Woods Cross, UT

"...we will hold you forever because families are forever."

Kris Parkin created a scrapbook "legacy" of wishes for her firstborn grandson, Shawn. She started with a simple list of 15 words (holding, belonging, kissing, crying, etc.), each word carrying a special meaning for grandmother.

Kris pulled out a her bounty of photos to find one single picture to capture each word she would use in a table of contents and as page headers. (See page at right.)

She chose to use black-and-white photos to match her serene ice blue and white color palette. By adding short, hopeful journaling adjacent to a single photo, Kris fashioned a simple bundle-of-love book for her first-born grandson.

"The words are timeless and the perspectives from the grandmother will grow and change just as the child will," says Kris, who also believes that her write-first, design-later approach could prove to be part of a longer legacy. "It would also be fun to make another album with the very same words and complete it for the toddler years, and maybe even one of grade school years and adolescent years, and compare the growth."

title page

Celebrating you. . .

. introducing
. holding
. bonding
. amazing
. touching
. belonging
. kissing
. crying
. sharing
. anticipating
. enjoying
. exploring
. loving
. remembering

kissing

Kissing you every time we're together and never enough. I know that I must give them now against the day you won't so willingly let me have them...

amazing

Amazing little feet, perfect little babe. We delight in every part of your being and can only guess where your feet will lead you and pray that we can always be a part of your journey.

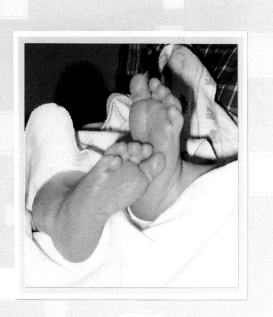

materials 6 x 6 album (Making Memories) • pattern paper (Patchwork Paper Design) foot punch (Carl) • square punches (Creative Memories) • CK Script font (Creating Keepsakes) • ribbon

Color me happy

CHILD'S PLAY

7 album ideas to preserve the fun

by Amy Sorensen

One morning, when I was sick in bed with a cold, my two-year-old son came into my room to find out why Dad was making breakfast instead of me. "Momma doesn't feel very good, buddy," I told him. He rubbed my cheek and smiled. "You're wrong, Momma," he said, "you feel so good."

If you're a mom, you've had plenty of moments like this, when you get a flash of insight about your kids' unique perspective on the world. The years between baby and kindergarten are such magical ones, when something as simple as a caterpillar's fuzz or a flower's bright color is enchanting. From talking to sharing, shapes to ABCs, kids learn something new every day. And don't forget personality—the temper tantrums, the stubbornness, the messes! No doubt about it, toddlers and preschoolers make us laugh, cry, shout, smile—and take pictures.

However, between building block towers and getting mustard stains out of white t-shirts, there's not much time for scrapbooking. And a chronological format sometimes fails to capture the texture of a child's days. A simple scrapbook that highlights an aspect of your child's experiences solves both problems.

Here are seven album ideas to help moms quickly assemble pages to enjoy and share, organized in a way that highlights personality and the joy of mastering new skills.

MATERIALS PagePaper/Priceless Paper Collections paper (Cock-A-Doodle Design) • CK Print font (Creating Keepsakes) • finger painted by hand

Two Cute

Jennifer Allen | Orem, UT

MATERIALS Enviro font (Microsoft Word) • O'Scrap! page accents (Imaginations!) • alphabet die cuts (Accu-Cut Systems) • tags, snaps and eyelets (Making Memories)

Who says twos are terrible? Not Jennifer Allen. She created an album to celebrate the traits of her two-year-old son, Trevor. Each page has a streamlined design, with squares of cardstock embellished with eyelets and preprinted accents. The journaling opposite each photo details one of Trevor's aged-two qualities, like happiness or busyness. An added perk is that the book is small enough for Trevor to look at often—and he does.

Title Page

Filler Pages

Trevor is a funny little boy. The picture is taken on the day of his birthday party. After he blew out the candle on his cupcake, he took the cupcake and ran into the other room. After just a minute we heard this hysterical laughing. When we got to his playroom, he was lying there laughing that the cupcake had fallen and the frosting was stuck to his neck.

Trevor does all kinds of funny things. He crawls into little spaces and then loudly says, "I'm stuck." He then waits for anyone to come and get him. He also likes to hide his toys and then act like he is looking for them. He will not eat his food hot. He likes it to be put into the freezer to cool down. If we count to ten two times he thinks that it is ready. When we are filling up the bath, he turns it very cold, backs up and says, "Ooooh, it's cold." Life is so great when you have a funny little boy in your home.

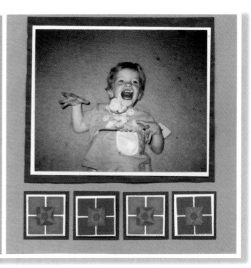

Trevor is happy. He has always been a happy boy. He has a great smile and we get to see it almost all the time. Of course he is happy in the picture; he has been outside running around with his friends all morning.

Other than being naturally happy, Trevor's life is full of happy moments. He gets to spend quite a bit of time with his grandparents, aunts, uncles, and cousins. He is happy when looking at the animals at the pet store, going to the library, playing with his friends, and splashing in the bathtub. Life is wonderful and bright when you have a happy, smiley boy in your home.

Rule #989

Grass on your clothes is bad. Very, very bad.

Every time you get grass on your coat, you'll want to
either brush it off immediately, or make a fuss until
your parents do it for you. Grass on your clothes is
not harmful; it's just one of those toddler things.

February 2002

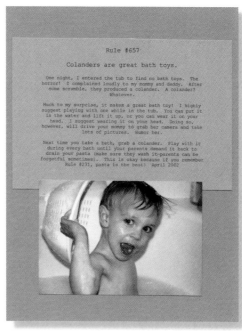

Rule #657

Colanders are great bath toys.

One night, I entered the tub to find no bath toys. The
horror! I complained loudly to my mommy and daddy. After
some scramble, they produced a colander. A colander?
Whatever.

Much to my surprise, it makes a great bath toy! I highly
suggest playing with one while in the tub. You can put it
in the water and lift it up, or you can wear it on your
head. I suggest wearing it on your head. Doing so,
however, will drive your mommy to grab her camera and take
lots of pictures. Humor her.

Next time you take a bath, grab a colander. Play with it
during every bath until your parents demand it back to
drain your pasta (make sure they wash it—parents can be
forgetful sometimes). This is okay because if you remember
Rule #231, pasta is the best! April 2002

The Rules:

How to Make the Most of
Your Toddler Years

(And Really Mystify Your Parents!)

by Jake Atkinson
as documented by his mommy

The Rules

Jessica Atkinson | Harrisburg, PA

MATERIALS Courier font
(Microsoft Word) • grass punch
(EK Success)

No doubt about it,
toddlers have their own
ideas about how to live
their lives. Jessica
Atkinson documented
her son Jake's quirks in
an album titled "The
Rules." Each page
describes one of the
unique ways Jake looks
at the world. The design
is easy: one picture per
page, two colors and a
wide swath of journal-
ing. One day, Jake will
love looking back at his
toddler antics.

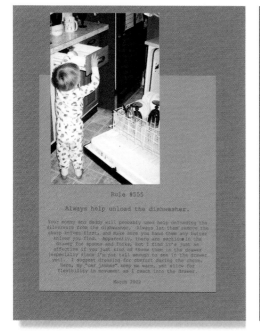

Rule #555

Always help unload the dishwasher.

Your mommy and daddy will probably need help unloading the
silverware from the dishwasher. (Always let them remove the
sharp knives first, and make sure you hand them any butter
knives you find. Apparently, there are sections in the
drawer for spoons and forks, but I find it's just as
effective if you just kind of throw them in the drawer
(especially since I'm not tall enough to see in the drawer
yet). I suggest dressing for comfort during the chore.
Here, my "car jammies" keep me warm, yet allow for
flexibility in movement as I reach into the drawer.

March 2002

Rule #776

Never nap alone.

Sometimes it's hard to fall
asleep. Reading books in bed
will help to make you drowsy.
If you just leave them open,
you'll see the page where you
left off when you awake.

It's important to have your
friends with you as well.
That way, you'll have some to
hug and kiss. I choose to
have Bob, Wormie, Rudolph,
Franklin, and Dumbo nap with
me on a regular basis. I
also like to nap with Turtle
Pillow, but he usually falls
on the floor.

Little was I to know that
this was one of my last naps
in my toddler bed. My Gram
soon brought me a car bed,
but the rules for that are
another story!

March 2002

Kieran's Toddler Dictionary

Jennifer Wohlenberg | Stevenson Ranch, CA

MATERIALS vellum (Autumn Leaves) • silver studs (Scrapworks) • hearts (Stringin' Things) • Simpson font for title and Adil font for journaling (Internet)

Learning to talk is an important process for toddlers, and it often yields funny results. Jennifer Wohlenberg made a scrapbook dictionary of her daughter's unique words. Each page features Kieran's pro-nunciation and usage of a word, plus a photo to illustrate it. Each layout includes a design element pulled from the pho-tograph. Kieran and her mom can "look up" her first words in the dictionary any time they want.

WackWack: Noun - anything with a beak. Kieran first applied this to ducks, as Mommy taught her that ducks quack. But as things evolved, everything be-beaked was a "wackwack." Here at the beach, there are many wackwacks for her viewing enjoyment.

Eeyaw: Noun - Ailie
See also *Eeyaw Meme*
Ailish is Kieran's primary playmate, chief tormentor and chief tormentee.

Haa: Noun -- Head or Hair Possible usages: "Ooh, ni, haa." (ooh, nice hair, as she combs it); or "Ow! Haa!" (she hit her head).

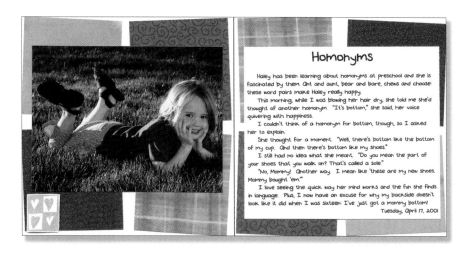

Homonyms

Haley has been learning about homonyms at preschool and she is fascinated by them. Ant and aunt, bear and bare, chews and choose: these word pairs make Haley really happy.

This morning, while I was blowing her hair dry, she told me she'd thought of another homonym. "It's bottom," she said, her voice quivering with happiness.

I couldn't think of a homonym for bottom, though, so I asked her to explain.

She thought for a moment. "Well, there's bottom like the bottom of my cup. And then there's bottom like my shoes."

I still had no idea what she meant. "Do you mean the part of your shoes that you walk on? That's called a sole."

"No, Mommy! Another way. I mean like 'these are my new shoes, Mommy bought 'em.'"

I love seeing the quick way her mind works and the fun she finds in language. Plus, I now have an excuse for why my backside doesn't look like it did when I was sixteen: I've just got a mommy bottom!

Tuesday, April 17, 2001

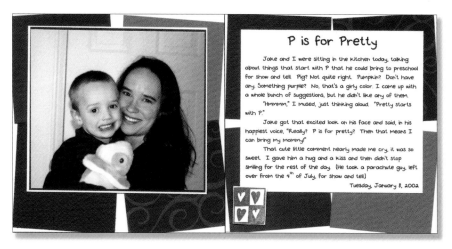

P is for Pretty

Jake and I were sitting in the kitchen today, talking about things that start with P that he could bring to preschool for show and tell. Pig? Not quite right. Pumpkin? Don't have any. Something purple? No, that's a girly color. I came up with a whole bunch of suggestions, but he didn't like any of them.

"Hmmmm," I mused, just thinking aloud. "Pretty starts with P."

Jake got that excited look on his face and said, in his happiest voice, "Really? P is for pretty? Then that means I can bring my mommy!"

That cute little comment nearly made me cry, it was so sweet. I gave him a hug and a kiss and then didn't stop smiling for the rest of the day. (He took a parachute guy, left over from the 4th of July, for show and tell.)

Tuesday, January 8, 2002

YOU CAN DO THIS

Creating a simple scrapbook for a toddler is as easy as 1, 2, 3.

1. Purchase a small album.
2. Pick up some snazzy coordinating accents.
3. Preserve an aspect of toddler life that you never want to forget.

Keep this combination album/journal by the side of your child's bed to record the quirky questions, silly insights and precious prayers that are a part of the bedtime routine. The cover serves as a title page, and there's a section for ages two through four. The closing page will be a photo of your toddler sleeping.

Album by Century Craft
available at
gonescrappin.com
3-ring binders with ribbon ties

Accents by Colorbök
800/366-4660
www.colorbok.com
Sesame Street stickers and frames

Sassy Speeches

Amy Sorensen | Orem, UT

MATERIALS Dear Diary font (twopeasinabucket.com) • pink and yellow papers (Karen Foster Design) purple paper (Doodlebug Design) plum paper (Close To My Heart) • rubber stamp (Hero Arts) • ColorBox stamping ink (Clearsnap, Inc.)

As soon as my kids spoke in complete sentences, they started saying the funniest things. Or sometimes they'd say something so sweet, I'd get a little teary. I kept all those stories in my journal, but realized one day that no one but me would ever hear them. So I turned them into a simple scrapbook. One picture, taken about the time the statement was made, illustrates each story. The color-blocked background, inspired by a rubber stamp, is a great way to use leftover scraps of paper and cardstock. Whenever I'm feeling frustrated with my kids, I pull out this album to remind myself why I love being their mom.

My ABC Album

Shan'l Parish | Boise, ID

MATERIALS ABC stickers (Provo Craft)
• embroidery floss • chalk (Craf-T Products)
• punches (Family Treasures) • Pigma
Micron pens (Sakura)

For kids, moving from lisping the ABC song to recognizing the written shapes of letters is a big step. An ABC album is the perfect way to get them excited about learning the alphabet. Shan'l Parish put a new spin on the traditional ABC book by writing a poem to lead readers through the album. Paired with pictures of family members and paper piecings that illustrate each letter, the poem keeps the book fun and interesting for her daughter.

is for Queen,

jewels sparkling in the sun

is for the need to

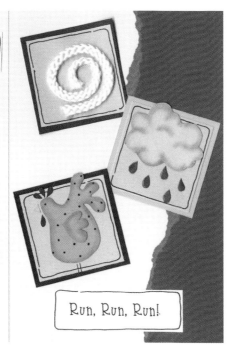

Run, Run, Run!

WRITE NOW

WRITE NOW

Writing a poem for an entire scrapbook might seem like a daunting task, but if you follow these steps, you can compose your pages and write an original verse in just a few hours:

- Pick out a photo to use for each letter of the alphabet.
- Organize them by letter.
- For each letter/photo combination, look for key words and possible rhymes
- Allow yourself to be funny or silly!
- Play, rearrange and rewrite until your lines rhyme

Shan'l wrote 13 rhyming couplets that connect the photos she used to the letter each photo represents. Her verse might help you get started with your own. If you get stuck, use the rhyming dictionary at rhymezone.com.

A is for animals, I think I'll eat a bear.
B is for bath time, jump in if you dare!
C is for circus clown, who makes the children grin.
D is for drivers, who are in a race to win.
E is for eating, a yummy pumpkin mess.
F is for flower, stuck here to my dress.
G is for green gun, ready, aim, fire!
H is for horses, of which we never tire.
I is for ice, falling to the ground.
J is for jumping, let's bounce, bounce around.
K is for kite, in the sky up high.
L is for love that can never die.
M is for marshmallows, an art project for you.
N is for night sky, red, yellow, and blue.
O is for orange smile, silly as can be.
P is for pioneer, crossed the plains for me.
Q is for queen, jewels sparkling in the sun.
R is for the need to run, run, run!
S is for superman, fast as speeding light.
T is for together, let's hold each other tight.
U is for uncle, who loves to tickle, tickle.
V is for Valentine, will you be my sweet pickle?
W is for getting wet in a water fight.
X is for Xtra tired and can't wait till night.
Y is for a young babe, new to our family.
Z is for zesty gal, to end our A to Z!

Colors
for Kevin

Amy Lowe | Hilton Head Island, SC

MATERIALS Century Gothic font for titles and Wendy font for script (Internet) • circle punch (Family Treasures)

Learning the names of colors is a quintessential toddler thing to do. Scrapper Amy Lowe made a simple scrapbook to teach her son, Kevin, the names of colors in English, Spanish and French. Each layout focuses on one color; the simple design includes punched circles and one photo of Kevin. Amy loves language, and she hopes her son will, too. She's teaching him simple concepts now to encourage it.

Little Cowboy

Aidan & his new cowboy hat - August, 2002

First Real Haircut

Aidan getting his first 'big boy' haircut.
February, 2002

Nana's Memory Book

Lisa Russo | Woodstock, GA

MATERIALS square punch (McGill) •
Garamouche font (P22 Type Foundry)

Scrapbooker Lisa Russo lives in Georgia, and her mom lives in New York. To keep her mom updated on her son Aidan's experiences, Lisa decided to make at least two scrapbook pages for her mom each time she has a roll of film developed. The result? "Nana's Memory Book," a fast and easy way for Lisa to share Aidan's activities.

The design is simple: the pages use the same font and are embellished only with color. Lisa saved the layout format on her computer, so when she wants to send new layouts to her mom, all she has to do is open the document, choose a color for the text, change the title and journaling, and print. She mats the photo or adds a colorful accent, and the page is ready to mail.

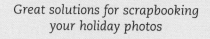

*Great solutions for scrapbooking
your holiday photos*

Christmas Past

by Gayle Humpherys

As Christmas rolls around each year, familiar sights, smells and sounds fill the air—twinkling lights, fresh-baked gingerbread, and the constant snapping of the camera shutter. The holidays bring out the photographer in all of us as we strive to capture a little of the season's magic on film. And since Christmas keeps coming year after year, chances are you've got a pile (or two or three) of holiday pictures waiting to be scrapbooked.

When you sort through your accumulated Christmas photos—whether they're from last year or twenty years ago—you'll likely discover three scenarios.

❶ LOTS OF PHOTOS. Some of us tend to take more pictures than we know what to do with.

❷ NOT-SO-GREAT PHOTOS. Bad lighting and poor colors are some of the problems you might encounter.

❸ NO PHOTOS. It's hard for a scrapper to believe, but you might have few or no photos for some holidays.

Santa's helpers are here to help you get your Christmas memories, past and present, into an album. We've created a Scrapbooker's Wish List for each scenario and gathered advice and top-notch Christmas layouts for great stocking-stuffer solutions!

LOTS OF PHOTOS With a multitude of things to take pictures of during the holiday season—from caroling and cooking to pageants and presents—it's no wonder so many of us end up with stacks of Christmas photos. Then we're left with the daunting—and sometimes overwhelming—task of scrapbooking them. But you might be surprised how many photos you can actually put on a page without it looking too cluttered.

Scrapbooker's Wish List:

✓ Incorporate lots of Christmas photos into one or two single layouts.

✓ Quickly size and position photos to fill up the available page space.

✓ Still include journaling with all the pictures.

The Night Before Christmas

Kim Heffington | Avondale, AZ

STOCKING STUFFER SOLUTIONS: Go ahead and crop your pictures! Cropping can help you get the maximum use of page space. Pictures cropped into small, equal-sized squares or rectangles can be used to create borders on the page.

In this layout, Kim was able to include 12 additional full-size photos by creating a "mini album" from individual Flip Pockets. The six pockets were stacked on top of each other, placed inside a cover created from folded patterned paper, and adhered to the page with a couple of small brads.

Mini album opened

materials embossed vellum (K & Company) • star brads (Scrapworks) • ribbon • tag • brads • CK Fresh font (Creating Keepsakes) • Memory Book Flip Pockets (C-Line Products) • ink for aging text blocks (Nick Bantock Collection)

Christmas

Shannon Watt | Van Nuys, CA

STOCKING STUFFER SOLUTIONS: A page layout template is a great tool for quickly cropping and positioning all the elements on a page so everything fits right the first time. The templates are very flexible, letting you pick and choose what to put in each area: photos, journaling blocks or embellishments. Shannon used the same template for each page of her layout but varied the placement of journaling and other embellishments.

Pre-made embellishments add a homemade touch without all the work, and they enhance your layout's theme.

materials Color Blocking template (Deluxe Designs) • Paper Bliss accents (Westrim Crafts) • Sonnets letter stickers (Sharon Soneff) • Angelina and Tribulation fonts (Internet) • eyelets

NOT-SO-GREAT PHOTOS It seems like there's always at least one photo in the bunch that never turns out quite right: the lighting is too dark, the subject is off-center, or the colors are a little too green or red. Older photos are also often not in the best of shape, with problems such as fading colors. Some photos can be altered for the better by either redeveloping them or by using photo-editing computer software. And sometimes, it's okay to just go ahead and use your bad photos—after all, the memories are still good even if the photos aren't!

Scrapbooker's Wish List:
- ✓ Create pleasing Christmas pages using poor-quality photos.
- ✓ Preserve older, faded photos.

Visits with Santa

Barbara Carrol | Tucson, AZ

STOCKING STUFFER SOLUTIONS: Quickly improve photos with color or lighting problems by scanning them and converting them to black and white with photo-editing software. Barbara found a faded Santa photo from 1960 and converted it to black and white. She also converted the remaining photos on the page to black and white for continuity. Using black and white helps focus attention on the people in the photos, and creating a second, modified copy of the picture allows you to keep the original preserved in a safe location.

m a t e r i a l s tree embellishment and black tag (Making Memories) • ribbon • Typewriter Rough font (Internet) • Flea Market font (twopeasinabucket.com)

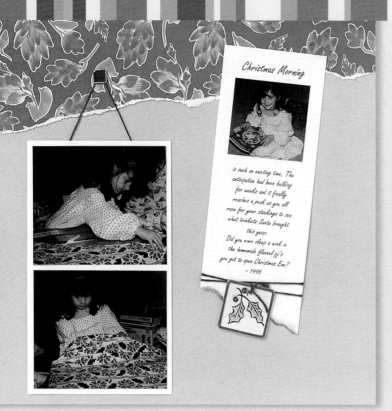

Christmas Morning

Kim Morgan | Pleasant Grove, UT

STOCKING STUFFER SOLUTIONS: Go ahead and use your not-so-perfect photos right on the page if you don't have the time or means to alter them first! Since your photos should still be the focus of the page—even if they're bad photos—try to keep your layout clean and simple. Try using a neutral color for the background, especially when using photos with dark or cluttered backgrounds. The white matting in Kim's layout provides some contrast for the darker photos without overwhelming them.

materials patterned paper (Sharon Ann) • tag and brad (Making Memories) • holly stamp (Close To My Heart) • chalks • Freestyle Script font (Microsoft Word) • embroidery floss

Christmas 1998

Brenda Cosgrove | Orem, UT

STOCKING STUFFER SOLUTIONS: When you have a group of so-so photos, or photos that don't go well together, choose the best one to mount on the page and create a small booklet for the rest. Brenda put photos in her booklet that were "cluttered" and contained a wide range of colors, since they would have been difficult to mat and group together in a layout. Store the booklet in a cardstock pocket created on the page.

materials Chestnut font (Two Peas in a Bucket) • Tree accent (O'Scrap) • eyelets and ribbon • Note, Brenda had her mini book bound at Kinko's

NO PHOTOS Despite the usual abundance of holiday photos, there might be a Christmas in your past when you didn't take any photos (or can't find them). Or, perhaps you simply didn't take pictures of everything you wished you would have. Pictures or not, it's still important to record those memories.

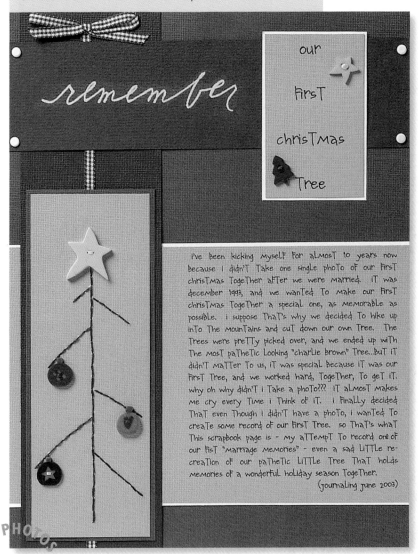

Scrapbooker's Wish List:
✓ Record Christmas memories when no photos are available.

Our First Christmas Tree

Wendy Sue Anderson | Heber City, **UT**

STOCKING STUFFER SOLUTIONS: A scrapbook page doesn't have to include a photo—sometimes the journaling is what's most important to convey a memory.

Page embellishments can correspond with the journaling memory and even recreate what the photo might have shown, as Wendy did with her embroidered "Charlie Brown" tree. (Note: A paper-piercer tool can make stitching and sewing buttons on cardstock easier.)

materials Simply Stated rub-on title (Making Memories) • Dotlets (Doodlebug Design) • Casual font (Stampin' Up!) • tree button • eyelets • thread • ribbon • stars • ornament buttons

DESKTOP Flip-Flop

BY CINDY KNOWLES

What's the best thing about a tabletop flip album? It's just asking to be opened! Flip photo albums make a great accessory to any room or office, and it's the perfect medium for an unconventional scrapbook.

Tabletop flip albums are a fun way to display photos, but have you ever thought of using one to make a scrapbook? The format is inviting and interactive — it can be much more fun to flip through than a traditional album. Take advantage of the unconventional format by taking an unconventional approach to a tribute album. You'll be glad you did!

Make a game of your album

I wanted to create a tribute album to my mother, whom my children call Gramma Sasse, so they could get to know her and the character traits, interests, and other things that she and my children have in common. Instead of making a chronological album of her life, I thought it would be fun to make use of a tabletop flip album that I'd had sitting on my fireplace mantel for more than a year.

How could I make the album a fun, engaging experience for my children (or anyone else, for that matter), while at the same time giving them a chance to learn more about their grandmother? The solution? Make it a mystery! I used one of our family's favorite car games, Twenty Questions, as the framework for the album. The trick, of course, is to see who can name the mystery subject with the least number of clues.

When a player answers a question correctly, she gets to guess the mystery person or turn the page for another clue. When she has solved the mystery person's identity, she turns to the back part of the album to see photos of grandma taken at various stages throughout her life!

Designing pages for the flip format

I had fun with the design challenges offered by the album's small size and flip format. I divided the album into two sections: the game, which includes questions and answers; and the photo section, which includes photos and fun facts about my mom. I set up a framework for the

MATERIALS Furio album (purchased at Target) • Serendipity patterned paper (SEI) • gingham ribbon (May Arts) • fibers and metal tags and shapes (Making Memories) • brads (Boxer Scrapbooks) • wire (Westrim) • 2 Peas Silly font (Two Peas in a Bucket) • Oldstyle Typewriter font (Internet) • charms (Hyglo, American Tag, Blue Moon Beads, and Westrim) • coin envelopes (Staples, Inc.)

question pages by creating four pocket designs, and I rotated those four designs through the entire section.

I began by writing a list of more than 30 questions (see page 83) that I asked my mom to answer. I asked more questions than I needed, so I could choose the ones with the best answers.

Next, I used my computer to make a page size that would fit in the album, and then I typed one question on each page and printed them on colored cardstock (see facing page).

On each page, I fashioned two pockets from coin envelopes; one pocket to hold the incorrect "no" answer and one to hold the correct "yes" answer. I attached the pockets to the pages at a slight angle (they needed to be slanted upward a little so the pull-out answer tabs wouldn't fall out) and then I embellished the pockets with one of my four designs, using charms, rubber stamps, tags, mesh, and fibers.

I then cut cardstock to fit the little pockets, and for each question page I wrote a correct answer on one piece of cardstock and an incorrect answer on the other.

Mystery solved!

The second section of my album begins with a picture collage of my mother with a "Who am I?" question printed atop the photo. Another page featured the same photo,

intact, with a vellum overlay. My mom's face is revealed with a square punch. Her signature also graces the vellum. These pages were followed by a page of fun facts about her —things my children would enjoy knowing. I filled the rest of the pages with photos of my mother at different points in her life: as a baby, at her wedding, with her children when they were young, and a recent photo of her as she is today.

Try it for yourself

Flip albums are easy to find at almost any store, and they're not expensive. This format lends itself to a quick, easy, rewarding tribute album. You don't have to scrap someone's whole life in order to make a meaningful album about someone you love. All you have to do is gather a handful of your favorite photos, create a simple theme and format, and put it together! The result is a priceless gift: sharing a loved one's life with others.

In the game of Twenty Questions, each question invites a "yes" or "no" answer. Choose questions from the list below to ask your Mystery Person. Or add some of your own.

1. What countries have you visited or lived in?
2. What is your favorite meal?
3. What career would you most like to have?
4. What is your favorite candy bar?
5. Which do you like better—the beach or the mountains?
6. What is your favorite season?
7. Are you a night owl or an early bird?
8. Did you grow up on a farm or in the city?
9. Which do you prefer, cake or pie? What kind?
10. What is one of your talents?
11. What do you collect?
12. What is your favorite outdoor activity?
13. What is something you want to do that you've never done before?
14. Who was your favorite pet?
15. What is your favorite hymn or song?
16. What do you like to do to relax?
17. What is your favorite color?
18. What is your favorite sport or exercise (to watch or to participate in)?
20. In what state were you born?
21. What was your first paying job (as a kid)?
22. Who is your favorite actor/actress/athlete/author?
23. What is your favorite children's bedtime story?
24. What is your favorite holiday?
25. Name one of your nicknames.
26. Name a good surprise.
27. Name one thing you want to be known for.
28. Tell me about your favorite gift.
29. What is your favorite book or movie?
30. What is your favorite store?
31. What is your favorite thing to shop for?
32. What is your favorite flavor of ice cream?
33. Do you have any fears or phobias?

HERE'S ANOTHER IDEA TO FLIP OVER

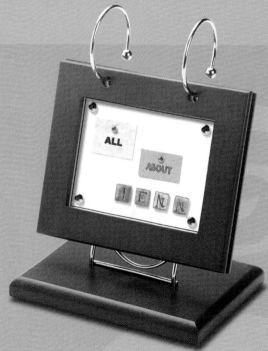

Tabletop flip albums don't need to be elaborate to be meaningful. Kris Parkin, a member of the Simple Scrapbooks Editorial Board from Centerville, Utah, created a tabletop flip album about her niece, Jenn, as a gift for Jenn's boyfriend. The album introduces him to Jenn and her family in a playful way.

Each page uses similar elements—a pen line outlining the page, a photo, and computer journaling strips attached with a simple silver brad. Background colors and journaling block strips are muted, focusing on the message of the album. The last page has an add-on flap with a picture of a frog. When the frog is lifted it reveals Jenn and her boyfriend, and the saying "She's found a real prince in you."

"I've always told her that she would have to go through a few frogs before she found a prince," laughed Kris.

For a family reunion, this album could spotlight a different family member every day and be the catalyst for fun getting-to-know-you family games.

MATERIALS Furio album (Target) + frog die cut (O'Scraps) + pewter alphabet letters (Global Solutions) + silver brads (Karen Foster Design)

This section is dedicated to you, our community of readers. It's a place to exchange thoughts, tips, ideas and inspiration. See what other scrapbookers are up to, and join in.

Share

DOGGY PADDLE

Willow and Dallas are so much fun to watch in the water. They love it when you throw a stick into the water. They'll swim out to it and bring it back. Dallas is smart through because she lets Willow swim all the way out for it and then just as she's back at the shore, Dallas will wrestle her for the stick.
- August 15, 2004 -

Fitting it in

10 busy women share how and why they find the time to scrapbook

✓ walk to the b
✓ Dine out
✓ Hit a move
✓ SCRAPBOOK
✓ Do a pu

by Angie Lucas

Children. Work. Grocery shopping. Friends. Laundry. Oil changes. Exercise. Laundry. Bills. "Survivor" reruns. Laundry.

It can be overwhelming just keeping up with life's daily tasks, let alone finding any extra time to recognize and record the special moments as they pass.

Millions of women face these same demands every day. And twenty years from now, they will want to remember this day, this month, this year, this home, this job, this baby, this circle of friends. And so will you. But there's just not enough time, right?

We found ten busy women who are somehow fitting it all in. Each has proven, in her own way, that it's possible to make room for this rewarding hobby. Whether you're a stay-at-home parent of two (or even five) children, or a criminal defense lawyer, or a waitress, one of the women featured here will speak to you.

If you need to simplify your pages, or let go of creative pressure, or grant yourself permission to leave most of your photos in the box, then do it. It's worth it.

Rebecca Cooper | Raymond, AB, Canada • Rebecca is a former dental assistant and the mother of a toddler and an infant. She spends about 20 hours per month scrapbooking in her home office, primarily during naptime.

"*To make the most of my scrapbooking time,* I keep a running notebook of random ideas (color combinations, page titles, journaling, photos I want to take, snippets of my daughter's speech) so that when I sit down and scrap, I don't have to waste time racking my brain for ideas.

I also find that keeping my photos organized helps simplify things for me. When I take a photo of someone, I jot down in my day planner a quick description of the photo—on the date I took it. As soon as I get my photos back from the developer, I pull out the day planner, date-stamp the back of my photos, and put them in a photo box that I've divided by months/years.

Additionally, I keep a binder filled with empty page protectors. When I come up with a layout idea, I place my photos and any notes for that page in one of the page protectors. This is my 'pages to do' binder, and it makes it easy to jump right in when I sit down to scrapbook."

Rebecca

Shauna Devereux | Athens, GA • Shauna is a supply chain manager at a manufacturing facility and a mother of two children, ages 10 and 2. She scrapbooks 45-50 hours per month, mostly on weekends, with her husband and children close by.

"This hobby just happens to be the perfect fit for me and my family. I used to be a little bit jealous of my husband for having so many hobbies, one of which is photography. And believe me, we have tons and tons of photos. Once I discovered scrapbooking, we found a great way to display both his work and mine. I've had several pages published, and he is just as proud to see them and show them off as I am.

The most important reason that I scrapbook, however, is to record the details that we tend to forget over the years. When I look at old photos of myself, I often wonder what was occurring in my life at the time the photo was taken. But when my son looks through our scrapbooks years from now, he'll know, for instance, just how much he loved dinosaurs when he was six, and what his favorite video games were at age nine."

Shauna

m a t e r i a l s patterned paper (K & Company) • large tag (Pebbles, Inc.) • small tag (KI Memories) • clip (EK Success) • rubber stamps (Making Memories) • vellum quote (DieCuts with a View) • stencil • ribbon • flower sticker

helping bake a Valentine's cake - 2003

YUMMY
SMILE
LOVE
SWEET
PUCKER

Kim Morgan | Pleasant Grove, UT • Kim has five children, ages 6 to 18, and she dreams of becoming an interior designer. Kim spends between 10 and 40 hours per month scrapbooking, usually at her kitchen table.

"I have to make time to scrap. Whenever I see a chance in the week to get a block of time, I'll plan ahead. If I manage to get dinner in the crock pot and the bathrooms cleaned before I run my morning errands, I can haul out my stash and get three hours in before I'm hit with the after-school frenzy of snacks, homework and music practice. And when I've completed a layout that I'm pleased with, I like to leave it out where I can glance at it as I go about my day. It makes me smile to know that I've created something worthwhile and lasting, something that will stay done, unlike the dishes and the laundry!

With the exception of an occasional get-away with my sister, I generally choose not to scrapbook on weekends or in the evenings. That time is reserved for my husband, Ron. But when he's out of town, the kids know that we'll be eating dinner at the counter, because I'm going to allow my mess to remain on the kitchen table until he gets home!"

materials word labels (Pebbles, Inc.) • flower punch (EK Success) • tiny flower punch (Fiskars)

Kim

"I'm not sure if I want to be a big brother, but I think having a baby will make my mom happy, and I want her to be happy."

Nigel, while we were at the pool today, I overheard you say this to Ryan, our eight-year old neighbor. It took everything I had to not burst into tears. You are my most sensitive boy. I cannot imagine you being any more kind, considerate, or thoughtful. I know you are worried about having a new sibling. I know that you have concerns about what will happen to our relationship when you are no longer an only child. You have asked if I will love you less once the baby comes, to which I always immediately & honestly respond, "Not possible!" I hope you believe my assurances that my heart will only grow and expand when the baby comes. In fact, I expect I will love you even more when I see what a great brother you are!! Truthfully, a small part of me worries more that I won't love the baby as much as you. How could I be so lucky to have another child who will say and feel such dear things? Nigel, thank you for being the kind of boy that thinks of others. Thank you for being willing to love your new role as a brother. Thank you for being more than I deserve. I am the luckiest mother in the world. I love you and will forever and for always!
xoxo, Mom

Marnie Flores | Madison, WI • Marnie is a former criminal defense attorney who is currently pursuing part-time legal work, and she's mother to a five-year-old and an infant. Marnie scrapbooks between 10 and 80 hours per month at a little table near her kitchen.

"*I scrap best when I design a bunch of layouts at a time.* Rather than do one layout from start to finish, I try to finish five or six basic layout ideas at my design table. This lets me get on a design roll without losing my momentum at the computer. I let the basic designs sit for a day before writing and formatting all of the journaling blocks on my computer. I then return to my table to put the layouts together.

Sometimes when a layout just isn't working, I either dream about it or I lie awake thinking of options. Rather than waste a whole night tossing and turning, I just crawl out of bed and head for the table! Once the basics come together, I sneak back to bed, hopefully to a more peaceful sleep. My neighbors probably wonder why my light goes on at 3 a.m. and stays on sometimes until sunrise. It's all in the name of a hobby!"

materials paper flowers, button and midori silk ribbon (Making Memories) • Sandra and Uncle Charles fonts • patterned paper (Rusty Pickle)

marnie

Amy Williams | Old Town, ME • Amy is a freelance designer and the mother of a 7-year-old and 3-year-old twins. She scrapbooks 30 to 40 hours per month in her family room, in the company of her three daughters.

"*My two main problems are overcoming the mess* and keeping little fingers away from my projects and supplies. To tackle the mess issue, I only work on one layout at a time, and I clean up and file all leftovers before beginning the next. As for the little fingers, when my kids show interest in what I'm doing, I set them up at a neighboring table and let them create their own works of art with leftover scraps.

Because I scrapbook in my family room, I don't keep all my supplies together. I keep the most used items in a basket on my project table, but everything else is organized in a closet. Keeping things separate has helped me be more productive: I focus more on the photos and journaling this way. I lay them out first and then go in search of the perfect embellishment. Consequently, I feel less overwhelmed by choices."

Amy

materials CK Toggle and CK Script fonts • sea stars (Li'l Davis Designs) • Zig Writer pen (EK Success)

Just You & Me

When you play checkers with Nate, you'd better **Watch Out!** He's pretty good and he's confident. When playing with him this time, he said to me, "OK, are you ready for me to win? Or do you want me to go easy on you?" Feb. 2, 2003

Mimi Porter | Plano, TX • Mimi is the mother of four children, ages 3 to 10 (the oldest are twins). She spends 40 to 90 hours per month scrapbooking in a spare room she equipped with two tables and a wall of shelves.

"*I love to make connections through my photos.* Last Thanksgiving, my siblings and I visited the Phoenix Zoo, and we piled 12 grandchildren onto a big red tractor for a picture. I later discovered a photo of my siblings and me on the very same tractor when we were children. I plan to use both pictures on a single layout—finding these types of connections makes this hobby meaningful for me.

Because my photos number in the thousands, it is very easy to forget what I have, or to use up all my scrapbooking time looking through photos. To remedy this, I bought a bulletin board to hang in my scrapbook room, and a package of transparent envelopes. When I find photos that go together, I place them in one of the envelopes on the board. Then, when it's time to scrapbook, I can decide at a glance which pictures I'm in the mood to work on. The red tractor photos are on my wall right now, waiting for the right moment."

materials eyelet (Making Memories) • yarn (Fibers by the Yard) • CK Summer font • patterned papers (Colorbök) • chalk (Craf-T Products) • Zig Writer pen (EK Success)

Oh, my sweet dear precious baby-love. You make me so happy. I look at you and a big goofy grin splashes across my face. I have so much fun being your mommy. You are so easy...so chill...so content. One of my favorite moments every day is when I go to get you out of bed in the morning. You don't cry when you wake up, you don't make a peep! You just roll onto your back and suck your thumb until someone is gracious enough to get you out of bed. So, after I get Mckenna ready for school and out the door, I rush to get you up. I peek over your bassinet and there you are, happily sucking away at your thumb. And when you see me, you do this wiggly-smiley thing with your whole body. And you lose the suction on your thumb. And I smile and gurgle at you, pick you up, smell your sweet morning smell, and relish the fact that you are all mine. Everyday.

i love you...

JUN 11 2003

Tara Whitney | Mission Viejo, CA • Tara is a stay-at-home mom with four kids, ages 2 to 9. She scrapbooks 20 to 30 hours per month in the comfort of her bedroom, with her husband close by.

"*One dilemma I faced was how to scrap-book and spend quality time* with my husband, without it conflicting with family needs. This is what works for us: After the kids have gone to bed, we go to our bedroom—also my scrap space—where I have a bookshelf filled with supplies and a desk for my computer. While my husband uses the computer, plays video games, watches TV or reads, I set up my small personal table (normally stored under the bed) and scrap away next to him. That way we can spend time together and talk... and my guilt is kept at bay."

materials metal word (Making Memories) • Caecalia font • brads

Tara

"*Most of my scrapbooking is done at a once-a-month get-together* with a group of friends. We meet in a big room with a lot of table space, fun snacks and great company. I expect to knock out quite a few pages in this one night, and I better, because I scrap almost all of my pictures! When I scrap at home, I work at my dining room table, so I can hang out with my kids and husband.

When I first started scrapbooking, I took enormous amounts of pictures, either to generate stuff to scrap or to match a page I had in mind. As my interest and skill level in photography increased, my focus shifted. I still take plenty of pictures, but now I think more about the quality and purpose of each shot, which makes my photos—and my pages—more meaningful."

materials • patterned papers (Autumn Leaves) • Zig Writer pen (EK Success)

Suzanne

"B" is for beautiful

Suzanne Lopez | Arvada, CO • Suzanne is a former travel agent and current mom of two girls, ages 6 and 8. She is a social scrapbooker who spends 6 or so hours per month on the hobby.

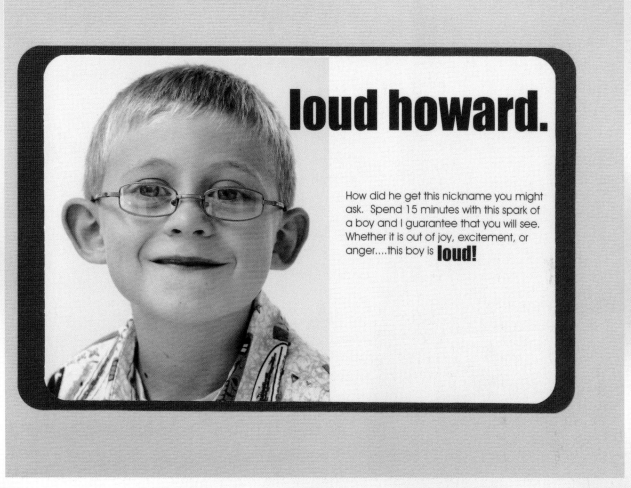

loud howard.

How did he get this nickname you might ask. Spend 15 minutes with this spark of a boy and I guarantee that you will see. Whether it is out of joy, excitement, or anger....this boy is **loud!**

Jill Beamer | Vancouver, BC, Canada • Jill is a labor and delivery nurse who now stays at home with her four children, ages 4 to 11. She spends 40 hours per month scrapbooking at a desk in the corner of her basement rec room.

"*While I love the look of the busier, more embellished pages,* 'simple' works for me for many reasons: I have four children to do albums for, and not a lot of time to get them done; keeping things simple frees me from the added stress and pressure (albeit self-imposed) of trying to work all these lumpy/bumpy, cutting-edge embellishments onto my pages; and my generally "flatter" pages are easier to store because I can fit more pages in each album.

I remind myself regularly that one of the reasons I am scrapbooking in the first place is to showcase my photos, memories, thoughts and feelings. I feel that this can be accomplished just as easily and effectively with simple pages.

I was adopted as an older child (age 10), and I have virtually no knowledge of my own childhood. I get a lot of grief now from my kids when I try to photograph them, but if one day they say a simple 'thank you' for my efforts to preserve some of their childhood memories, that's all I can hope for."

Jill

materials photopaper (Ilford) • Impact and Decker fonts • corner rounder (EK Success)

We tried. Oh, we tried, when the kids were young to have a steady date night. We struggled with finding the right babysitter. Sometimes, we felt guilty spending the money. It just never seemed to work out. We always thought when they got older, it would be easier. Then, it seemed that all our spare time was spent at swim meets and basketball games. We talked a lot about a regular date night, but again, it just never seemed to work out. Well, now the kids are away to college and we finally have our date night. It is as important as it was years ago. Every Friday night, we go for an early dinner at El Charro. Winter and spring, we eat on the porch. In the summer and fall, we are inside. We always order the same thing, guacamole, a plate of carne seca tacos for you and a plate of ground beef tacos for me and if it is cold, two cups of tomato soup. Dinner comes and we immediately swap a taco with each other. Then we catch up. Isn't it amazing that after all these years, we still haven't run out of things to say?   2004

at last...

DATE NIGHT

Barbara Carroll | Tucson, AZ • Barbara is a former elementary school teacher who has two children, ages 20 and 23. She loves to scrapbook on her dining room table, near the computer and stereo, an average of 40 hours per month.

"*I try not to get hung up on the 'shoulds' of scrapbooking.* I use many different styles and approaches, from filling a whole page with journaling to including just a simple title or a quote. Some of my pages contain several photographs, but more often I select the single best image for that particular layout. Sometimes, I use several embellishments, but other times I place just a single photograph on cardstock and add a few words.

I let my photographs inspire me, both in choice of what to work on and how to scrap. A single week can find me scrapping an 80-year-old heritage photo, a picture from when my children were small, a photo I took last week of my niece, and a shot of the prettiest rose in my garden that I took a few minutes ago. This method, which may seem haphazard to some, allows me the freedom to work on what inspires me."

m a t e r i a l s Times New Roman, 2Peas Champagne and 4YEOSTAMP fonts

Barbara

my boy

Jeannie Leiterman | Berrien Springs, MI

JEANNIE IS AFRAID OF SPIDERS AND FAILURE.
She drives a Mitsubishi Galant, and she's a sucker for a good massage and/or a 20-oz. white chocolate mocha espresso from Starbucks.

my boy,
my hope,
my love,
my life,
my joy.

materials patterned paper (Chatterbox, Inc.) • metal plaque (Making Memories) • CK Plain Jane font

smile
Rosemary Waits | Mustang, OK

ROSEMARY MET HER HUSBAND, JUSTIN, *in a German language class at Oklahoma State University. He later showed up at a charity date auction and bought Rosemary for $6. If Rosemary's life were made into a movie, she says Garfield (the cartoon cat) would play her best.*

materials patterned paper (Making Memories) • Slick Writer pen (American Crafts) • stamps (MoBe' Stamps!) • stamping ink

doggy paddle
Cherie Nymeyer | Cambridge, ON, Canada

CHERIE IS A NEWLYWED. *Dallas and Willow are her mother-in-law's dogs, and she has known and loved them for more than four years. When she was young, Cherie dreamed of being a writer or owning a bookstore. Her favorite vegetable is the potato.*

materials mesh (Magic Scraps) • eyelets (The Happy Hammer) • paw print punch (EK Success) • alphabet stamps (FontWerks) • stamping ink • Cargo D and Rock It! fonts • fibers

a girl's room

Joy Bollinger | Midlothian, VA

JOY HAS A CHIHUAHUA NAMED BAILEY and a pit bull named Rudy. Her daughter Rachel struggles with the blunt safety scissors she has to use in kindergarten, as she's been using mom's scrapbooking scissors since age three!

materials patterned paper (Creative Imaginations) • metal rimmed tags (Making Memories) • letter stickers (Colorbök) • ribbon • embroidery floss • Optima font

Mommy started planning Rachel's new room a few months before the baby was born. We moved her bedroom to the end of the hall so we could use her current room as the baby's room. We wanted her to have her own **BIG GIRL ROOM** - Mommy wanted it to be very pretty and special for her. We bought new white furniture and Mema and Papa bought her bedding for Christmas (Mommy picked it out at Company Kids). Daddy painted the walls and ceiling white and Mommy painted the bottom of the walls a pale lime green with scallops and daisy wallies at the top. Mommy designed the window treatments and Mema made them. Everything turned out so pretty and Rachel really likes her new room - she wants to show it to everyone who visits. She even has a small TV and VCR so she can watch her favorite videos. She loves her Disney Princess calendar - she doesn't care about what month it is, she just wants to change the Princess pictures every so often. Rachel picked out her 'Bee Happy' picture all by herself. Mommy still has some decorating to do but we think her room turned out perfect and special - for a special little girl (although not so little anymore).

A Girl's Room

have fun

Marie Cox | Springfield, MA

MARIE STARTED SCRAPBOOKING as a way to cope with her mother's death in 2003. She's now addicted to the hobby. Marie and her daughter, Zavia, are both outgoing and somewhat impatient. Marie hates seafood, and she longs to travel to Africa.

have fun

materials patterned paper (SEI) • monogram (My Mind's Eye) • rub-on words (Making Memories) • flower eyelet (Creative Imaginations)

uncharted territory

Kimberly Kett | St. Catharines, ON, Canada

KIMBERLY, A SALES ASSOCIATE *at a children's clothing store, says her favorite fictional character is Winnie the Pooh. If Kimberly could have a superpower, she would choose the ability to heal.*

m a t e r i a l s patterned paper (Chatterbox, Inc.) • paper frame (Bazzill Basics Paper) • flower cut-out (The Beary Patch) • flower punches (EK Success) • rub-on words (Making Memories)

my life at 25

Erin Roe | Hampton, VA

ERIN HAS A BIRTHMARK *that looks like a capital E, and she loves photography. She is terrified of flying, which makes it hard to visit her husband, Tim, who is stationed in San Diego with the Navy.*

m a t e r i a l s patterned paper (Scrappy Cat) • snaps (Making Memories) • letter stickers (KI Memories) • circle punches • Dirty Headline and Two Peas Hot Chocolate fonts

true love

Ramona Lockwood | Amery, WI

RAMONA, WHO HAS MET THE CLINTONS AND THE GORES, *currently teaches high school business classes. Her grandparents, Bud and Lucille, fell in love in high school and stayed very much in love all their lives.*

digital tools Adobe Photoshop Elements 2.0 (Adobe Systems) • CK Wellington font • **note** Ramona scanned a doily with cardstock behind it as well as a strip of cardstock and three ivory buttons. She assembled the pieces digitally.

glorious success

Andrea Chamberlain | Penfield, NY

ANDREA HAS BEEN SCRAP-BOOKING FOR FOUR YEARS.
A year ago, this computer-illiterate scrapbooker taught herself a photo-editing program, and she's 100 percent digital today. Andrea's favorite book is To Kill a Mockingbird by Harper Lee.

digital tools Microsoft Digital Image Pro 9 (Microsoft Corp.) • CK Cosmopolitan font • **note** Andrea created a "vellum" overlay by duplicating her layer and reducing the top layer's opacity. She then deleted a small section covering Lilly's little foot.

TERRI'S FAVORITE VEGETABLE IS CARROTS. *She likes Agatha Christie novels and other mysteries. Her son, Nathan, loves to make faces and wear the color yellow.*

january
Terri Davenport | Toledo, OH

materials january sticker (EK Success) • embossing powder

KATIE LOVES THIS STORY, TOLD IN HER GRANDMA'S WORDS,
because it proves grandma Phyllis, who grew up poor during the Great Depression, had some normal childhood moments. Katie loves the funky fishing hat her grandma wears and admires her take-it-as-it-comes attitude.

knowingness
Katie Watson | Corpus Christi, TX

There is a long story to this picture. I am sitting on the cement stairs of a swanky (in it's day) apartment house where the "rich" folks lived. We (Mother, Billie, Gene and I) rented a small house across the street. On occasion my big brother, Gene and sister, Billie would sit me there & hide over to the side. When the people came in and out they would talk to me and give me a nickel, dime or a quarter. Sometimes even a silver dollar. Then we would all go over to Christy Market and buy Pop & Candy. Who could resist such an (obviously) poor little girl with a head of curly hair and a big smile. *Joyce Toohey 2003*

Joyce Shea   Butte, MT

The knowingness of little girls, is hidden underneath their curls
Phyllis McGinley

materials patterned paper (C-Thru Ruler Co. and K & Company) • photo corners (Pioneer) • chalk (Stampin' Up!) • Little Days font

DR MARTIN LUTHER KING

Remembering

I HAVE A
Dream
DREAM
dream

OUR MOTHER OF MERCY CATHOLIC SCHOOL
PREK4
FEBRUARY 2004
BLACK HISTORY MONTH

I have a dream
Raquel Joseph | Beaumont, TX

RAQUEL LOVES TO TRAVEL,
and her favorite destination is the Bahamas. She works for an airline and is a mother of two. The first thing she'll do if she wins the lottery is go on a scrapbooking cruise.

materials patterned paper (SEI and 7 gypsies) • dream sticker (Creative Imaginations) • alphabet stickers (EK Success) • rub-on letters (Making Memories) • labels (Dymo Lablemaker) • die cut

marry me?

Kelli Lawlor | Norfolk, VA

IF A MOVIE WERE MADE ABOUT KELLI'S LIFE, *she'd like Holly Hunter to play the title role. Kelli's favorite book, Stolen Innocence, was written by her aunt. It's about the two-time kidnapping of her cousin, Jan, who is now a television actress.*

materials stickers (Club Scrap) • Nostalgiques letter stickers (EK Success) • stamping ink (Clearsnap, Inc.) • date stamp (Making Memories) • Antique Type font

just the 2 of us

Stacy Yoder | Yucaipa, CA

STACY IS MARRIED TO A *Los Angeles County firefighter, and her favorite colors are fire-engine red and other vibrant hues. Stacy homeschools her three children.*

materials patterned paper and stickers (KI Memories) • safety pin, heart eyelet, metal label holder, ribbon charm and ribbon (Making Memories) • buttons (Junkitz) • nails (Chatterbox, Inc.) • flower (EK Success) • ribbon (May Arts) • Baskerville Old Face and SandraOh fonts

hapa baby

Margaret Scarbrough | South Lancaster, MA

MARGARET AND HER SON MATTHEW (*Kwang Soo in Korean*) *enjoy eating breakfast cereal any time of day. Margaret loves watching reality television, organizing her home, and staying awake until the sun comes up.*

materials handmade paper (Artistic Scrapper) • conchos (Scrapworks) • patterned paper (The Paper Patch) • alphabet page pebbles (Making Memories) • felt flowers (Hirschberg Shutz & Co.) • Two Peas Chicken Shack font

kurz boys

Laura Kurz | Gambrills, MD

IN HER TEENS, *Laura was a competitive figure skater who trained six hours a day. She currently works for the U.S. Naval Academy in Annapolis. Laura and her husband Ken love to vacation on Bethany Beach, Del., with their extended family.*

materials patterned paper and stickers (Chatterbox, Inc.) • fabric label (me & my BIG ideas) • photo turns (Making Memories) • monogram stencil

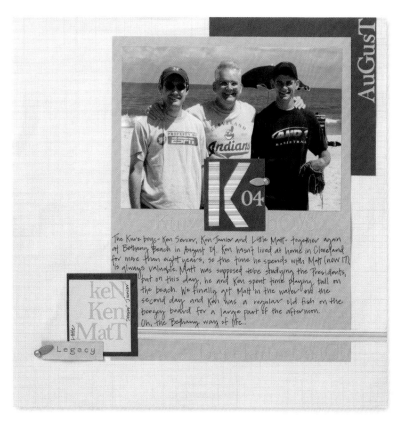

LIFE BRINGS SIMPLE
PLEASURES TO US
EVERY DAY. IT'S UP
TO US TO MAKE THEM
WONDERFUL MEMORIES.

———

CATHY ALLEN